# Running an Effective Investor Relations Department

# Running an Effective Investor Relations Department

## A Comprehensive Guide

STEVEN M. BRAGG

WILEY

John Wiley & Sons, Inc.

***Library of Congress Cataloging-in-Publication Data:***
Bragg, Steven M.
    Running an effective investor relations department: a comprehensive guide/ Steven M. Bragg.
        p. cm.
    Includes index.
    ISBN 978-0-470-63030-3 (cloth); 978-0-470-64253-5 (ebk); 978-0-470-64254-2 (ebk); 978-0-470-64255-9 (ebk)
  1. Corporations—Investor relations. 2. Corporations—Public relations. I. Title.
    HD2744.B727 2010
    659.2—dc22                                                      2010004699

10  9  8  7  6  5  4  3  2  1

# Contents

## Chapter 4: Event Management   37

## Chapter 5: Public Communications   57

## Chapter 6: Publications   69

## Chapter 7: Investor Relations Web Site   83

## Chapter 23: Investor Relations Metrics    239

## Index    **250**

# Preface

NVESTOR RELATIONS IS AN extremely complicated activity, because it requires an intensive level of communications with an unusually broad range of constituencies—analysts, brokers, investors, investment bankers, credit rating agencies, and the board of directors. The type of communication used is broad, requiring considerable skill in producing a multitude of written documents, Web site pages, press releases, conference calls, road shows, and other meetings. However, these communications are tightly controlled by government disclosure requirements that could land a company in a great deal of trouble if it violates them.

*Running an Effective Investor Relations Department: A Comprehensive Guide* was designed to assist the investor relations professional in creating a message for the investment community, navigating through the various constituencies, handling many forms of communication, and knowing how to operate within government disclosure guidelines. The first two chapters address the management needs of the investor relations function, covering the goals and objectives of investor relations, how to budget for it, several specific management issues, and how to build an investor relations officer (IRO) job description.

Chapters 3 through 7 address every aspect of communications with the investment community. They cover how to create a viable company story, as well as how to conduct a road show, conference call, and annual meeting. There is also a lengthy discussion of the proper formatting of a press release, and how to write a fact sheet, annual report, and many other reports. Chapter 7 specifically addresses the various elements of an investor relations Web site and refers the reader to a number of company sites that have taken the presentation of investor relations information to a high level.

Chapters 8 through 11 cover multiple aspects of disclosure rules. Chapter 8 reveals the requirements for management discussion and analysis (MD&A) reporting, while Chapter 9 covers Form 8-K event reporting, Regulation Fair Disclosure, and disclosure compliance policies. Chapter 10 addresses the origins of class action lawsuits, as well as the proper way to handle forward-looking statements. Chapter 11 discusses the reasons why guidance is used, as well as its format and timing, and the proper level of aggressiveness to be communicated.

Chapters 12 through 18 cover the various investor relations constituencies—the buy side, sell side, credit rating agencies, board of directors, and short sellers. These chapters primarily describe the nature and needs of each constituency and how to deal with them. Special topics are also addressed, such as the requirements for being an accredited investor, how to handle short sellers, the fee structures and requirements of the various stock exchanges, and how to monitor the markets.

Chapters 19 through 23 cover a broad range of miscellaneous topics. Chapter 19 addresses blue sky laws, while Chapter 20 shows how to conduct both traditional and electronic proxy solicitations. Chapter 21 discusses the intricacies of dividends and stock buy-backs, while Chapter 22 covers how to outsource a variety of investor relations activities. Finally, Chapter 23 reveals a broad range of metrics that can be used to measure a company's investor relations activities, as well as its performance for presentation to outside investors.

Taken as a whole, *Running an Effective Investor Relations Department* is intended to be the daily reference source for the investor relations professional.

# About the Author

**Steven Bragg, CPA,** has been the chief financial officer or controller of four companies, as well as a consulting manager at Ernst & Young and auditor at Deloitte & Touche. He received a master's degree in finance from Bentley College, an MBA from Babson College, and a bachelor's degree in Economics from the University of Maine. He has been the two-time president of the Colorado Mountain Club and is an avid alpine skier, mountain biker, and certified master diver. Mr. Bragg resides in Centennial, Colorado. He has written the following books:

Accounting and Finance for Your Small Business
Accounting Best Practices
Accounting Control Best Practices
Accounting Policies and Procedures Manual
Advanced Accounting Systems
Billing and Collections Best Practices
Business Ratios and Formulas
Controller's Guide to Costing
Controller's Guide to Planning and Controlling Operations
Controller's Guide: Roles and Responsibilities for the New Controller
Controllership
Cost Accounting
Cost Reduction Analysis
Essentials of Payroll
Fast Close
Financial Analysis
GAAP Guide
GAAP Policies and Procedures Manual
GAAS Guide
Inventory Accounting

Inventory Best Practices
Investor Relations
Just-in-Time Accounting
Management Accounting Best Practices
Managing Explosive Corporate Growth
Mergers & Acquisitions
Outsourcing
Payroll Accounting
Payroll Best Practices
Revenue Recognition
Run the Rockies
Running a Public Company
Sales and Operations for Your Small Business
The Controller's Function
The New CFO Financial Leadership Manual
The Ultimate Accountants' Reference
The Vest Pocket Controller's Guide
Throughput Accounting

 **FREE ONLINE RESOURCES BY STEVE BRAGG**

Steve Bragg issues the Accounting Best Practices podcast, which is available on
iTunes and at www.accountingtools.com.

# Running an Effective Investor Relations Department

# CHAPTER ONE

# Managing Investor Relations

T HE WORK OF THE investor relations officer (IRO) centers on communicating the company's current and potential market value to investors. IROs achieve this by targeting a specific set of goals and using a broad range of tools to attain them. They must also be conversant with the methods for constructing a viable investor relations budget. Furthermore, proper management of bad news defines the character of the IRO, and is a key driver of investor faith in a company. All of these topics, and more, are addressed in this chapter.

## WHY HAVE AN INVESTOR RELATIONS DEPARTMENT?

A public company is not required to have a public relations department at all. There is no legal requirement to engage in any communications with the investment community, outside of the required SEC filings. However, when there is no investor relations function, investors must rely solely on media, Internet, and SEC reports, which are all based on historical information or sometimes on conjecture. With this limited pool of information, investors are less inclined to acquire a company's stock, and will certainly not bid it up above the average market valuation of the peer group against which the company is usually compared.

Given this lower stock price, a company's cost of capital tends to be higher, since it will obtain fewer funds per share sold. Also, without strong demand for a stock, its price will tend to be more volatile, with many upward and downward transactions over short periods of time. Further, without a consistent investment message being promulgated by a company, short sellers will be more inclined to feed erroneous information into the marketplace in order to trigger short-term price slides from which they can earn profits.

A low stock price will also attract hostile takeover bids. A case can be made that management's primary objective is to obtain the highest possible stock price for investors, so it should welcome even a hostile tender offer. The problem is that the potential acquirer will undoubtedly offer a price below what the company could have obtained if it had actively worked to achieve a higher stock price!

Thus, the key reason for building an investor relations department is to maximize the company's market value. The IRO does this by continually communicating a company's unique value proposition to the investment community, and specifically through the goals noted in the next section.

## INVESTOR RELATIONS OBJECTIVES AND GOALS

The first step for the IRO in creating an investor relations department is to determine its objectives and supporting goals. The IRO should be very clear about these issues in order to avoid wasting resources in the pursuit of other activities.

Ultimately, the only objective of the investor relations function is to maximize a company's market value. By doing so, the company can obtain the maximum amount of cash in exchange for the fewest number of shares. Also, a strong stock price will keep away hostile takeovers, because the company is too expensive to buy.

IROs should therefore direct considerable attention to the goals that support higher market value:

- ▪ *Alter perception of the company.* If a company has historically been compared to a peer group whose valuation multiples are low, then the IRO will have a difficult time increasing the stock price to a level above that of the peer group. One solution is to reposition the company story to align it with a different peer group whose multiples are higher.
- ▪ *Increase analyst coverage.* The opinions of analysts carry considerable weight with investors, so obtaining coverage from a moderate number

of analysts is a key objective for the IRO. Favorable analyst reports will very likely increase average sales volume, which, in turn, tends to drive up the stock price.

- *Increase geographic coverage.* If a company's stockholders are limited to a few geographic areas, then it does not take long before everyone who wants to hold the stock is already doing so. This results in reduced stock trading and minimal upward pressure on the stock price. The IRO can avoid this by scheduling road shows in new regions to meet with an entirely new group of analysts, brokers, institutional investors, and retail investors.
- *Reduce stock price volatility.* If there are institutional investors who constantly buy and sell large blocks of company stock, then the stock price may swing considerably. Volatility is not a desirable condition, since it drives away some investors and attracts short sellers. To reduce volatility, the IRO can work on attracting retail investors, who hold smaller blocks of stock and tend to retain their holdings longer.
- *Manage existing investors.* If current investors sell their holdings, then the increased supply of stock will likely cause a price reduction, as well as increased price volatility. The IRO can reduce this risk by generating a high level of communication with them, using one-on-one meetings and newsletters. The result should be longer-term retention of investors.

Clearly, the IRO must delve into a broad array of activities to achieve a high market value. The tools available to reach this objective are described in the next section.

##  INVESTOR RELATIONS TOOLS

We have established that the primary investor relations objective is to maximize a company's market value. Before attempting to enhance the price, we must first determine what factors influence it. Two key factors are the condition of the general economy and the condition of the industry in which a company competes. Neither one can be altered by specific company actions, which means that a stock's price will, to some extent, fluctuate irrespective of any investor relations activities. In addition, a stock's price will be governed by a company's operating and financial results, its strategic direction, and the quality of its management team. The IRO can do a great deal to favorably present these later items to the investment community using the tools described in this section.

IROs have a broad array of tools at their disposal, which can be categorized as basic, intermediate, and advanced tools. A basic tool is one needed to accomplish the basic investor relations goals, while more advanced ones are layered on top of the basic tools to achieve the highest possible level of communications with the investment community. The basic tools are as follows:

- *Annual report.* The IRO is expected to manage the creation of an annual report that shows a company's results for the past year and explains its goals and future prospects. A more basic variation on this report is the *wrap report*, which is the annual SEC Form 10-K, accompanied by a letter from the chief executive officer. The wrap report is increasingly common, but conveys no investment message to stockholders.
- *Annual meeting.* The IRO is responsible for organizing the stockholder annual meeting, at which stockholders vote for a board of directors. The IRO can greatly expand on this minimal agenda by including manager presentations, additional decisions to be voted upon, and question and answer sessions.
- *Proxy solicitation.* The IRO is responsible for issuing the annual proxy solicitation, in which the company asks investors to vote for a slate of candidates for board of director positions, and possibly a variety of other motions involving corporate governance.

These basic tools achieve only the most modest level of communication with the investment community. The proxy solicitation and annual meeting are designed to fulfill legal requirements, rather than to enhance communications, while the annual report tends to be a dry recitation of historical facts. Thus, the IRO should use an additional set of intermediate tools to engage in a more active level of stockholder communications:

- *Press release.* A key IRO tool is the press release. This is a brief summary of information about a key company event, such as an acquisition or a major contract award. It is issued through a press release distribution service. The IRO may choose to also issue the same information through a Form 8-K filed with the SEC.
- *Web site.* The investor relations section of a company's Web site is capable of imparting an enormous amount of quality information to investors. If properly constructed and maintained, it can be the primary source of investor information.

- *Fact sheet.* This is a two- to four-page document that lists the essential facts about a company, including its key customers, managers, recent press releases, and mission. The fact sheet can be posted on the company Web site and is also a useful document to bring to external meetings of all kinds as a handout.
- *Reports.* The company Web site can include an offer for any site visitor to sign up for a variety of reports, such as new product notices, product pipeline reports, management newsletters, and earnings releases.
- *Speech transcripts.* If a company officer makes a major speech or presentation, then the investor relations staff can record it, have it transcribed, and post it on the company Web site.
- *Advertising.* An advertising campaign can introduce a company to an entirely new group of potential investors, though it can be expensive in relation to the number of new stockholders obtained. It is not an effective tool for smaller firms with limited investor relations budgets.

These intermediate-level tools are primarily designed to create new information and present it passively for consumption by the investment community. However, an additional level of activity is needed to bring the company face to face with investors and analysts. This requires much more personal involvement by the senior management team, since management must be involved in the presentations. Also, the company is (in some cases) paying for meeting rooms and meals for all participants, which can involve a considerable expense. The advanced tools are as follows:

- *Road show.* The most effective of the advanced investor relations tools is the road show. This is usually a series of meetings in which the CEO, CFO, and IRO present the company to a variety of audiences. The expense of an ongoing series of road shows can be considerable, but it results in the best possible face-to-face contact with the investment community.
- *Conference calls.* It is standard practice to schedule a conference call immediately following the release of a company's quarterly 10-Q report. During this call, company officers discuss the earnings release, and usually allow some time to field questions from attendees.
- *Investor day.* The company invites investors and analysts to a formal series of presentations by company managers. This may be located near the investment community, or at a major company location (in which case a facility tour is expected).

All of the tools noted in the preceding bullet points are described in more detail in Chapters 5, 6, and 7 on public communications, publications, and Web sites.

Once an IRO has set up the most appropriate mix of tools to achieve the objective, the IRO should also create a measurement system to evaluate the effectiveness of those tools. Examples of appropriate metrics are changes in the stock price, the number of requests for financial information, changes in the mix of investors, the number of analysts following the company, trading volume, and the price/earnings ratio in comparison to the market or a peer group. Investor relations metrics are addressed in Chapter 23.

## INVESTOR RELATIONS BUDGET

When constructing a potential budget for investor relations, the best approach is to build it in layers that are based on the need for a variety of activities. The bottom-most layer of the budget should always address entitlements. These are the bare-minimum activities required of any public company. The key item is SEC compliance, where a company must pay for adequate attorney, auditor, and valuation services to file the required number of SEC reports within the designated timelines. The cost of this item may be located within the budget of the accounting department, rather than the investor relations budget—but it has to be addressed *somewhere*.

The minimum-level investor relations budget should also include a salary sufficient to retain the services of a qualified IRO. A company may try to reduce costs by hiring a clearly unqualified person or by promoting a low-level manager into the job. Since the IRO is the primary interface between the company and the investment community, the company is clearly stating how poorly it values investors! If the IRO is of exceptionally low quality, investors will either sell off their holdings or find alternative means of communicating with the company through other managers.

A minor item that is generally included in the bottom layer of the budget is the cost of buying back stock from excessively small stockholders. There are significant proxy costs associated with each share held, including the printing and mailing of a proxy statement and the tallying of annual votes for directors. Depending on the proxy cost per share and the market price per share, it may be cost-effective for a company to offer to buy back its stock from smaller stock-holders. For example, if the total proxy cost for a single stockholder is $20 per year, and the market price of the stock is currently $4, then the IRO can reasonably conclude that buying back the holdings of all stockholders owning five shares or less will result in full payback within one year.

The next layer of the budget is for the minimum amount of investor communications required to keep the investment community aware of the company. This usually includes the cost of responding to investor inquiries, a stockholder hotline, an annual report, a Web site, periodic press releases describing major events, conference calls, and occasional media contacts. Many companies budget only to this level and stop.

At the top layer of the budget is active communications, such as road shows, investor days, and a plethora of reports that are pushed out to a mailing list of investors, analysts, and media contacts. This level of budgeting can be expensive, but also can propel a company into the upper ranks of public companies in terms of investor perception.

An additional defense for a fully funded investor relations department is that the investment community may extrapolate the performance of this department to how well the entire company is run. If the company handles its customers as well as its treats its investors, then it would appear reasonable to an investor that the company's customer base must be satisfied and loyal. When the investment community's sole point of contact is the investor relations staff, it is not unreasonable for them to make this assumption. Thus, a small but well-funded investor relations department can have an inordinate impact on investors.

The layering approach to the investor relations budget is the most logical and easily defended budgeting technique, since it directly ties expenditures to the performance of a specific set of activities. There are other methods for setting the budget, such as a percentage of the total company market capitalization, or a cost per stockholder. However, these methods are far too general, and cannot be tied to specific performance. Also, they fluctuate too much—for example, a company's market capitalization can change so much from year to year that the IRO could see her budget, to which it is tied, slashed or doubled from year to year.

There *is* a defensible high-level justification for an investor relations budget, which is to compare it to the cost of a line of credit or an investment banking relationship. Both activities are also used to acquire funds, so one could make the case that the investor relations budget should be calculated as a percentage of the incremental funds obtained through stock sales, and then compared to the same calculation for these other funding activities. However, a company does not go to the capital markets every year to obtain funds, so there will be years when this comparison will not be functional.

When initially budgeting for investor relations, the IRO should set expectations by pointing out that the program will have little impact in the short term. Investor relations activities require a cumulative long-term effort, with multiple "touches" of the investment community, before a discernible increase in investor interest becomes evident. In the short term, other effects—such as economic downturns, political disturbances, and currency valuation changes—will have such a large impact that they overwhelm the initial effects of a nascent investor relations program. Instead, there must be a long-term, consistently applied budget. Also, there is very little long-term residual value to investor relations activities if they are halted. Even if such a program has been in existence for years, its cumulative effect will vanish once it is stopped. Thus, a public company must permanently commit to a consistently applied and well-funded investor relations department.

 ## FLOAT MANAGEMENT

The primary objective of the IRO is to maximize a company's market valuation. A key driver of this valuation is the number of shares available for trading by the investment community (commonly known as the *float*). If there is a large float, then investors can easily move in and out of stock positions with a minimal impact on the stock price. As noted in this section, there are a number of actions the IRO can take to properly manage the float.

When a company is in need of cash and has a choice of obtaining it through either debt or equity, the IRO should point out to the chief financial officer that increasing the amount of stock outstanding will increase the float (once it is registered). This is especially important if there is currently a small float, since the proportional impact on the float would be significant. When the IRO takes this position, she will likely be arguing against the advice of the CFO, who will note that debt is less expensive than equity, and that issuing more stock will drive up the cost of capital. The CFO is correct in this reasoning, but it is more important for a public company with minimal float to increase that float than it is to maintain a low cost of capital.

The IRO should also be active in having stock registered. If a public company privately issues stock, such as through a Private Investment in Public Equity (PIPE), then those shares cannot be publicly traded until the company files a stock registration document, which must be approved by the SEC. This can be a torturous process, since the SEC may issue multiple iterations of comment letters prior to approval, requiring a company to modify its application and quite possibly other public documents that it had previously filed. The registration process is very expensive and may require well over three months to complete. Despite these obstacles, the IRO should make continual efforts to register stock that cannot currently be publicly traded, in order to increase the float.

If the number of unregistered shares is relatively small, then the registration cost will be prohibitive. In this case, the IRO should wait for additional private stock placements to increase the total number, until such time as the registration process will no longer be cost-prohibitive on a per-share basis. Some private stock placement agreements will require best efforts for a stock registration within a certain period of time, which may force the IRO to file registration documents for a small amount of stock.

If the IRO is successful in having a large amount of privately placed stock registered, she will now be at risk of having the holders of these newly registered shares dump their holdings on the market. If they do so, the sudden overwhelming supply of stock will put significant downward pressure on the stock price. The best way to avoid this problem is to require the stockholders to sign a *lockup agreement*, under which they cannot sell their shares for a certain period of time, or can only sell a certain number of shares within predetermined time blocks (e.g., 50,000 shares per month). A lesser alternative is to recommend to investors that they have their holdings liquidated in an orderly manner through a single brokerage firm, which can attempt to sell stock over a longer period of time. Of the two methods, the first is mandatory, and so tends to function better, especially if the lockup agreement allows the gradual sale of stock, rather than suddenly allowing all shares to be sold at the end of a predetermined holding period.

An overly complex capital structure can also effectively reduce the amount of float. For example, if a company has multiple types of stocks, bonds, warrants, and other equity instruments, then it is diffusing the amount of tradable equity among all of the various equity instruments. A better approach is to simplify the equity structure by trading common stock for all of the other types of stock. This centralizes all equity into a single large pool of tradable stock.

A related issue is that investors tend to avoid owning multiclass stocks, on the grounds that they only have access to nonvoting stocks or stocks with minority voting rights. Investors prefer to have all voting rights centered on the common stock that is available for sale, so that they can vote out a board of directors in the event of inadequate company performance. Thus, having a single class of common stock with full voting rights can increase the pool of stockholders, thereby indirectly increasing the stock price.

Another difficulty is when a company has achieved a large float, but holdings are centralized in the hands of a small number of institutional investors. If these investors are not actively trading stock, then the effective float of the company may be far smaller than the standard float calculation may indicate. The IRO can meet with the larger stockholders to persuade them to sell some portion of their holdings, though an investor who is optimistic about the future performance of his holdings will be unlikely to do this. A better long-range approach is to initiate an ongoing series of road shows to present the company either to brokers or directly to retail investors in order to encourage stock placements with the types of investors who are more likely to create an active trading market.

The IRO should offer advice to the board of directors if it is considering the repurchase of stock. A stock repurchasing program sends a signal to the market that the company considers its stock to be undervalued. It also tends to prop up the stock price, if the company makes it clear that it will buy back stock if the price drops below a predetermined level. Further, it increases earnings per share, since there are fewer shares to divide into earnings. However, it also reduces the volume of stock outstanding, which reduces the float. In most cases, the number of shares authorized for repurchase is so small that the float reduction will be minimal. Thus, the IRO should advise against a stock purchase *only* if the contemplated repurchase is so large that the float will be seriously reduced.

It is also useful to monitor the public filings of competitors to see how they are managing their floats. If they use an innovative approach that appears to work well, then copy it. Conversely, if they have difficulty with float management, learn from their experience and try an alternative method.

In short, there is no such thing as an excessively large or widely distributed float. The IRO should always strive to simplify a complex capital structure, register stock, and persuade retail investors to buy stock, thereby improving the float.

## MANAGING BAD NEWS

Bad news will arise from time to time, and the IRO must be prepared to deal with it. The exact nature of bad news is extremely difficult to predict, since it can come in many forms and may involve a new scenario that has never arisen in the past. Examples of bad news include a hostile takeover attempt, many types of lawsuits, the failure of a key patent application, conflicts with a labor union, and so on. The investment community will adjust a company's stock price not only in reaction to the actual news, but also in accordance with how the company handles the news.

If a particular type of bad news has happened in the past, and there is a reasonable possibility of its recurrence, then the IRO should develop a contingency plan for dealing with that specific item. This plan should encompass a contact list that itemizes which managers and investors will be contacted, where to contact them, who to contact if they are not available, a list of actions to take, and a media contact list. This can include a boilerplate set of press releases. The IRO should include in her schedule of activities an annual review of all contingency plans, to ensure that all responses are still reasonable, and that contact information is still up-to-date. Also, an attorney should periodically review the plans to determine the need for any SEC filings if certain actions are taken.

An excellent way to prepare for bad news is to constantly monitor the affairs of other companies in the same industry. If they fall prey to a particular problem, the IRO should monitor how they deal with it. If a competitor creates an unusually effective response to a situation, then the IRO should copy it directly into her contingency plan for the same scenario.

The IRO should also develop an early-warning system in order to learn about bad news as soon as possible. This means cultivating contacts in the business media and investment community, who will forward any rumors they hear. Also, the IRO should immediately examine company financial statements as soon as they are available for internal distribution, to see if they contain any issues that might prompt queries from investors or analysts. In addition, the IRO should be on the distribution list of any auditor letters outlining potential concerns about company controls. If there is even a slight chance of a strike, then the IRO should be in constant contact with the company's labor negotiator. If there is upcoming legislation that may negatively impact the business (such as pollution controls or import restrictions), then the IRO should be receiving regular updates about the prospective law from a lobbyist or attorney. Even an insider stock sale can be considered bad news. If a manager sells off a massive stock position, the stock price is likely to dive as a result. Consequently, the IRO should be aware of upcoming stock sales and be prepared to discuss the reasons for the sales. Thus, an early warning system should include input from a broad array of information sources.

The early warning system should also monitor the appearance of the *contagion effect*, which sweeps through industries from time to time. In essence, if one company in an industry suffers from a problem, investors will suspect that its competitors may suffer from the same problem, and drive down the stock prices of the entire cluster of firms. Thus, an IRO may find the company caught up in the contagion effect, even though it has done nothing wrong. In these cases, a company's stock price will likely fall, irrespective of any investor relations actions taken. However, it may be possible to quickly drive the price back up by using the early warning system to spot the contagion starting with another company and immediately take steps to tell investors that the company does not suffer from the same problems. For example, if one company suffers a massive loss from not using hedging to cover its foreign currency investments, the IRO should immediately sponsor a press release detailing the extent of hedging activities used by her company, and how this has kept the company from incurring similar losses.

The contagion effect may begin at the IRO's company. If so, the IRO could deliberately unleash the contagion effect on competitors by being the first one to issue bad news to the investment community. By being first, the IRO has the time to craft the best possible message for how the company is dealing with the bad news. Competitors will hopefully be caught off guard by the announcement, and will therefore appear less prepared than the initiating company.

Whenever an early warning system uncovers a potential issue, the IRO should immediately draft a plan to deal with it, along with associated press releases. The plan may never be needed, but it is important to create the plan before any inquiry ever arrives from the public, so that the management team can spend more time considering the appropriate response and level of disclosure, and less time ruminating over the basic plan.

The IRO can also take an extremely proactive approach to bad news by recommending mitigation plans to the CEO, and publicizing the implementation of those plans. For example, if there is no obvious successor to the CEO, the IRO can recommend the enactment of a succession plan, and set up media interviews with division presidents to show the depth of management. As another example, if an oil company is at risk of having an oil tanker cause a pollution incident on the high seas, then enact a plan to convert to double-hulled ships, and create a media campaign to advertise this action.

If the bad news involves allegations that an employee or the company itself has done something illegal, then the IRO (after suitable discussion with counsel) should immediately announce the situation, point out that a mitigation plan is being developed to reduce the risk of the event reoccurring, actively cooperate with the justice enforcement authorities, and promptly pay any fines imposed. The worst thing a company can do in this situation is to appear defensive; the media love to report on conflict and so will keep the story in front of the investment community for far longer than would have been the case if the company had simply revealed the situation at once and taken mitigation steps.

If bad news occurs and there is no contingency plan for it, then the IRO should first assess the extent of the damage caused by the news. In many cases, the "damage" will disappear within a few days or weeks, as the stock price returns to historic levels. However, if the damage appears to be impacting key stockholder beliefs about the company, such as its brand name or product quality, then further action will be necessary. The IRO should focus on mitigating the lingering effects of the bad news that threaten to permanently impair the stock price. For example, if a company product causes the death of a consumer, then the company should immediately announce the hiring of a quality assurance consultant to independently investigate the cause of the problem. Without this sort of prompt action, it would be reasonable to expect investors to put downward pressure on the stock price.

If there is a solid block of bad news that the IRO must reveal to the marketplace, then the best approach is to issue all of it at once, rather than dribbling it out over a period of time in the hope that the company can mitigate some of the damage before needing to publicize it. By addressing the problem in its entirety at one time, the stock price will suffer a one-time drop, but the IRO can then focus on informing the market about remedial actions, which will gradually bring the stock price back up. If the alternative method of spreading out the bad news were to be used, then investors would gradually form the opinion that the management team is not credible, ultimately resulting in a longer and more profound price dip.

Also, when releasing bad news, present it prominently and clear of any other items that may distract readers from the underlying issue. By doing so, investors gain the impression that the company is maintaining a high level of candor in revealing its problems. The worst way to release bad news is to bury it in the financial statement footnotes, in the hope that no one will see it. A diligent investor or analyst always reads the footnotes, and will not appreciate having to dig so deep to uncover potentially critical information. Also, a company's propensity to mask bad news will trickle through the investment community, eventually resulting in the departure of some investors and downward pressure on the stock price.

The IRO should periodically keep investors updated on the company's progress in resolving its issues. This does not require continual communications if there is no change in the underlying situation – only a notification when there is a material change.

In many bad-news situations, the IRO should plan to contact a select group of the largest stockholders to discuss the situation and the company's planned response to it (within the bounds of the SEC's disclosure rules). This is particularly important in the event of a proxy battle or hostile takeover attempt, when the concurrence of key stockholders will be vital. For these events, the IRO should prepare in advance a rough draft of a message to be sent to the key stockholders, preferably by e-mail, with a follow-up by express mail. This means that the IRO must collect e-mail address information in advance from the major investors, and continually update this list.

If a company has suffered through a string of bad news over a protracted period of time, then it is possible that investors are fleeing the stock, whose price is therefore dropping. Under this scenario, there is no easy way to win back the existing shareholder base. Instead, consider repositioning the company story and selling it to an entirely new audience. This may require a corporate name change, the sale of whichever divisions were causing the bulk of the problems, and a series of road shows into entirely new geographic regions in order to attract a new base of investors.

In short, the primary goal when dealing with bad news is to handle it in such a manner that a company's long-term market capitalization is preserved, or even enhanced. Short-term pricing dips are not especially important, as long as the long-term value is not damaged.

##  RESPONDING TO RUMORS

A rumor may arise that circulates through the investment community and noticeably impacts the stock price. If a company waits long enough, the rumor will likely die out and the stock price will return to its normal level. If asked about the rumor, the IRO can simply state that the company does not respond to rumors and speculation. This lack of action may harm shareholder value in the short term, but is unlikely to do so over the long term.

However, there may be cases where the rumor is so egregious that it impacts customers' view of the company and may cause a sales decline. In this case, the IRO may be tempted to refute the rumor, either through a press release or some other public means. While this may seem like a judicious response, it can create a precedent where investors now expect the company to refute rumors. If it does not do so, then investors will think that the rumor is correct, which may prolong its impact. Thus, it is generally best *not* to respond to rumors except under extraordinary circumstances.

## SUMMARY

Ultimately, the IRO is responsible for maximizing a company's market valuation over the long term. This requires the use of a multitude of tools to communicate a company's unique value proposition to the investment community. It also calls for the proper handling of bad news in order to avoid an artificially low stock price, which many IROs would consider the most difficult part of their jobs. The net result of a consistently applied communications campaign and adroit handling of bad news should yield a higher stock price than would be the case without an investor relations department, as well as prices that vary within a relatively narrow price range. These results justify the investor relations budget.

2

# Investor Relations Officer Position

A WELL-RUN INVESTOR RELATIONS function can add a massive amount to a company's market valuation, and so should be viewed as a strongly value-added area. Accordingly, a company should hire into the IRO position a very highly qualified individual. This chapter discusses the key aspects of the IRO position, expands upon those criteria with a formal job description, and then addresses the uses to which additional investor relations staff can be put.

## KEY ASPECTS OF THE IRO POSITION

Several of the most important aspects of the IRO position are noted in this section, touching on the IRO's experience level, knowledge base, and reporting relationships.

Experience with the company is a key consideration for an IRO candidate, since this person should have a detailed understanding of how the company operates and should know the managers who run the various divisions. Otherwise, the IRO will be dangerously dependent on other people for information to pass along to the investment community, and will be unable to discern which information might be misleading. There are two ways for an IRO to obtain a sufficient level of experience. One is to promote an internal person to the position who has been in a series of responsible positions with the company for many years. The alternative is to bring in an outsider with strong IRO skills, and to then force this person through a detailed company review process that includes multiple meetings with all key company personnel.

Even if an IRO already has a strong operational background with a company, this does not mean that the IRO can afford to stop keeping close contact with all aspects of the company. On the contrary, the IRO should regularly attend a broad range of operational, executive, and board meetings. By doing so, the IRO will stay in close touch with both upcoming and ongoing issues that may impact the message being given to investors.

The IRO is in the unique position of having a valid demand on the time of both the CEO and CFO. These individuals are responsible for making presentations to the investor community through road shows, conference calls, and the annual investor meeting. Since IROs are responsible for the management of all these activities, they must work closely with company CEOs and CFOs to schedule their time, as well as to assist in crafting their presentations.

The IRO must set herself up as an internal critic on behalf of investors. In this role, she keeps track of the investor messages that have been used in the past and the responses received from investors about the company's strategic positioning. By doing so, she can critique changes to that message and give the CEO and CFO feedback regarding the positioning of the company in a manner that will yield the highest possible stock valuation. This can be an extremely difficult role, requiring a considerable amount of backbone to point out a flaw in a company's strategic direction that no one else wishes to discuss.

Given the need for an IRO person with considerable experience, contacts throughout the company, a close relationship with senior management, and independent standing as a critic, it is apparent that the IRO position can only be given to someone with the experience and expertise of a senior-level employee.

An IRO must have a solid grounding in finance and accounting principles. Investors expect and deserve to have someone in the IRO role who knows what financial information they need, why it is useful, and how to obtain it. This does not mean that IROs must have a college degree in accounting or finance, but such a background should certainly be considered a plus for the position. There are also several master's degree programs specifically targeted at investor relations that provide an excellent grounding in the financial and accounting concepts needed for this position.

At a minimum, IROs should have a demonstrated knowledge of not only accounting and finance principles, but also of the unique aspects of accounting terminology and rules for the company's industry. For example, there are unique accounting terms used in the oil and gas exploration business that are used nowhere else, as well as industry-specific accounting standards. Investors will expect the IRO to know the "lingo," and to have a firm grasp of how the company interprets industry-specific accounting standards.

IROs should have a detailed knowledge of a company's short-term and long-term financing needs, so that she knows approximately when the company plans to offer new debt or equity instruments to the public, and can be prepared with the appropriate message to the investment community.

IROs must also have an excellent knowledge of the capital markets and how they operate, which should include experience in dealing with representatives of both the sell side and buy side of the investment community. This requirement is usually a weak point for anyone promoted into the IRO position from an accounting position, and is the main reason why so many IROs have Wall Street backgrounds.

The ability to write is a key requirement of the IRO position. There is a continual need for press releases, investor reports, and speeches by top-level management, and the IRO is expected to provide this information. If there is no other staff, then the IRO will be expected to either do the writing herself, or outsource the task to a press release or speechwriter. However, even if all writing chores are outsourced or handed off to someone else within the company, IROs are still responsible for the final product, and so must be capable of editing any written materials to be issued to the investing public.

IROs need some communication skills, though they do not need to be as highly honed as was the case for writing skills. IROs are mostly involved in introducing the CEO or CFO during road shows or formal presentations, and in coordinating conference calls where (again) the CEO and CFO are doing the talking. IROs are not really expected to make lengthy, solo presentations or speeches on behalf of the company.

Also, IROs should be available on extremely short notice to answer questions from the investment community. The company always has a core set of investors with whom a strong and ongoing dialog is essential, and it cannot afford to have protracted delays in responding to their queries. Accordingly, an IRO should be a frequent user of voicemail and e-mail, even when on the road. Also, the IRO should have an administrative assistant who can efficiently respond to minor queries while proactively tracking down the IRO to handle more critical responses.

IROs must also have considerable planning expertise. This includes the ability to audit the existing investor relations function, determine its strengths and weaknesses, and to then craft an investor relations plan that will optimize both the company's message to the investor community and its mix of investors. A key part of this planning requirement is the ability to manage several staff, and quite possibly the services of one or more investor relations consulting firms.

Finally, to whom should the IRO report? There are three common alternatives, which are the CEO, CFO, and director of public relations. The CEO is the best choice, because the IRO gains the authority of the top company manager to obtain access to information throughout the company, and to construct the best and most consistent investor relations message. The CFO is the next best choice, since the IRO inherits slightly less authority, but gains a supervisor with a good knowledge of the investor community. The director of public relations is the worst choice, because the message the IRO is trying to create and maintain may be in danger of being subordinated to the public relations function, which typically alters its messages about the company with considerably greater frequency than a more independent IRO would consider reasonable.

Having pointed out that the IRO should not report to the director of public relations, the issue also arises of having the public relations function issue a message that varies from that being issued by the IRO. To avoid having diverging information reach the public, consider having both the IRO and the public relations function report to the same position. By doing so, the supervisor of both activities can ensure that a common message is being delivered.

##  IRO JOB DESCRIPTION

The IRO job description will vary by company, depending on the specific requirements of the situation. Nonetheless, the following job description contains the key requirements generally expected of an IRO, to which one can then make alterations to match the circumstances.

Reports to: chief executive officer or chief financial officer
Responsibilities include:

- Develops and maintains a company investor relations plan.
- Performs a comprehensive competitive analysis, including financial metrics and differentiation.
- Develops and monitors performance metrics for the investor relations function.

- Establishes the optimum type and mix of shareholders, and creates that mix through a variety of targeting initiatives.
- Monitors operational changes through ongoing contacts with company management, and develops investor relations messages based on these changes.
- Provides Regulation FD (Fair Disclosure) training to all company spokespersons.
- Creates presentations, press releases, and other communication materials for earnings releases, industry events, and presentations to analysts, brokers, and investors.
- Creates the text of the quarterly earnings statement.
- Oversees the production of all annual reports, SEC filings, and proxy statements.
- Manages the investor relations portion of the company Web site.
- Monitors analyst reports and summarizes them for senior management.
- Serves as key point of contact for the investment community.
- Establishes and maintains relationships with stock exchange representatives.
- Organizes conferences, road shows, earnings conference calls, and investor meetings.
- Provides feedback to management regarding the investment community's perception of the company.
- Represents the views of the investor community to the management team in the development of corporate strategy.
- Provides feedback to the management team regarding the impact of stock repurchase programs or dividend changes on the investment community.

**Qualifications:**

- 10+ years accounting/finance experience. Must be able to explain financial statements and footnotes in detail.
- 5+ years experience in managing the investor relations department of a company with at least a $___ market capitalization.
- BA/BS degree
- Excellent written and verbal communication skills
- Excellent relationship-building skills with the investment community
- Excellent collaborative skill in working with the executive team
- Ability to maintain a 50 percent travel schedule

##  INVESTOR RELATIONS TEAM

The investor relations team varies in size from 1 to as many as 20 employees. In a small-cap company, the IRO will be expected to fulfill most investor relations functions with minimal support. In a Fortune 500 company, the IRO can expect up to 10 staff, while the largest multinational firms may employ as many as 20 people within the investor relations department.

Larger investor relations departments usually allocate work based on those serving institutional investors and those dealing with retail investors; the typical result is that most of the investor relations staff focuses on the buy side. Other IROs assign some staff to servicing the sell side and others to the buy side. The work assignment decision is driven by the following factors:

- ■ *Current shareholder mix.* If there is currently a large proportion of one type of investor, then the IRO should assign more staff to servicing that group. Thus, a large institutional investor presence will logically require more staffing to serve them.
- ■ *Budgeted shareholder mix.* If the IRO decides to alter the shareholder mix, such as to obtain more long-term retail investors, then this may call for a substantial shift in resources to market to the target investor group.
- ■ *Analysts.* If the company is large enough to attract the attention of a large number of analysts, then it makes sense to shift more staff into handling the sell side.

Those investor relations staff assigned to institutional investors are responsible for managing the release of financial information at the end of each quarter and year-end, which includes the quarterly conference call, and any press releases as needed. This group also arranges any on-site visits from analysts and fulfills analyst requests for information. Further, it handles relations with any stock exchanges where the company's stock is listed. A manager who reports to the IRO may supervise this group.

The staff assigned to retail investors develops retail marketing campaigns, and handles interactions with the company's stock transfer agent. It also updates information on the investor relations section of the company Web site (since the primary user is the retail investor), creates the annual report, and manages all meetings with stockbrokers. Another manager who also reports to the IRO may supervise this group.

Most sell-side firms direct their activities at institutional investors, and so are best serviced by the company's institutional investor group. In the rare cases where a sell-side firm markets to retail investors, it makes more sense to support them with the company's retail investor group.

It is less certain which of the two groups should manage road shows, since a single road show may market the company to both institutional and retail investors. Thus, the road show is more likely to be a jointly managed activity, unless road shows are to be separately organized for each type of investor.

A final consideration is to ensure that some work is shifted to the company's stock transfer agent, who is responsible for maintaining the company's stock records. The transfer agent should handle all investor calls regarding such issues as purchasing stock directly from the company, reporting lost stock certificates, gifting of stock, and responding to proxy voting materials. The transfer agent's contact information should be prominently displayed on a company's printed materials and Web site, so that investors will not contact the investor relations department about these issues. In cases where large companies experience a massive amount of shareholder contacts, it may even make sense to have the transfer agent base an employee in the corporate headquarters, next to the investor relations staff. This person acts as the liaison to the transfer agent, and can also respond to investor issues that are routed through the company.

The IRO should monitor any complaints received from investors about the quality of service they receive from the stock transfer agent, and take remedial action as needed. This is an important issue, since the transfer agent represents the company. In rare cases involving unusually poor customer service, it may be necessary to switch to a new transfer agent.

## IRO AS MANAGEMENT REPRESENTATIVE

The IRO acts as the go-to person for the bulk of all inquiries from the investment community. This means that the IRO can directly answer most questions, with the rest of the management team never having to be involved, and probably not even knowing the nature of the inquiries. This is entirely appropriate behavior for most external interactions. However, the IRO should not act as an impenetrable shield behind which the management team hides. In such a situation, investors will be more likely to turn their attention to other companies that provide more open access to management.

To avoid turning away investors, the IRO must selectively provide access to other managers. This can occur at scheduled events, where the managers know they must be prepared to make presentations well in advance. Investors and analysts should be made aware of when additional management access will occur, so they can prepare accordingly, and be ready with questions targeted at those individuals. By providing access on a scheduled basis, the investment community still gets access to management, while the IRO still handles the bulk of investor inquiries on an ongoing basis.

## SUMMARY

This chapter has outlined key aspects of the IRO position that are critical to the proper performance of investor relations. The primary issue to be aware of when selecting someone for the IRO position is that she will represent the company with the investment community, and for that reason, must be of the highest quality. This is one of the worst possible positions in which to employ an inept or inexperienced person.

The job requirements noted here make it clear that the IRO position requires such a broad array of knowledge that very few individuals are capable of filling the position. Given the difficulty of the position, consider the extensive use of consultants to bolster the weaker skills of the IRO. This can include the use of press release writers, investor relations consultants, accountants, and public relations consultants. The proper mix of these professionals will depend on the resources available in-house, the IRO's initial skill set, and the varying needs of the company over time.

Companies with larger investor relations budgets can support the IRO with more staff, who are usually split into two subgroups—one to service institutional investors and one to service retail investors.

3

# Creating the Company Story

NVESTOR RELATIONS IS ESSENTIALLY a marketing function that uses public relations tools to further the financial goals of a company. In public relations, a broad array of information is being transmitted to the public. In investor relations, the information being issued is much more narrowly focused, centering on the company story. The story must be succinct, because investors may not invest in a stock if they have difficulty understanding it—they equate a complex story with a high level of risk. In this chapter, we will address how to create and package the company story, as well as how long to retain it and the extent to which the company should be altered to match the story.

##  CREATING THE STORY

Creating the company story can require a considerable amount of time. To do so requires a methodical process called the *investor relations audit.* First, the IRO gathers information about the company from its public filings, interviews the management team about the company's strengths and weaknesses, notes industry trends, and identifies peer companies and their stories. Based on this preliminary set of information, the IRO creates several one-sentence stories for the company, each one succinctly stating what the company does. The story generally focuses on the key product line or service provided. Here are some examples:

- The company creates fine stemware for discerning wine drinkers.
- The company retrofits helicopters as air ambulances.
- The company builds environmentally friendly homes.

This process invariably results in a multitude of iterations before the management team can agree on the most simple and direct message that clearly conveys the company story while maximizing its valuation. For example, the first message, "the company creates fine stemware for discerning wine drinkers," implies that the company focuses on high-priced crystal that is sold at only the best retail establishments. This firmly positions the company as a purveyor of luxury goods (with a correspondingly high market valuation comparable to that of such companies as Christian Dior and LVMH Moet Hennessy). If the message had instead been, "the company sells glassware," the story might still accurately describe the company, but positions it with investors as an ordinary manufacturer of kitchen supplies, with a lower market valuation.

Alternatively, if a company were to use the preceding story example of "the company retrofits helicopters as air ambulances," then it could attempt to position itself as a helicopter manufacturer in order to gain multiples similar to those of Textron or Boeing. However, since this is a considerable conceptual stretch, it is entirely possible that the marketplace will ignore this positioning, and instead assign a valuation closer to that of the suppliers of automobile interiors, such as Lear, Visteon, and Delphi. Thus, it is important to create a story that realistically links the company to a valid peer group.

A key part of the story creation process is to compare the story to those of other companies to see how the story impacts valuation. For example, a geospatial services company found that its production services business only had a multiple with comparable businesses of 1.0 times revenues in the marketplace, while its geospatial databases business had a multiple of 3.5 times revenues. Given this massive disparity in comparable valuations, it created a story line around its databases business and applied it to the entire company, promptly tripling its market valuation. Thus, the single most important factor in the development of the story is to identify those factors most closely associating the company with an enhanced valuation, and then leverage those factors through the initial formulation and subsequent packaging of the story.

Another issue that arises for many companies is the presence of disparate divisions that make it difficult to create a coordinated, seamless story. In this case, don't try—instead, break the company into separate reporting segments in order to clearly identify the results of the divisions, and then formulate a separate story for each one. This allows investors to more easily focus on the results and prospects of each one. However, this may also lead to a lower overall valuation; each segment will have a different peer group, likely with different valuations, and investors may elect to assign a total valuation based on the peer group having the lower valuation. In these cases, a possible alternative is to sell off the division having the lower peer valuation (see the "Matching the Company to the Story" section).

An integral part of the story creation process is to obtain feedback from the investment community. Specifically, if there is a relationship with investment bankers, then obtain their input to craft a message that resonates best with the investors from whom the company may eventually seek funding. Investment bankers are ideal for this task, because their job is to assist companies in obtaining funding, which requires packaging a presentation to investors that is most likely to raise capital. Thus, investment bankers have considerable experience in determining what stories are least or most likely to result in a high valuation.

When developing the company story, remember that a single sentence should be sufficient. Do not burden investors with a confusing array of detail that may span multiple paragraphs. This can be difficult for the CEO who likes to bury the audience with a vast array of information. Too much information creates noise that interferes with investors' ability to grasp the underlying dynamics of the business. If the story is too long, then throw out all extraneous details until the core message is clearly visible.

##  PACKAGING THE STORY

Once the basic story line is completed, the IRO must carefully build upon it to emphasize how this is an excellent prospective investment opportunity. To properly package a story, start with the story line, and amplify and enhance it with supporting information.

For example, a company may have a number of high-profile customers. If so, the story can borrow from the credibility of those customers. The following example begins with the story line, and enhances it by itemizing key customers:

> The company is the primary provider of drilling platform maintenance services in the Rocky Mountain region to such major oil and gas exploration companies as Anadarko, ExxonMobil, and ConocoPhillips.

As another example, a company may have patented a superior form of technology that places it in a defensible competitive position. It can supplement its basic story line to incorporate the technology, as in the following example:

The company creates advertising programs in public spaces. It is rapidly acquiring market share through its patented use of wrap-around LCD displays, which can be mounted on columnar kiosks.

A variation on the use of patents to package the story is to state the percentage of company products or sales that are covered by patents. An example follows:

The company produces laser rangefinders for commercial surveyors. Of its product sales, 80% are covered by a series of interlocking patents that make it difficult for competitors to produce similar devices.

Another possibility is to emphasize a company's ability to enter new geographical regions by rapidly opening new stores. This capability is of the greatest value in the retail sector. An example is:

The company sells chai tea latte drinks through portable kiosks. It grows through cooperative agreements with national retail chains that allow it to position the kiosks outside their store locations, resulting in hundreds of new locations per agreement.

It is also possible to emphasize the size or quality of a company's sales capability. This can be a subtle and not especially valuable distinction—"our salespeople are better than your salespeople"—so it is better to emphasize the sheer number of sales staff, which is more easily verifiable. An example is:

The company creates drugs targeted at skin cancer patients. The company's products outsell all competing drugs because of its direct sales staff, which is as large as the sales departments of all other competitors combined.

A variation on the sales angle is the sales channel being used. For example, Dell Inc. has spent years touting its direct sales model that allows customers to custom-order a computer directly through the Dell web site. In Dell's case, this sales channel turned out to be unusually difficult to duplicate, generating a significant differentiating factor. However, Dell is also an unusual case—for most companies, the sales channel is not a differentiating factor, so be careful about packaging it with the company story.

Marketing can also be included in the story packaging, but only if there is a significant long-term investment in product or company branding that results in strong name recognition. An example is:

> The company creates a variety of dental products under the WhiteNow! brand name. It has spent 10% of revenues on a branding campaign for the past five years, and plans to continue that effort in the future.

The competence of the management team can be included in the story packaging. This element must be used with care, since there must be a clear differentiating factor that separates a management team from those of other companies, and which provides the employing company with a clear, long-term competitive advantage. An example follows:

> The company represents the products of its commercial clients to the Department of Defense. It employs retired generals and admirals for this work, who leverage their federal government networks to achieve consistently excellent sell-through results for clients.

An overused type of story packaging is an emphasis on low costs. This approach should only be used by larger, high-volume companies who have long-term sustainable cost advantages in their industries. Any other company who wraps its story in a low-cost package will likely be forced to back away from this approach over time, as larger companies take away its cost leadership. If a company insists on this approach, then consider emphasizing such highly specific cost-reduction topics as an unusually small number of corporate personnel, the use of telemarketing or Web site sales, or capacity constraint analysis. An example is:

> The company produces low-cost footwear for third world countries. Since low prices are the key to success in these markets, the company maintains low cost leadership by developing highly advanced and patented rubber sole molding equipment.

Another option is to use that segment of the business considered the most attractive by investors as an initial storyline "hook," which then draws them into a discussion of the company's core business. A classic example is Ball Corporation, which is primarily in the stodgy business of making vast numbers of cans. However, its small Ball Aerospace subsidiary builds instrument packages for satellites, as well as the Deep Impact probe that was deliberately rammed into a comet in 2005. What a great story line an enterprising IRO could build from this scenario!

The same approach applies to any attractive or high-demand product, regardless of its contribution to earnings. As long as it is the most readily recognizable product to investors, then it makes sense to package the product into the story as a hook to spark investor interest.

Story packaging must also involve the integration of current and projected financial results into the basic storyline. This is necessary, because investors must be able to view the story in the context of the actual operating entity. Here is an example:

> The company sells chai tea latte drinks through portable kiosks. To concentrate on this aspect of its business, we sold our coffee-vending segment during the last quarter, resulting in a $280,000 loss. Absent that segment, we expect ongoing gross margins of 45% and net income of 12%.

The preceding example tells investors a great deal—that the company has elected to be narrowly focused on what it believes to be a profitable niche, and that its sale of an unrelated segment has caused a loss (which otherwise could have been interpreted as a loss from the remaining segment). Also, the company is now willing to provide earnings guidance, which speaks to its confidence in the future results of its chosen segment.

When creating packaging to enhance the core story, be sure to include only information that shows how the company is an excellent investment. For example, if a company has developed a franchising model that is proven to result in profits and is repeatable, then this is excellent packaging from the viewpoint of a prospective investor. As another example, point out the maintenance revenue stream from the latest line of production equipment, if the product life span is lengthy, and the associated maintenance revenue is equally long-term. In short, hone the story packaging to highlight what the company does, and specifically how this translates into an excellent investment opportunity.

## STRATEGIC CREDIBILITY

When designing and packaging the company story, an enormously important factor to consider is the company's credibility in having met its goals in the past.

If a company continually swaps out stories, trying and failing to operationally attain each newly crafted image, the investment community will collectively yawn over any new stories, and ignore the company.

If this has happened in the past, the IRO must work on regaining the trust of investors by sticking with a story and then issuing a stream of detailed press releases about how the company is consistently following through on what it stated in the story. Investors will still be cagey about investing, so this may require several years of effort before investors conclude that the company has mended its investor relations problems, and can now be relied upon to reliably define itself and act in a predictable manner.

Even if a company has reliably stood by a defensible story in the past, it may still make the mistake of creating a new story that it does not have the strategic capability to attain. For example, a startup telecommunications company has no chance of attaining market leadership in such a massively entrenched industry, and so should not say as much in its story. Instead, the IRO should focus the management team's attention on what the company is currently capable of achieving, and use that information to craft a story that has some degree of strategic credibility.

## CLARIFYING AND MITIGATING RISK

The primary focus of a story and its packaging is to reveal an investment opportunity. However, investors are also concerned with investment risk. If a company has problems, they could result in poor future results that in turn yield investment losses. These problems can take a variety of forms. For example, a company may be second in market position in its key industry, or several of its products may be reaching the end of their life cycles, or it may be faced with lawsuits from a faulty product. If investors cannot quantify these risks, then they will probably discount the company's stock price by an inordinate amount.

To avoid an excessive stock price reduction, lay out the key problems as part of the company story, and describe how the company intends to resolve them. For example, having reduced market share also means that there is considerable opportunity to capture a bigger share by a variety of techniques. If products are becoming too old, then describe the product development pipeline and how new products are poised to replace the old ones. If there is a product-related lawsuit, then describe the steps the company has taken to bolster product quality. By formally addressing problems as part of the company story, investors can now see how the company is clarifying and mitigating risks. This extra level of explanation tends to cap the amount by which investors will reduce a stock's price to compensate for risk, which has the added benefit of reducing stock price variability.

An unusual problem is having *too much* market share. Though a management team may be vigorously patting itself on the back for owning 95% of a market, investors will take a different view—that there is no room for further growth in that market. To mitigate these concerns, always emphasize the steps being taken to maintain the existing market share. Next, describe how the company intends to expand the range of products sold, in order to expand the overall size of the market. Finally, describe any steps being taken to encroach upon related markets in which the company can use its existing strengths to garner market share. Thus, a variety of techniques must be used to allay concerns about an excessively high market share.

Using market share as part of the company story may not even be a good idea. In some industries, the scope of a market is not clearly defined, and may be difficult for an investor to verify. Also, if a company does not expect to achieve consistent, measurable increases in market share over a long period of time, or if there is a risk of losing market share, then it makes little sense to even mention the topic.

As another example of how to deal with problems, some element of a company's business may be seasonal or subject to outside factors that make its results vary considerably over the course of a year. If so, it is better to forewarn investors of fluctuating results as part of the story packaging, so they are not surprised when results sometimes vary considerably from their expectations. Here are some examples of how to deal with seasonality:

- The company sells jet-turbine snow blowers to municipalities, with most sales during the fall. It is creating a distribution network in Australia, New Zealand, and South Africa to expand its sales season.
- The company manufactures premium patio furniture for the summer selling season and retro wooden skis during the winter season.

In both examples, the company does not reveal that there is a problem—it only clarifies when most sales occur, and lets the investment community draw its own conclusions from that information. These examples typify how to deal with problem areas—clarify the information and, if necessary, state what the company plans to do about it.

Another option for clarifying risk is to develop a worst-case scenario based on past business cycles, and create a contingency plan for how the company would deal with such a situation, preferably while keeping it profitable. The management team can discuss the plan during road shows and conference calls, and even post it on the company Web site. The contingency plan is useful not only for defining how bad the worst case is likely to be but also for reassuring investors regarding how the company can potentially deal with it. Of course, the company has to be clear in stating that this is merely a *scenario*, not a *forecast* of upcoming conditions!

##  COMPANY REPUTATION

When creating and packaging a company story, the primary emphasis is on the potential return to the investor, followed by the clarification and mitigation of risks, as previously addressed. A third element to consider is the company reputation. This is less clearly linked to company valuation, and so generally receives considerably less attention from IROs. Nonetheless, proper long-term attention to a variety of reputation-enhancing issues can potentially result in some increases in a company's market value, and so should not be ignored. Here are six ways to enhance a company's reputation:

1. *Corporate governance.* Address the steps the company has taken to comply with the provisions of the Sarbanes–Oxley Act, as well as the independence and experience level of the board of directors and its various committees.
2. *Compliance with accounting standards.* It is possible to enhance a reputation by adopting new accounting standards before their use becomes mandatory, thereby establishing the company as a leader in this area. At a minimum, try to follow the interpretation of accounting standards generally used by peer companies. The worst impact on reputation occurs when a company adopts an aggressive stance on an accounting standard that inflates its reported results, since this sets up the company as a target for action by the media and the SEC.
3. *Local community support.* One of the best ways to burnish a reputation is to endorse active, long-term involvement in local community activities wherever the company has a facility. Such efforts are remembered not only by local citizens but also by the local media, who are more easily swayed to write favorable stories about the company. A useful side benefit is that people living near company facilities are more likely to become

investors, and to hold their shares for longer periods than the norm. Examples of local community activities are the support of local arts events, road cleanup campaigns, and contributing to the funding of civic buildings.

4. *Customer loyalty.* If a company retains its customers for many years, then this implies that some aspects of its reputation have impressed the customers, and so is an indirect indicator of reputation. To report on customer loyalty, emphasize that portion of the customer base with the longest retention, or describe the customer dropout rate, if it is unusually low.

5. *Pollution controls.* Point out if the company has complied with environmental regulations ahead of time, if its pollution control standards exceed those mandated by law, or if it has recently upgraded to the latest pollution control equipment. If the company is actively developing "green" technologies, is using environmentally friendly facilities, or has a comprehensive recycling program, then publicize these activities.

6. *Corporate culture.* The corporate culture is an extremely "soft" aspect of a company's reputation that can be easily besmirched with something as insignificant as the threat of a harassment lawsuit, even if no lawsuit materializes. Consequently, most companies do not invest a great deal of time in promoting their culture as part of the investor relations function. However, it can be quite useful for attracting new employees, especially if there is an emphasis on promoting from within, an employee stock ownership plan, flexible work hours, and the like. Thus, if the human resource department wants to promote the company's culture, then the IRO should certainly consider riding on the coattails of this effort.

A company's reputation will only yield a discernible increase in valuation if its efforts in this area have yielded extraordinary recognition in the marketplace. In most cases, reputation is considered to drive *reductions* in valuation, rather than improvements. In other words, the IRO must ensure that publicity efforts, at a minimum, position the company to have a reputation no worse than those of its peers. Conversely, investing too much in publicizing a company's reputation will not usually be cost-effective in increasing its valuation. There are rare cases where a company achieves such noteworthy success in its field (usually in consumer goods) that it becomes a *cult stock* that investors will pay a premium to invest in, and will hold for an inordinate period of time. However, the number of such companies is quite small, so the probability of attaining and maintaining such status is quite poor.

##  MATCHING THE COMPANY TO THE STORY

It is not at all necessary to have a company story that matches current circumstances. Instead, the story should tell where a company intends to go, rather than where it is now. Stock prices are driven by the prospect of future performance, rather than historical results, so where the company intends to go is the most crucial part of the story.

The real driver of long-term improvements in the stock price is to gradually alter the company to match its story. For example, a company's story says that it will expand its consulting services to the federal defense agencies, but it is currently burdened with two unrelated divisions. The appropriate management action would be to sell off those two divisions and use the proceeds to acquire companies in the targeted market space.

All actions taken to more closely align a company with its story should be promptly and continually communicated to the investment community. This creates a favorable opinion of the company's ability to eventually fulfill the promise indicated by its story.

If a company creates a new story, then investors will closely observe how well the management team transitions the company to match the story. A briskly efficient transaction will bolster confidence in the company, while a bumbling execution will be guaranteed to reduce investor confidence and yield a reduced stock price.

##  DURATION OF THE STORY

The management team should stick to its story for as long as possible, because investors like consistency. If the story varies every few months, then the impression in the marketplace will be that the company is continuing to cast about for a strategy that works. Instead, concentrate on refining a core message that does not deviate for years. This shows consistency, the ability to focus on the same strategy, and attention to a specific market niche for which the investment community can easily develop comparative stock price valuations. The result will be consistent stock price performance, with reduced price variability.

If it becomes apparent that the company must change its story, then the IRO should explain why the old story became obsolete, and how the management team is now using the company's core capabilities as the foundation for a new story. For example, if a large national competitor moves into a company's retailing niche, this is an understandable reason to alter the story to state that the company is now shifting its retailing operations solely into smaller markets where large competitors cannot cost-effectively compete.

Selling off a subsidiary is a relatively common event that can be construed as a departure from the company story. When negotiating for a subsidiary sale, or investigating its closure, the IRO should say nothing, on the grounds that the contemplated event may not occur. Once the sale or closure is completed, the IRO has several options for presenting this information. The best option is to show how the company is now focusing on its story even more by having eliminated a subsidiary that was unrelated to the core business. The most difficult option is to confess that the company was unable to integrate the subsidiary or experienced poor profitability from it; but if this was the case, then say so at once in order to avoid speculation by the investment community, and then focus on how much better the company would have been and will be without the subsidiary.

 ## COORDINATION WITH PUBLIC RELATIONS

There is nothing more frustrating for the IRO than to create and disseminate a finely tuned story, and then see the public relations staff launch a publicity blitz that contravenes that story. Furthermore, the public relations function generally does not have as long-term a focus as the investor relations function, and so has difficulty maintaining a consistent story for as long a period of time.

At a minimum, the IRO should certainly spend a great deal of time coordinating activities with the director of public relations, in order to minimize these issues. The IRO's influence over public relations will be significantly more weighty if the IRO reports directly to the CEO, since the CEO may occasionally intervene directly to ensure that public relations works in lockstep with investor relations.

Better yet, both the public relations and investor relations functions should report to the same manager. By doing so, the manager can require the two functions to work together, and can regularly monitor their activities to ensure that they do so.

 ## SUMMARY

The discussion of how to create the company story does not mean that this is a vast effort to create a positive spin on a company that has no prospects, of "putting lipstick on a pig." If so, it will quickly become apparent that the company cannot deliver on its story, and the stock price will decline as disappointed investors sell their holdings. Instead, concentrate on creating a story and related packaging that is reasonably within a company's strategic capabilities to support.

The best way to create a story is to ensure that all information about a company is presented in a way that is clearly understandable, so that investors can see what the management team is trying to do. Investors then form their own opinions about the company's ability to deliver on its story. Ultimately, the story should persuade an investor that a dollar invested in the company will have a greater return than a dollar invested elsewhere.

# CHAPTER FOUR

# Event Management

E VENT MANAGEMENT IS A primary duty of the investor relations function, since it directly connects members of a company's management team with the investment community. This direct interface is extremely important, because analysts and investors have a chance to meet with or listen to a company's management team, which plays a large part in their evaluation of the company. The most common events are the quarterly conference call, the road show, and the annual meeting. This chapter describes how to practice for and run each of these events, as well as other events.

## CONFERENCE CALL

The conference call gives the investment community an opportunity to interact with the management team to learn about the latest quarterly results and hear any guidance updates for future projections. It is best to schedule conference calls to be held immediately after the latest 10-K or 10-Q filing, so there should be at least four conference calls per year.

The IRO should prepare an extensive set of written remarks for every conference call. If the management team instead delivers off-the-cuff remarks from a short outline of topics, then listeners will not think that the management team is taking the conference call seriously. Also, using a script gives the IRO plenty of time to develop a thoroughly clear presentation, so that no information is missed that would be left to interpretation by analysts. A prepared script also allows the IRO to develop a central theme to the call that participants can state clearly and repeatedly.

When constructing the formal remarks for a conference call, pay particular attention to the informal rule of keeping them under 30 minutes. If the formal remarks extend even longer, then listeners will have less time to ask questions, since most IROs prefer to limit the total length of a conference call to one hour. The trend for the duration of formal remarks is dropping below the 30-minute mark, so that remarks lasting as little as 20 minutes are increasingly common. If the call runs too long, expect to have participants drop out of the call or to shift the task over to an associate.

If a company faces a difficult issue, such as a decline in sales or the departure of a key employee, always address the issue within the conference call script. By doing so, the IRO can formulate a considered answer to the issue and present it in the best possible light. Otherwise, someone might ask about it during the question and answer (Q&A) section of the call, and then the management team will have to answer it without a script.

In addition to the scripted remarks, the IRO is also responsible for compiling an extensive set of answers to every question that can possibly be asked during the Q&A portion of the conference call, which reduces the risk that the management team will appear to listeners to be unprepared. An excellent source of questions is the conference calls conducted by peer companies; listen to them to determine what questions are being asked of those companies, and be prepared to respond to the same questions. Also, review analyst reports to determine the areas in which they have concerns about the company. Another possibility is to scan the chat rooms on financial Web sites to see what questions investors are asking, or what issues appear to be of most concern at the moment. Finally, prepare a list of the most troublesome questions that may be asked and spend extra time preparing answers to them.

An excellent way to organize the questions and answers is to post them around the meeting room on white boards or sheets of paper; this makes it easier to quickly find and read off an answer without any shuffling of paperwork that would be apparent to anyone listening over the phone. The team needs to show a very high level of operational knowledge during conference calls, since this gives investors a higher level of confidence in their ability to run the company; prewritten answers are a good way to give this impression.

Be prepared for speculative questions, such as, "What would you do if the price of oil doubled next week?" The correct response is to initially state that the company does not engage in speculation, and then answer the underlying question. For example, in response to the last question, the CEO might say, "We forward purchase key supplies for 180 days in advance, in order to stabilize our raw material costs." Or, if the underlying question is difficult to discern, ask the questioner to restate the question.

The conference call is not a good place to extol the virtues of a company. This is a forum in which listeners want to hear about a company's immediately preceding results, how it interprets those results, and any changes to its guidance for future results. Thus, this is a mostly factual discussion, and is not the right place to make generalized claims about future performance.

The IRO should schedule conference calls at least three days in advance (preferably a week), and send out notifications by press release, e-mail, and fax, itemizing the time when the call will be conducted and the phone number to call in order to participate. If sent by fax, the notifications should be on corporate letterhead. No matter what form of distribution is used, the notice should come from the CEO, state the purpose of the call, which company managers will be on the call, and whether a question and answer session will be conducted. Some companies include in this notification a summary of the information to be covered during the conference call, which allows participants extra time to think of questions to ask during the Q&A part of the call.

When scheduling the conference call, it helps to place it immediately *after* those of peer companies (based on either their historical or scheduled release dates and times), since the IRO can listen to their conference calls and see what questions are being asked, as well as to learn their results. However, if the company will impart bad news during its conference call, then it may be better to schedule your call *before* the calls of peer companies, so that analysts will badger them during their conference calls about the issue that impacted the company. Also, it is better to schedule both the earnings press release and conference call for after the markets have closed. Otherwise, the market might improperly react to the earnings release before hearing what the company has to say during its conference call.

Company employees attending the conference call should be the CEO, CFO, and IRO. It may occasionally be necessary to bring in an expert, such as the manufacturing manager, to answer any anticipated questions that call for a deep level of expertise. However, use additional people infrequently, because listeners may think it is now acceptable to call the new person directly for additional information. Also, have a staff person on hand who writes down questions from listeners on a white board. By using this extra staff assistance, the main meeting participants can concentrate on answering questions.

Under no circumstances should a meeting participant call in on a cell phone. There is too much background noise and variability in signal strength to make that person consistently intelligible. Anyone wanting to use a cell phone is not giving sufficient priority to the conference call, and needs to put off whatever activity is preventing him from calling in on a land line.

When the conference call begins, the IRO should introduce everyone from the company who will be participating in the call, and then read a safe harbor statement (See the Forward Looking Statements chapter). She then introduces the CEO, who is the main speaker, and who should speak exclusively from the scripted remarks. The CEO may hand off to the CFO to discuss numerical results, or present the entire scripted comments personally. After 20 to 30 minutes of prepared remarks, the CEO turns the meeting back over to the IRO, who accepts questions from callers and moderates the discussion until the conference call concludes after about one hour. The IRO may sometimes call back some of the conference call participants for feedback on how the call was conducted.

If there are still callers in the queue when the IRO decides to stop the call, then the team should restructure the next conference call to permit more time for questions. This can involve limiting each analyst to fewer questions or reducing the amount of time allocated to the prepared remarks at the beginning of the call.

Once a conference call is complete, have a post-meeting review to determine which elements of the call can be improved. The IRO should chair this meeting, since she is not presenting during the bulk of the call, and so is in the best position to evaluate it. This meeting should result in an improvement memo that is carried forward to the next conference call, and which is the foundation of an advance meeting to improve that call. In addition, members of the presentation team should listen to a recording of the call to see how to improve their individual presentation skills.

A variation on the standard interactive conference call is a shorter one where the management team conveys a specific set of information and then terminates the call. This call is designed for a specific, scripted message and is similar to a press release. It is not advisable to use this shortened version very frequently, since listeners gain the most value from the Q&A portion of the conference call and will stop attending if the Q&A section is permanently removed.

Another variation on the conference call is to either have a separate call that focuses on a specific topic or to add a theme to each conference call where there is special emphasis on one topic. The intent is to increase the knowledge of the investment community about some special aspect of the company, such as a new product release, or an expansion into a new country, a post-acquisition update, or a patent that was just granted. If the call focuses entirely on the special topic, rather than earnings, then consider including in the call the operational managers in charge of the subject area.

In case people are unable to attend a conference call, consider recording the call (see the "Podcast Dissemination" section) and posting it on the company Web site. There is no need to retain conference call recordings for very long, since the information presented in them will become stale once the next conference call occurs.

##  ROAD SHOW

The road show is a repetitive series of meetings with the intent of raising money, where a team of company presenters gives essentially the same presentation multiple times over several days, and frequently in multiple cities. The road show is the most versatile event tool at the IRO's disposal, because its subject can be altered to match the audience. For example, it can be an informational meeting with current shareholders living in a specific area or a sales pitch to a group of local brokers, or one-on-one meetings with institutional investors or large stockholders. Each of these audiences requires a different presentation based on its specific needs, so the management team will impart a different set of information to each one.

Given the repetitive nature of the presentation and the heavy travel schedule involved in a road show, there are several best practices to be aware of that can lighten the overall level of participant stress:

- *Preparation.* The presentation should be thoroughly prepared in advance. By doing so, the speakers can relax between meetings and spend more time mingling with attendees. This usually calls for a practice session prior to each road trip, to ensure that the presenters are thoroughly familiar with their materials.
- *Starting point.* Begin the road show in a regional market, not with major prospects. By doing so, the management team can become comfortable with its presentation and learn about the most likely questions being posed by investors. The team should then be well prepared by the time it presents to key investors.
- *Duplication.* Given the intense travel schedule of a road show, there is a high probability that something will be lost or fail at some point. To

mitigate this risk, keep a separate set of backup speaker notes and copies of the presentation. Also, bring chargers for cell phones and laptop computers, and consider bringing spare batteries and projector bulbs, too.

- *Arrive early.* If the first meeting of the day starts late, then this will probably roll forward into all of the meetings that day. The solution is to do whatever it takes to be early for the first meeting of the day.
- *Buffer time.* Always leave enough time between meetings for travel between locations and on-site setup time. If this means that there will be room for fewer meetings during the day, then fine—schedule a longer road trip.
- *Building passes.* Getting through building security can substantially delay the presentation team. This is a particular problem in New York City, where security is especially tight. To reduce the security wait, send one of the team members ahead with the driver to obtain building passes for the next meeting.
- *Shipping.* The presentation package for each attendee may add up to a considerable amount of shipping weight. If so, pre-ship the presentation materials in advance to each meeting location. If this is not workable, then store the materials within the group's carry-on luggage, which minimizes the risk of it being lost in transit.
- *Audio/visual equipment.* Only bring presentation equipment if it is not available at the various meeting locations. Bringing a laptop computer and projector is not only a hassle, but there is a risk of breakage. Thus, always call in advance to verify what equipment will be on hand.
- *On-site branding.* Assign a subordinate the task of branding the company name at each location. This can involve using the company logo on attendee nametags, presentation materials, and signage. This person does not have to go on the trip, but must have overall control over the design of the materials brought on the trip.
- *Trip logistics.* The speakers need plenty of time to decompress between meetings, so have someone else handle all luggage for the group, as well as travel connections. If possible, hire a van and driver during the group's entire stay in each city. A van is particularly useful if there may be a need for the management team to assemble between meetings in order to refine the presentation. A van equipped with a small conference table, adequate lighting, and presentation monitors is ideal for this purpose. Further, the IRO should have the name and cellphone numbers of chauffeurs at least one day in advance, in order to properly coordinate pickups.
- *Phone list.* A road show may involve dozens of meetings, as well as multiple hotels, drivers, and other people involved in logistics. Put the

contact information for all of them on a single document, and keep spare copies of this document where it is easily accessible. The chances are good that the team will have an emergency at some point during the road show and will need this information.

- *Specialists.* If a road show involves an unusually large number of meetings, participants, and/or cities, then consider hiring a road show specialist. This person reviews the itinerary for trouble spots and advises on how to optimize the schedule.
- *Backup planning.* Anything can go wrong during a road show, and frequently does. To guard against these problems, have a backup team that can assist with such issues as sending additional equipment on a rush basis and providing rerouting information in the event of traffic delays.

During a road show presentation, the CEO is the primary speaker and is responsible for telling attendees about the investment opportunity presented by the company. The CFO presents the financial aspects of the business and may repeat any guidance that has already been issued elsewhere. The IRO is responsible for the logistics of each road show and may bracket presentations with introductory and concluding comments.

This group should be absolutely consistent in making the same presentation in every meeting. This creates a rhythm to the meetings, which allows the team to operate almost on autopilot, except for those times when an attendee interjects a question. By doing so, the group will experience much less stress through the day, and can avoid looking tired or discouraged toward the end of the day.

The CEO, CFO, and IRO may not feel comfortable presenting to a large number of people. If so, a PowerPoint presentation projected onto a screen shifts the audience's attention away from the speakers and to the screen, which may alleviate some speaker nervousness. However, if a presenter is comfortable with the audience, and especially if he can speak "off the cuff" from limited notes, then by all means eliminate the projection equipment and let the audience focus directly on the speaker. A team of skilled speakers is a powerful tool, and the IRO should work hard to polish the management team's speaking skills to reach this level of expertise.

Irrespective of the speaking ability of the presentation team, it should still use a PowerPoint presentation, if only to control the sequence of topics covered. It is critical to reduce the *number* of these slides to the bare minimum, while also keeping the *contents* of each slide as minimal as possible. Presenters may be so eager to tell the company's story that they bury attendees with too much information. The IRO can draw on the assistance of any investment bankers being used to arrange the road show to provide some weight to the argument that a reduced presentation has a greater impact on participants.

The contents of every presentation are different, depending on what type of message a company wants to impart. However, it should contain the following nine points:

1. *Overview.* States what the company does in as few bullet points on one slide as possible.
2. *Investment highlights.* Investors will pay attention to this slide, so spend time constructing four or five points, and be prepared to discuss them at length, if asked.
3. *Market size.* State the size of the market, any subcategories, and the source of the information.
4. *Customers.* Either name the general type and characteristics of the target customer, or (better yet) name better-known customers and their proportion of total company sales.
5. *Growth strategy.* State how the company plans to grow, such as through an industry roll-up, new store rollouts, new geographic markets, and so forth.
6. *Competitive positioning.* Show the company's positioning in relation to its main competitors. This may be best presented in chart form. In addition, and on a separate slide, state the company's competitive advantages, such as its technology, intellectual property, regulatory approvals, or low-cost structure.
7. *Financial statements.* Show financial results for at least the past three years, with projections for the next year. Attendees will be particularly interested in the trend of gross margins and net profits, so provide this information. The balance can be in summarized format, and for just the most recent year-end.
8. *Management team.* Note the name, title, responsibility, and experience of each member of the senior management team.
9. *Summary.* In four or five bullet points, state the key points that a prospective investor should remember.

An IRO that can restrict the number of PowerPoint slides to just 10 is to be applauded, while 30 slides should certainly be considered the upper end of the acceptable range. When there are too many slides to cover and the presentation is limited to an hour or less, the management team becomes driven by the need to ram through the presentation as fast as possible, which leaves little time for a question and answer session.

If a road show presentation is to brokers, the presentation is simplified and uses a considerable amount of repetition. Brokers want to know how they can make money from the stock, so present the investment message at the beginning of the presentation, reinforce it several times as the talk progresses, and finish with a reiteration of the same message.

If, during a road show, there is a meeting with a small number of participants (as would be the case with an institutional investor), consider keeping a recording of the conversation, to prove that no material, undisclosed information was imparted. Also, institutional investors expect more information than brokers, so send them a fact sheet in advance of the meeting, and provide a duplicate at the beginning of the meeting. This does not necessarily mean that they also receive a complete copy of the full presentation at the beginning of the meeting, since they may read ahead and therefore pay less attention to the speaker.

If there is an attendance sheet for a presentation, then the IRO should use it to send to each attendee a thank-you note, an invitation to make further inquiries or attend a plant tour, and a request to put them on the investor relations mailing list. Also, offer to send investor materials, such as a fact sheet, to their associates. Finally, include an evaluation sheet, in case anyone has suggestions for improving the presentation. The response rate on these materials will be low, but it is still worth making the effort in order to add a few people to the investor relations mailing list.

Of all the various types of investor relations events, the road show presents the greatest risk of overcommunication. The problem is that the IRO may fall into the habit of visiting the same people on a repetitive basis, which is roughly comparable to "preaching to the choir." Realistically, there is no justification for meeting with the same people even once a year, since they already know the company's story and do not need to hear it again. If the IRO persists in meeting with the same people too frequently, then everyone who has heard about the company will have already bought its stock, resulting in no new demand. Instead, shift the road show to new cities on a regular basis, or at least use different sell-side contacts to arrange meetings with new people who have not heard of the company before.

A final note about road shows—how effective are they? The CEO, CFO, and IRO may be spending a considerable proportion of their time on the road, meeting with the investment community. This is a considerable investment in executive time, so there must be a discernible tradeoff between the labor and out-of-pocket cost of road shows and the number of shares placed that are directly related to them. A reasonable goal over the long term is to stay below a road show cost of $0.05 per share placed. If the cost increases beyond this benchmark, then the IRO should work on targeting a smaller group of road show attendees whose investment interests are more closely aligned with those of the company.

## NON-DEAL ROAD SHOW

While the standard road show is designed to raise money, the *non-deal road show* is a presentation to investors with the objective of spreading information about the company. Non-deal road shows are generally scheduled four times per year, immediately after the quarterly conference call (though some companies schedule a dozen or more per year) and never during the earnings blackout period that typically covers the last two weeks of the third month of a quarter. During the blackout period, company participants will very likely know the quarterly results, and may let slip some hint about those results. Given the resulting disclosure problems, it is best to completely avoid any road shows during the weeks when quarterly results have been compiled but are not yet released.

When scheduling non-deal road shows, consider setting them up in a broad range of geographic areas. The reason is that many IROs focus their attention on the region near company headquarters, which eventually results in saturation of the local market. By shifting presentations away from this home market, the company can tap a much larger pool of investors.

When arranging a non-deal road show, it is best not to present directly to buy-side investors without the involvement of a sell-side firm. The reason is that the sell-side can earn commissions from the eventual purchase of company stock that may result from the road show. The potential earnings may result in additional sell-side analyst coverage, which, in turn, yields more positive press, and therefore an even higher stock price. To maximize this effect, have a different sell-side firm arrange investor presentations in each city, so that more sell-side firms are beholden to the company, resulting in more analyst coverage. Also, having a sell-side firm arrange meetings eliminates a great deal of the same type of work that the IRO would otherwise have to perform. For these reasons, sell-side firms are involved in some manner in nearly 100 percent of non-deal road shows.

If there is currently no interest from sell-side firms, then consider employing an investor relations firm with contacts in the targeted geographic regions to arrange for investor presentations. The company will have to pay a fee for this service, whereas a sell-side firm will arrange meetings for free. However, the cost is well worth the effort if the investor relations firm has good contacts within the investor community.

When deciding on where to schedule non-deal road shows each year, the IRO should meet with the CEO to discuss what worked during prior trips, where investor requests are coming from, and which sell-side firms or investor relations firms are interested in providing trip support during the coming year. It is difficult to reschedule these trips, given the large number of participants, so the presentation team should block out the meeting dates on their calendars at the beginning of the year, and avoid alterations to the schedule.

There may be a number of non-deal road shows in a year, so be sure to obtain feedback from each trip that can be used to upgrade the presentation in the next road show. The sell-side firm should provide this information on an anonymous basis. If the firm is not providing any or insufficient feedback, then it may be necessary to switch to a different firm for the next road show.

Non-deal road show presentations are short and to the point, which means that there are *a lot* of meetings per day—up to eight meetings in a day is optimal. Participants are the IRO, CEO, and CFO, with occasional attendance by a senior manager from some key part of the company. The IRO may present alone, especially when the company schedules so many non-deal road shows per year that it would be burdensome for more of the senior management team to attend.

If it is too difficult to schedule the senior management team for a road show, then there are alternatives available. One option is to schedule presentations around industry events, such as trade shows, which managers already plan to attend. Another possibility is to schedule a *reverse road show*, where investors come to the company to meet managers. Finally, consider a series of one-on-one conference calls, which can be inserted into gaps in the schedules of senior management.

## ANNUAL MEETING

At far too many annual meetings, the meeting is considered a minor event that neither stockholders nor directors are expected to attend. Instead, the company chairman rapidly pushes through a number of formulaic motions, as required by law, and shuts down the meeting as expeditiously as possible.

Though certainly an efficient way to deal with the annual meeting, it does not provide for any interaction between the company and its stockholders. An improvement on the situation is to release during the meeting a variety of information, such as the results of the first quarter, highlights of events during the past year, and the CEO's opinion of the current economic climate. Also, start making major corporate announcements at the event on a regular basis. Though this requires the coincident issuance of a press release to fulfill disclosure requirements, investors and analysts may now consider it more worthwhile to attend, in case they can glean extra insights from the associated Q&A session.

Also, require all directors to attend the annual meeting, or at least pay them an attendance fee to encourage them to sit through the meeting. Also, have them stay after the meeting, along with as many company executives as possible, to talk to any attending investors.

To encourage media attendance, give reporters a press kit and have a company representative sit with them to answer questions. Including a description of the last annual meeting in the company newsletter may be useful for drawing more attendees to the next meeting. Similarly, post notices in multiple newsletters prior to the next annual meeting, and also prominently display the meeting date and location on the company Web site. If there will be prominent speakers during the meeting, list their names in the notices. Further, if the company issues dividend checks directly to investors, then include a meeting notice in each mailing.

To make the annual meeting available to more investors, consider creating a video of the event, and posting it on the company Web site. This is a particularly useful technique if the chairman plans to make extensive remarks about the company during the meeting, but less so if the meeting is designed to only address the legal minimum number of motions. If a video is created, consider editing it down to the smallest possible size while still retaining the bulk of the content; this reduces the download chore for those investors having slow internet connections.

Any annual meetings that are designed to be completed as a formality are usually not very well run, since there is no expectation of having attendees. However, if the preceding recommendations are implemented, then the level of event planning must be ratcheted up considerably higher, in order to give the impression that the company cares about the annual meeting. This is particularly important if the meeting is being taped, since a large number of people may eventually view or listen to the recording.

In short, use every form of corporate communications available to ensure that investors are fully aware of the annual meeting. Hopefully, a combination of these enhancements will attract more attendees over time.

## PLANT TOUR

A plant tour can be a multi-hour affair that includes formal presentations to the participants. It is a useful event not only for key investors, analysts, and members of the media, but also for environmental groups who might otherwise voice concerns about a company's pollution controls.

The IRO should arrange each plant tour, but should not lead the tour. This task is given to the local facility manager, who has the most knowledge of the facility and who can therefore provide answers to visitor questions with the greatest authority.

The IRO should brief the facility manager in advance regarding fair disclosure requirements, as well as those questions that are most likely to arise. Also, be aware that any analysts included in a plant tour may attempt to contact employees who they meet during the tour. If so, be sure to contact these employees regarding the same disclosure information given to the facility manager, and advise them to refer questions to a designated manager, if there is a disclosure policy in place.

## ANNUAL ANALYST MEETING

If a number of analysts follow a company, it can arrange an annual event for them. This is normally held at the corporate headquarters location, where the senior management team, selected operational managers, and even the company's customers make presentations to the analysts. An alternative to a meeting at company headquarters is to do so in New York, where many analysts are located. This also makes it easier for European analysts to fly in, given the large number of available flights between Europe and New York and the reduced time differential from Europe.

The event can include product demonstrations, speeches by outside experts regarding industry trends, and a variety of breakout sessions. It can sometimes be added onto the annual shareholder meeting, so that participants can attend both events.

This can be a logistically intense event for the investor relations staff to coordinate, especially if there are multiple sessions, accommodations, meals, and transportation to be arranged for dozens of participants. Given the company's investment in this event, it is important to commit to it for a number of years, so that the company gradually builds up relations with its analysts. A one-time event is not worth the trouble, and also sends the message that the company is not being consistent with its investor relations programs.

## ANALYST AND INDUSTRY CONFERENCES

Any industry that has its own trade group will likely sponsor an annual conference. Also, sell-side analysts sponsor their own conferences. Buy-side analysts and portfolio managers attend both types of meetings, so this is a good opportunity for the IRO to request a keynote speech or panel discussion for the company CEO, thereby giving the company good exposure with the buy side. The IRO of a larger or better-known company has some leverage in arranging for a keynote speech.

These conferences are especially easy for the investor relations staff to arrange (as opposed to the annual analyst meeting), since the sponsoring organization is making most of the arrangements. The investor relations staff only has to arrange for company personnel to travel to and from the conference.

The IRO should not accept any engagements for conferences during the earnings blackout period that typically covers the last two weeks of the third month of each quarter. This prevents a company presenter from inadvertently letting slip any earnings information for the current quarter that has not yet been reported to the SEC.

## PODCAST DISSEMINATION

Any of the preceding events can be recorded and converted into either an audio or video podcast, which the IRO can post on the company Web site or iTunes, where they will be universally available for downloading. A number of large companies are now listing their investor relations podcasts on iTunes, including Merck, IBM, Johnson & Johnson, and Dell, so this is becoming an accepted practice.

A key factor for a podcast is to ensure a high level of audio quality. There are several types of recording equipment needed that will ensure high audio quality. They are as follows:

- ▪ *Microphone.* The best-quality microphone type is the condenser microphone. Expect to pay at least $200 for one of sufficiently high audio quality. A high-end microphone, such as a Neumann, that costs well over

$1,000, is not necessary. Good-quality brands are Shure, Sennheiser, and Electrovoice.

- *Microphone preamplifier.* A condenser microphone requires a 48-volt power source, which comes from a preamplifier. The preamplifier can cost anywhere from $200 to $4,000, but the low end of the range contains a sufficient number of features for an adequate recording session. Good-quality brands are dbx, Studio Projects, and PreSonus.
- *Compressor.* A compressor pushes down any excessively high or low audio signals, which would otherwise result in annoying static in the recording. Better yet, it smothers any sibilance (strong "S" sounds), which can be annoying if not suppressed (some preamplifiers also contain sibilance reduction technology). A sibilance reduction feature is called a "de-esser." Compressors can cost from under $100 to about $9,000, with something in the $200 to $300 range being sufficient for investor relations recordings. Good-quality brands are dbx, Presonus, and Samson.
- *Equalizer.* A multiband equalizer allows for the modification of recorded voices, to give them higher or lower emphasis throughout their signal range. For example, an equalizer can give someone a deeper voice than is really the case. The equalizer is not necessary for investor relations recordings, but can be added to enhance the overall sound quality. The equalizer starts at $200 and can be fabulously expensive for a high-end system (which is completely unnecessary). A $300 two-channel equalizer should be sufficient. Good-quality brands are dbx, URS, and Mackie.
- *Digital recorder.* A digital recorder eliminates the need for a personal computer, and the unwanted background noise associated with its fan and hard drive. Instead, it silently records audio onto a computer chip. This approach is highly recommended. Expect to pay about $900 for a recorder. The main supplier of this equipment is Marantz.

The author's recording equipment is a Shure KSM 27 microphone, which is attached to a dbx 286A preamp, and which is then linked in series to a dbx 266XL compressor, dbx 2215 two-channel equalizer, and a Marantz PMD560 digital flash recorder.

Once an audio recording is made onto the digital chip in the digital recorder, insert the chip into a chip reader that is attached to a personal computer. The audio file is now available for downloading into any of a variety of sound production software packages, such as Audacity or Adobe Audition. Use this software to chop out any unnecessary parts of the recording, add introductory and outgoing comments or music, and reduce unnecessary sounds. Once completed, use the software to convert the audio file to an MP3 format, and upload it to the company Web site or iTunes for downloading by anyone with access to an MP3 reader.

The equipment and production steps described here may sound complex, but are actually not difficult to master, following some likely initial fumbling in the setup and production phases. Assume that the first few podcasts will have inadequate sound quality, so do not post anything on the company Web site or iTunes until the sound quality is adequate.

 ## VIDEO DISSEMINATION

The most widely used form of information dissemination by video is of a speech by a company officer, particularly from a shareholder meeting. However, the concept can be expanded further. For example, consider creating a corporate video, featuring a company officer responding to the top questions asked on recent quarterly earnings calls, or explaining the company's underlying business model. Such videos can be posted on the company Web site, which carries the additional benefit of driving more investors to the company site.

 ## BLOG DISSEMINATION

A small number of companies have an investor relations blog. The most common uses of a blog are to notify readers of the issuance of SEC filings and to amplify upon those filings. If readers respond with a comment, this also gives the investor relations team an opportunity to create a direct dialog with them.

A key aspect of an investor relations blog is its level of organization. It should not just be a lengthy string of blog posts. Instead, the blog page should offer to reindex blog postings by type of comment. For example, it can allow reindexing by the following categories:

| | | |
|---|---|---|
| Acquisitions | Corporate social responsibility | Operations |
| Analyst meetings | Dividends | Sales channels |
| Capital allocation | Earnings | SEC filings |
| Customer issues | Management team | Shareholder meeting |

If possible, also allow readers to sort by the most viewed blog entries and those receiving the largest number of comments.

## EVENT DISCLOSURE ISSUES

When planning the information to be released during an investor relations event, the IRO should be aware of seven issues regarding the types of information allowed:

1. *If a conference call is readily accessible by the public and is nonexclusionary, then it is acceptable under Regulation FD (Fair Disclosure) as a vehicle for full and fair disclosure.* Thus, it is not necessary to find an additional vehicle for material information disseminated for the first time during a conference call.

2. *If non-GAAP (Generally Accepted Accounting Principles) information is to be released during an event, then post the reconciling information on the company Web site.* The posted information should itemize the differences between the non-GAAP information and fully GAAP-compliant information. Be sure to announce where the reconciling information is posted.

3. *Schedule meetings after the most recent earnings release.* There is a significant risk of inadvertently disclosing material information during a road show presentation, especially when the meeting is with an institutional investor who can be expected to ask a number of detailed questions. To mitigate this risk, schedule meetings immediately after the most recent earnings release, so that all material information is public knowledge.

4. *Prepare a response for questions you cannot answer.* Anyone listening to a company-sponsored event generally expects to ask questions and receive answers. However, there will be times when a complete response to a question is not possible, either due to a disclosure issue or because it will result in the release of information that could aid competitors. In these situations, it is acceptable to decline to answer the question. However, to avoid being impolite to the questioner, state in general terms why the question cannot be answered.

5. *To make sure that all event participants are well aware of disclosure issues, develop a brief company policy for material disclosures, and read it to them just prior to each event.* A sample policy is, "The company does not allow the disclosure of new material information during investor relations events. Instead, all discussion during these events should be limited to the reinforcement of information that has already been made public." Another way to avoid disclosing material information is for the IRO to prepare a list of items not to be discussed, and to go over it with all event speakers just prior to an event.

6. *If a first-time disclosure will be made, also issue a press release.* Events are generally not the place to make a formal, first-time disclosure of material information to the marketplace. However, if the IRO chooses to do so, then always have a press release prepared in advance that contains the same information, and issue it at the same time as the disclosure during the event. This is an easy matter to arrange, since most press release services allow for the automatic, timed issuance of press releases.

7. *Do not bring up topics that should not be discussed.* There are several issues that it is best not to speak about at all. For example, it is generally best during any event to avoid stating that the company will do something in the future. Instead, the presenter should state that she believes or expects that certain events will occur. This avoids the risk of setting expectations excessively high. Similarly, keep away from any discussion of the proper stock valuation; the speaker should deliver earnings and strategy information, and let the investment community figure out the proper valuation.

Thus, there are a multitude of ways in which an event can result in the unexpected release of material, undisclosed information. The IRO can reduce this risk by using disclosure-related training, notifications, and policies, as well as through the proper scheduling of events.

 ## PRACTICING FOR EVENTS

The CEO and CFO are the main speakers at most events, and must be thoroughly prepared not only in regard to their presentations, but also for any questions that may arise. In particular, the CEO must project a sound grasp of the company's strategic direction and exactly how he intends to manage the company to match that strategy. In addition, both the CEO and CFO should practice their answers to the most difficult questions, covering such uncomfortable topics as:

- Aggressive interpretations of accounting standards
- Antidiscrimination practices
- Conflicts with regulatory authorities
- Executive compensation
- Layoffs
- Manager and director qualifications
- Political contributions

- Pollution issues
- Relations with questionable foreign governments
- Safety issues
- Stock option grants
- Succession planning

When preparing answers to these topics, it will become apparent if one individual is most capable of answering a specific question. If so, designate that person to answer all related queries.

When practicing for a speaking event, the CEO and CFO should stand behind a podium to practice their speeches, preferably with the IRO listening and providing feedback. Though this may seem uncomfortable at first, it is better to be uncomfortable in private than to duplicate the experience in front of a live audience!

A common problem for the IRO is including nonexecutive company managers in any investor relations event for which they are not adequately prepared. Many managers are uncomfortable in a public speaking role, and also have no idea what information could cause disclosure problems with the SEC. Accordingly, the IRO should assemble a training document for all senior managers, and walk through it with anyone asked to participate in an investor relations event. In addition, initially limit the role of anyone who is making a presentation for the first time, so they can gradually become accustomed to the experience.

No matter what event is in progress, the IRO should have someone jot down all questions asked by participants. The management team can later discuss them and devise the best answer to have available during the next event.

In short, the best event presentations involve in-depth preparation and the anticipation of questions. By spending sufficient time on these issues in advance, a company can regularly complete flawless investor relations events.

## SUMMARY

Investor relations events are extremely important for the IRO, since they are an exceptional tool for putting the management team in front of the investment community. However, this does not mean that the IRO should immediately schedule a full range of events. Instead, consider the experience level of those managers who will be expected to present information during events, as well as the profitability of the company. If it is well funded and its managers are polished speakers, then it is acceptable to launch a full event schedule. However, a more common option for a smaller company with moderate funding and less experienced speakers is to gradually ramp up, first using smaller and less frequent meetings, and gradually progressing to more elaborate affairs with advanced audio-visual equipment and larger audiences.

Another concern for the IRO is excessive saturation of the marketplace with too much of the same information about the company. If the company engages in a large array of activities, it should consider introducing some variation in the content of its presentations over time. However, this does not mean that it completely changes the tenor of its information package; instead, it should continue the same underlying themes while overlaying it with sufficient new information to retain the attention of the investment community.

# CHAPTER FIVE

# Public Communications

THE IRO IS CONTINUALLY in the position of having to draw attention to her company, because a single news item will fade quickly in the eyes of the investment community. Consequently, the IRO must issue a never-ending stream of information. This is done directly through press releases, or indirectly through the media. This chapter addresses how to handle both forms of public communication.

## CONSTRUCTING A PRESS RELEASE

A press release is initiated by the IRO and brings significant company events to the attention of the investment community. Examples of events worthy of a press release are the award of a large new contract, the hiring of a new CEO, or a new product launch. It is also frequently used to release the most recent company earnings information.

Though a press release can be structured in many ways, in reality it follows a regimented format from which few companies deviate. The general structure of a press release is as follows:

- *Header.* The header line is intended to grab the attention of the reader with the shortest possible number of words. The font is usually in bold to add emphasis.

- *Dateline.* When creating a press release, always include in the dateline the city and state where the company headquarters is located, because the business editors of local publications will give coverage preference to local firms. Also, list the stock exchange and ticker symbol in parentheses after the company name, since a variety of search engines will search the press release specifically for this information.
- *Story.* Summarize the story in the first sentence, so that the reader does not have to dig through the release to locate the kernel of the story. Also, keep the entire story short—very short! In addition, it is customary to include a quote from a company officer. The quote is useful for articulating the significance of the news event, putting it in the context of the company's overall strategy, and showing that a key milestone has been reached.
- *About the company.* A brief statement about the company is a useful extract for a reporter to use in writing about it, and also gives sufficient information for the reporter to decide if the issuing company is one worth writing a story about.
- *Forward-looking statement.* To avoid legal liability, always include a forward-looking statement (also known as a *safe harbor* statement) in the press release. An example is shown in Chapter 10. Given the bulk of this statement, it frequently contains the largest amount of verbiage of any part of a press release.

An example of a press release that incorporates these elements is as follows:

**Industrial Donut Corporation Awarded a $10 Million Contract**
Denver, Colorado—Industrial Donut Corporation (NASDAQ: DNUT), a producer of really large donuts, today announced that it has been awarded a $10 million contract by the Department of Defense. The contract provides for the inclusion of Industrial's donuts in the standard Meal, Ready to Eat (MRE) that is provided to soldiers in the field.

Richard Jelly, President of Industrial Donut, said, "This contract is a strong vote by the nutrition experts in the federal government that really large donuts are an excellent emergency meal supplement for intense battlefield situations."

**About Industrial Donut Corporation**
Industrial Donut Corporation produces industrial-grade donuts for high-volume applications. It distributes its donuts throughout North America, with applications in large-headcount organizations such as Fortune 500 companies and the federal government.

**Forward-Looking Statements**

The statements included in this press release, other than statements of historical fact, are forward-looking statements. Forward-looking statements generally can be identified by the use of forward-looking terminology such as "may," "will," "expect," "intend," "estimate," "anticipate," "plan," "seek," or "believe." These forward-looking statements, which are subject to risks, uncertainties, and assumptions, may include projections of our future financial performance based on our growth strategies and anticipated trends in our business. These statements are only predictions based on our current expectations about future events. There are important factors that could cause our actual results, level of activity, performance, or achievements to differ materially from the results, level of activity, performance, or achievements expressed or implied by the forward-looking statements, including, but not limited to our ability to win additional government business. In particular, you should consider the risks outlined under the heading "Risk Factors" in our most recent Annual Report on Form 10-K. Although we believe the expectations reflected in the forward-looking statements are reasonable, we cannot guarantee future results, level of activity, performance, or achievements. You should not rely upon forward-looking statements as predictions of future events. These forward-looking statements apply only as of the date of this press release; as such, they should not be unduly relied upon as circumstances change. Except as required by law, we are not obligated, and we undertake no obligation, to release publicly any revisions to these forward-looking statements that might reflect events or circumstances occurring after the date of this release or those that might reflect the occurrence of unanticipated events.

When issuing a material event in a press release, try to quantify the news. Otherwise, analysts will have difficulty translating it into revenue, profits, and earnings per share, and may issue estimates of altered company performance that are highly inaccurate. For example, rather than stating "Industrial Donut Corporation was awarded a $10 million contract," say "Industrial Donut Corporation was awarded a $10 million contract that comprises a $2 million base year and four one-year contract extensions." Using the later wording will keep analysts from misconstruing the news and assuming that the company will realize $10 million of revenue in a single year.

An earnings release is a highly formulaic press release that itemizes a company's earnings results, usually for the last quarter. It follows the generally outline just noted for a press release, but earnings information takes the place of the story. A bare-bones earnings release merely itemizes a company's revenues, profits, and earnings per share for the past quarter and in comparison to the same quarter in the preceding year, with no other supporting information. An example of the story follows:

> Denver, Colorado—Industrial Donut Corporation (NASDAQ: DNUT), a producer of really large donuts, today announced financial results for the first quarter ended March 31, 2010: (1) first quarter 2010 net revenue of $2,777,000, up from $2,601,000 in the first quarter of 2009, (2) net income for the first quarter 2010 of $503,000, compared to net income of $80,000 in the first quarter 2009; and (3) basic and diluted net profit per common share of $0.02 and $0.02, respectively, in the first quarter 2010, as compared to basic and diluted net profit per common share of $0.01 and $0.01 in the first quarter 2009.

A more informative alternative for an earnings release is to include the income statement, balance sheet, and statement of cash flows, as well as a summary-level management discussion and analysis (MD&A) section (see Chapter 8). The MD&A section should include a brief description of the company, primary trends impacting revenues and expenses, changes in accounting policies, an explanation of special charges, discussion of liquidity, any FASB accounting changes impacting the company, and current guidance. Also, if the earnings release contains pro forma results, then put GAAP results in front of the pro forma results and reconcile any differences between the two.

Since a press release of this size can be expensive to issue, consider using a reduced version that summarizes only a portion of the earnings information. For example, place the financial information in a summary table, including bulleted highlights of the MD&A section, and finish with a quote from the chief executive officer. An example follows:

> Denver, Colorado—Industrial Donut Corporation (NASDAQ: DNUT) today announced financial results for the first quarter ended March 31, 2010. Highlights for the first quarter compared to the same quarter a year ago were as follows:
>
> ▪ Total revenue increased 7% to $2,777,000
> ▪ Federal government sales rose 11%
> ▪ Earnings per diluted share increased 100% to $0.02
>
> Richard Jelly, president of Industrial Donut, commented, "We are pleased with our first quarter performance, which shows the strength

of our recurring sales, as well as continued penetration into the federal market. The doubling of earnings per share reflects our strong commitment to advanced procurement technologies, as well as the rationalization of our distribution channels."

First quarter 2010 net revenue was $2,777,000, up from $2,601,000 in the first quarter of 2009, primarily due to an increase in our federal government segment. First quarter 2010 net income was $503,000, compared to net income of $80,000 in the first quarter of 2009, which was caused by both the use of forward contracts to reduce our wheat costs by 15 percent and the elimination of our direct sales force. Our fully diluted net profit per common share was $0.02 in the first quarter of 2010 as compared to $0.01 for the first quarter of 2009.

For the second quarter ended June 30, 2010, we expect total revenue to be in the range of $2.8 million to $3.0 million. This revenue assumption is based on the continuing demand for our products within the Department of Defense, especially due to the roll-out of our new Combat Donut®, which is designed to survive intense fire fights. We also believe that fully diluted earnings per share for the second quarter will range from $0.02 to $0.04, which is driven by the revenue assumptions noted above, and 9.2 million diluted weighted average shares outstanding.

We are hosting a conference call today, April 5, 2010, at 5:00 p.m. EDT to discuss these results. A replay of the call will be available until June 30, 2010 on our Web site at www.industrialdonut.com.

Whatever format is used for the story section of an earnings release, the header should reveal the contents of the release in the fewest possible words. For example:

Industrial Donut Corporation Reports First Quarter Financial Results

An alternative is to add a subheading that highlights a key factor in the release. Here are three examples:

Industrial Donut Corporation Reports First Quarter Financial Result
**Management raises guidance for fiscal 2010**
Industrial Donut Corporation Reports First Quarter Financial Results
**Earnings increase 25% over preceding quarter**
Industrial Donut Corporation Reports First Quarter Financial Results
**Improved results driven by three acquisitions**

A press release can be enhanced with links to additional information. For example, it can contain a link to a video in which a company officer explains some aspect of the information contained within the release, or a video in which a technical expert explains the features of a new product release or approved patent. The press release can also contain links to white papers that are stored elsewhere, and that expand on the information in the release. Further, it is possible to tag earnings releases with XBRL in the same manner used for SEC filings; this enables users to more easily search for financial information. A few wire services are even issuing press releases in a social media format, so that users can submit comments about the news directly on the press release. This extra information tends to build stronger connections with readers.

Rather than issuing a full-featured press release, some companies have experimented with the reverse—just a headline or brief summary of an announcement, along with a Web link to the full text of the announcement, which is located on the company Web site. There is no safe harbor language in the press release at all. There are several advantages to this *notice and access* version of the press release. First, it reduces the fees charged by the wire service, since those fees are based on the number of words included in the release. This can be a substantial savings, since a press release with supporting tables and safe harbor language contains enough words to result in a wire service charge exceeding $1,000. Second, it drives traffic to the company's Web site, which improves the opportunity for investors to browse through the site and learn more about the company.

Do not have the company attorneys write a press release. Their orientation is to protect the company from liability, so they will strip out as much information from the release as possible. Instead, they should be the last ones to review a press release, and their role should be strictly limited to disclosure compliance.

Every press release should go through a standard approval process. First, the IRO attaches a standard approval form to it. The company attorney should review every press release and sign the approval form. If the release contains financial information, the auditors or at least a senior in-house accounting manager must review it, and also sign the form. Once approved, the IRO notes on the form the date and time when it should be disseminated, how it is to be released, and signs it to indicate final management approval. He then forwards the press release for distribution and files a copy of the approval packet.

Once a press release is written and approved, the next order of business is to disseminate it to the investment community. The best approach is to do so through a reputable wire service. Though there are many wire services, the two most established ones being Business Newswire and PR Newswire, which will send a press release to all major financial publications in the United States, a massive number of publications and newspapers, and many brokerage houses. Thus, they offer an extremely rapid way to disseminate news. They also notify the sender by e-mail that they have received the press release, and issue another notice when they have sent it to the designated distribution list, which can encompass a variety of publications, radio and television broadcasts, Web sites, investors, journalists, and so forth. In addition, they assign at least one proofreader to check every press release for spelling, punctuation, and format before it is issued, and who sometimes recommend changes to improve readability.

Once a press release is issued, be sure to send it by fax or e-mail to everyone who needs to see the information, since many people will not see the initial issuance. The trouble with press releases is that thousands of them are issued every day, so a specific corporate release is very likely to be lost in the flood of information. And besides, issuing an extra copy represents another opportunity to push the company's name into the marketplace. Also, send a copy of the press release to the board of directors, senior managers, and anyone else in the company who might be contacted by an outsider regarding the issue noted in the release. Finally, post a copy of each press release in the investor relations section of the company Web site.

At a minimum, any outside investor relations firm retained by a company should receive all press releases, as well as its market makers (for over the counter stocks) or specialists (for national exchanges). These people should be made aware of every press release within minutes of their being formally released (though sending it early is neither acceptable nor legal).

Issuing information to the investment community through the media (see the next section) can yield sporadic results, whereas the use of press releases is entirely within the control of the IRO. Consequently, the press release is by far the most common public communications tool used by companies.

##  DEALING WITH THE MEDIA

The IRO's goal in dealing with the media is to build credible, long-term relationships with those reporters at key publications who are in the best position to provide favorable coverage. This can be an extremely difficult goal to achieve, since reporters have tight deadlines that call for rapid response times, and also do not always provide favorable coverage. A few publications, such as *Forbes* magazine, pride themselves on issuing critical, if not downright acidic, coverage.

Some companies do not even try to deal with the media, instead avoiding all contact with them. The reason is that a reporter with a negative opinion of a company will quite possibly put this opinion in print, causing some damage to the company's reputation. Moreover, if an analyst does not like a company, he simply loses interest, which has no publicity impact on the company at all. Also, some types of news can cause problems for a company, such as a glowing story about its massive profitability that appears in the middle of a cost-reduction negotiation with a supplier or a labor union. Hence, there are sound reasons for avoiding the media.

If an IRO elects to deal with the media, then the first priority will be a high level of responsiveness to media deadlines, which are extremely short. Typically, a reporter will call regarding a press release that was just issued, and will need a story to accompany it the same day. If the IRO dawdles and does not return the call for several days, then the opportunity for a favorable story is lost, and the reporter may not even remember the company. Thus, the IRO must return media calls immediately to respect their deadlines.

After the story is published (in print or online), the IRO should call back and congratulate the reporter for a well-written article. Doing so is extremely rare, so the reporter may remember the company and be more inclined to write another story about it in the future.

On a longer-term basis, it is useful to invite reporters to the company for plant tours and interviews with company officers. Though these visits may not immediately result in media coverage, they do provide reporters with background knowledge about the company. Reporters can then write more accurate stories in the future. In addition, they will be in a better position to evaluate any rumors circulating about the company.

Also, try to develop ongoing relations with reporters by keeping them on a formal media mailing list. To do so, obtain their e-mail addresses and copy them on company press releases and newsletters. This mailing list need not contain too many names, since it can be difficult to satisfy the informational demands of a large group of reporters. Thus, restrict the mailing list to less than one hundred names, and preferably considerably less than this number.

The IRO should also consider an ongoing program of actively developing story lines and pitching them to the media. By doing so, a company can control the types of stories being written about it. Under this approach, first obtain the name of the most relevant editor or reporter at a publication by calling it or reviewing its list of employees on the publication masthead. Then contact that person to determine what types of stories the publication is looking for, and develop several possible story lines to meet its needs. Then write a brief letter to the targeted reporter, separately describing each story and why it is newsworthy, the availability of staff for interviews, and whether the company has any graphic materials available that can be used to supplement the proposed story. If the publication responds favorably, then assign a staff person to assist the reporter in collecting information for the story.

When developing a story line, keep in mind that a reporter wants to write a story about a significant change or special capability, not about how a company has maintained the status quo (which does not contribute to an exciting story!). For example, a story line might address how a company is building the largest dump truck in the world, or the new facility it just built, or its recent patent on laser technology. Conversely, don't even try to propose a story line about how a company has been building the same product since World War II—no reporter will ever follow up on *that* letter!

Reporters usually want to interview the CEO. If so, spend some time in advance, preparing the CEO for all possible questions (such as those noted in the "Practicing for Events" section of Chapter 4 on event management). In addition, point out to the CEO the information the IRO has already given to the reporter, in order to avoid duplicating it or stating conflicting information during the interview. When possible, the IRO should sit in on the interview to spot areas of miscommunication, note the topics covered or missed, and jot down any additional information to be sent to the reporter. Finally, the IRO and CEO should spend a few minutes immediately following the interview to evaluate it and determine how to improve upon it the next time.

During an interview, it is quite likely that a reporter will ask for information that is not readily available. If so, promise to obtain and forward the information within a reasonable period of time. This assists the reporter in meeting what is probably a tight story deadline and also avoids the perception that the company is withholding information.

If the IRO is not able to attend a media interview, then anyone participating on behalf of the company should write a memo itemizing the topics discussed and forward it to the IRO. The IRO should use it to verify if any material, undisclosed events were addressed during the interview, and to make an immediate, public disclosure if that was the case.

In short, the IRO must first decide whether to deal with the media at all. For smaller companies, the media may have no interest in the company, which makes this decision a moot point. For larger companies, it is nearly always useful to develop an ongoing media relations campaign, which requires regular contact with key reporters, as well as periodic interaction between senior management and the media.

## DEALING WITH ELECTRONIC MESSAGE BOARDS

A message board is an anonymous forum on which anyone can post messages that can be read by anyone visiting the site. There are numerous message boards on which people pass along tips, comments, and outright lies about a company. Examples of Web sites containing such boards are Yahoo!, Motley Fool, and Raging Bull.

The vast majority of all messages on these boards are posted by a small minority of people using the site. The theme of messages posted generally trend toward the extremes, with short sellers posting negative comments and bulls posting the reverse. Thus, the "information" in these postings is strongly slanted toward the needs of the posting individuals, and does not necessarily reflect any form of reality.

Given the unusual nature of the message boards, it is extremely unwise to "sink into the muck" and engage in any form of message exchanges on them. Indeed, this can have adverse legal implications, since any message posted by a company officer on a message board can be considered an official form of guidance by the company, and is therefore subject to control (and penalties) by the SEC. Thus, the primary external message board issue for an IRO is to create and enforce a policy prohibiting employee participation in message boards.

However, it may make sense for the company to sponsor its own electronic forum for investors. The SEC allows such sites under its Rule 14a-17. This rule provides that the company, a shareholder, or a third party working for the company or shareholder that operates an e-forum will not be liable for another participant's postings, even if they provide the medium of communication. This protection is available as long as the forum is conducted in accordance with federal securities laws.

Operating a forum can attract investors, especially if company managers participate in the forum. Managers can use the forum to distribute information and explain the company's position on various issues. The IRO can use it to determine support by investors for various company initiatives, and even learn in advance of rumors that she can then deal with before they spread through the investor community. Having an active and well-supported forum of this type may also drain investors away from other forums not supported by the company.

Although having a company-operated electronic forum might seem like a good idea, there are also some downsides to consider:

- *No participation.* What if few investors participate? The company is committing management time to monitor the site, but this may not be a good use of the monitors' time if they are only engaging with a small group of investors.
- *Poor behavior.* The message board could be taken over by a vocal minority with its own activist agenda, driving away other investors.
- *Staffing.* The company must commit staff time to monitoring the site, responding to comments, and legal guidance to ensure that postings do not contain disclosures that should not be released.
- *Tone.* While the ideal situation is for a large volume of reasoned discussion, the message board may degenerate into claims and accusations, with the company on the defensive.

If a company elects to create its own electronic forum, it also has to resolve several management issues. First, how frequently should it respond to postings? Daily monitoring may be too great a burden for the management team. Second, will the site be restricted to just a few topics, or left wide open to any topic? Third, will it be available only to current shareholders (which requires a login), or to all and sundry? Fourth, how much censorship will the company exercise over posts that attack the company or criticize other posters? If the company elects to require a login, this forces participants to be identified, whereas general access allows for anonymous participation.

## INVESTOR RELATIONS ADVERTISING

Some companies use advertising as a form of investor relations. It is not recommended for any but the largest companies, for several reasons. First, it is a scattershot approach that impacts many more people than those who are likely to invest in a company. Second, advertising requires repetition in order to firmly lodge a message in the minds of potential investors, so long and expensive campaigns are necessary. Third, it is not entirely clear that people make investment decisions based on advertisements, rather than by other means, such as discussions with an opinion leader.

For these reasons, advertising is well outside of the investor relations budgets of smaller companies. Also, the number of tradable shares that these smaller firms have available is usually so small that potential investors would have a difficult time obtaining the stock, even if the advertising were to persuade them to make a purchase. Finally, advertising across multiple states by an over-the-counter firm can cause conflicts with state blue-sky laws (see Chapter 19), which can present liabilities for anyone selling the company's stock.

However, there is one case where advertising can be useful. If a company is involved in a takeover contest or proxy fight, the most effective means of quickly sending messages to shareholders is through an advertising campaign. An advertisement can be placed overnight with a daily publication for immediate distribution, whereas it could take a week or more to distribute a letter directly to stockholders. Also, during these contests, stockholder turnover is higher than normal, so that stockholder lists become outdated so quickly that mailing lists are no longer accurate. Thus, advertising can be the best form of investor communications during a takeover contest or proxy fight.

## SUMMARY

Although this chapter has addressed how to issue news to the public, this does not mean that the IRO should continually flood the market with announcements. There is a risk that investors will not discern the most important announcements, so adopt a policy of only issuing information about events above a predetermined, materiality level. For example, only publicize a new contract win if it exceeds $1 million, or a product launch only if it is for an entirely new product, or a hiring only if it is at the executive level.

Public communication falls into the realms of both investor relations and public relations. If the public relations department is constantly issuing messages that interfere with the IRO's job, then consider having a board-level policy that the public relations department always copy its messages to the IRO prior to release. Other alternatives are to use a coordination committee or to assign management of the two functions to the same person. Any of these methods allow for better coordination between the two functions.

Of the various forms of public communication noted in this chapter, the IRO's primary tool is the press release. Its content and the timing of its release are completely controllable, which is certainly not the case with the other main communications tool, the media story. Consequently, the IRO should devote a disproportionate amount of her communications time to the formulation of press releases.

# CHAPTER SIX

# Publications

B ASED ON THE VOLUME of information that it disseminates, the investor relations department can in some ways be considered an in-house publications department. It can create fact sheets that summarize a company's current situation and prospects, issue a vastly more elaborate annual report, or generate specialty publications such as product pipeline reports and welcome kits. This chapter describes each of the various investor relations publications.

## FACT SHEET

The fact sheet is a short compilation of the key information that describes a company and its operations. It is extremely useful, both as a reference tool and as a handout to a variety of constituencies. It does not involve fancy production work; instead, it is intended to have a low production cost and be easily updated on a regular basis.

The fact sheet usually covers four pages, and is designed to be mailed as a pamphlet. The usual contents of the four pages are as follows:

*Page 1.* The name of the company is presented at the top of the page, followed by "Fact Sheet" on the next line, to identify the document. Next, centered on the page, is the ticker symbol and the name of the exchange where the stock is located. Most of the first page is left blank, so the reader can clearly identify the company and its ticker symbol.

*Pages 2 and 3.* These two pages contain all of the key information on the fact sheet. Page 2 contains a standard set of information, while the contents of page 3 tend to be more variable. Page 2 should include these items:

- Quick Reference Header
- Company name
- Ticker symbol
- Shares outstanding and management ownership
- Recent stock price and market cap
- Web site address
- Business Summary. A one-to-three paragraph summary that states what the company does, and key investment highlights.

Page 3 contains additional information about the company, which can vary based on individual circumstances. A common inclusion is a summary of recent press releases, usually using headlines and excerpts from the actual press releases. Other options include descriptions of key subsidiaries, management resumes, products, the market opportunity, and the company's competitive advantage. The footer on this page lists the contact information for the CFO, IRO, and corporate counsel. All information provided should be as succinct as possible.

*Page 4.* The fact sheet is intended to be folded into thirds and then mailed, so the bottom third of the back page is reserved for an address label, return address, and postage. The top two thirds of the page is mostly blank, leaving room for key identifying information, such as the company name, its ticker symbol, and its Web site address.

The fact sheet is also produced in a two-page format, in which case it contains the information shown on pages 2 and 3 of the four-page version. The format uses the front and back of a single sheet of paper, so that it makes an excellent handout for meetings. An example of a two-page fact sheet is shown in Exhibit 6.1.

Investors will be particularly interested in the investment highlights section of the fact sheet, since this will form the basis for their continued interest and investment in the company. Given the importance of this section, here are some sample highlights to consider:

"Revenue growth has exceeded the industry average by 10 percent for the last five years."

**Exhibit 6.1**   Sample Two-Page Fact Sheet

Industrial Donut Corporation

Investment Profile

(September 20XX)

| | |
|---|---|
| Trading Symbol: DNUT | Recent Price: $12.10 |
| Shares outstanding (fully diluted): 26,304,000 | Market Cap: $318.3 million |
| Management Ownership: 12,718,000 | Web Site: www.industrialdonut.com |

### Industrial Donut at a Glance

Industrial Donut Corporation produces industrial-grade donuts for high-volume applications, including provisioning the U.S. military and the special forces of other countries. Its core competency of delivering high caloric-density foods in large volumes has become increasingly important in national security initiatives. Industrial Donut's expertise positions the company on the leading edge of organizations qualified to benefit from greatly increased federal government expenditures committed to soldier nutrition.

Industrial Donut became publicly held in December 20XX, and trades under the DNUT symbol on the NASDAQ.

Industrial Donut has acquired four companies that bolster its high-caloric offerings, and is actively evaluating additional opportunities in the same market.

In addition, Industrial Donut has garnered multiple new federal contract awards, and has also received a five-year SmartBUY contract from the General Services Administration, to be the sole provider of donuts to the federal government.

### Corporate Goals and Strategy

Industrial Donut's management has set revenue and earnings goals to achieve annual revenue in excess of $50 million and profitability

### Investment Highlights

- Excess manufacturing capacity availability limits the cost of additional growth opportunities.
- Top secret and polygraph clearance requirements limit competition for donut provisioning.
- Federal commitment to high-caloric nutrition in battlefield situations makes significantly increased funding likely.
- Deep bench of ex-military advisors with strong federal government and industry contacts improves the odds of obtaining additional federal contracts.

### Management Team

The company's top leadership team comes from Fortune 500 backgrounds in which managers have executed strategies similar to Industrial Donut's in the past. President Richard Jelly and other top managers have extensive experience with food production systems, as well as long-standing relationships within the federal defense establishment, corporate America and the owners and managers of many companies that Industrial Donut has identified as strategic acquisition candidates.

The leadership team is supported by a strong board, including several Top Chef advisors.

### Competitive Advantage

Industrial Donut believes it brings several competitive advantages to the very large markets it is seeking to penetrate:

(*continued*)

**Exhibit 6.1**   *(continued)*

in FY 20XX. The company says it expects to reach these goals through 15% annual revenue growth from operations and accretive acquisitions.

**Market Opportunity**

The market for Industrial Donut's products and services is large and growing. The principal driver is the long-term federal government commitment to use high-caloric foods for prolonged battlefield assignments to protect against terrorist risk to civilian populations and key economic infrastructure in the United State and abroad.

A recent estimate by FedFoods, a Washington think tank, set the market for federal high-caloric purchases at $12 billion over the next five years. This is just one category of federal spending for which Industrial Donut's capabilities qualify it to compete. Industrial Donut's potential market also includes many large U.S. companies, which have worldwide operations.

Taken together, the public and private sector market opportunity for Industrial Donut over the coming five years is conservatively estimated in excess of $20 billion.

- Industrial Donut is an established vendor in the market sectors it is seeking to exploit. Current customers include the Departments of Defense and Homeland Security. These agencies control a significant portion of the future opportunities for which Industrial Donut will compete. In addition, Industrial Donut's existing private-sector customers include many Fortune 500 companies. These organizations deploy staff in the field in numbers rivaling those of the federal government.

- Industrial Donut's acquisition strategy adds products, services, development capabilities, marketing and sales expertise that help it move to a leading position as a prime contractor for the largest available federal and private-sector contract opportunities.

**Contact Information:**

| CEO | Investor Relations | Legal Counsel |
|---|---|---|
| Richard Jelly | Kim Krueller | Carl Custard |
| 303-990-0870 | 415-233-7020 | 303-773-0111 |

"The revenue run rate for this year is 20 percent greater than the previous year's revenue."

"The backlog of $25 million is 50 percent higher than at the end of the last year."

"The Board has authorized a 10 million share buyback, which is 8 percent of outstanding shares."

"The company has increased the annual dividend by at least $0.10 in each of the past 20 years."

"The company has a no debt and $100 million of cash on its balance sheet."

"The company invests 5 percent of its revenue into research and development activities."

"The company has successfully acquired and integrated two companies per year for the past five years, yielding an annual net increase in earnings per share of 12 percent."

"Administrative expenses have been reduced by $5 million in each of the past three years."

"The company has sufficient production capacity to support a doubling of sales."

Each of these investor highlights will appeal to a different type of investor, so the IRO should carefully consider which selection of highlights to include in the fact sheet. For more information about investor types, see Chapter 13, "Dealing with the Buy Side."

The fact sheet can be issued to a variety of entities besides the investment community. It may also be useful for presentations to customers and suppliers, as well as prospective recruits, local government officials, the media, and employees. The company CEO can use it to prepare for a variety of meetings, such as road shows and the annual meeting.

A variation on the fact sheet is the *fact book*, which is intended to be a research document for the investment community. Its layout can resemble that of a research report, though no stock price target is ever included. It presents an investment thesis and then expands on it with a comprehensive description of the company that includes the following items:

- Company overview
- Company history
- Strategy
- Products and services
- Financial results
- Total shares and float
- Stock exchange listing
- Stock transfer agent
- Stock trading range
- Operating and financial ratios
- Officer biographies
- Director biographies
- Auditor contact information
- Employees
- Facilities
- Product development planning
- Marketing campaigns
- Investor relations contact information

The fact book is a more elaborate production than the fact sheet, and so is updated less frequently (though no less than once a year).

## ANNUAL REPORT

When first constructing an annual report, the IRO needs to establish a baseline for the content and presentation of the report. A good starting point is the reports issued by peer companies. If these reports consistently contain the same types of information, then the IRO should assume that the company's first report should be similar to them in most respects. Then, over time, the IRO can gradually add to and subtract from the report in order to more closely match how the company wishes to present itself to investors and analysts.

Though the contents of annual reports can vary by types of peer companies, some common elements are found in most reports:

- *CEO letter.* Addresses the general results of the past year and plans for the future. The intent is to show investors that the company has a strategic plan and is following it, and will advance toward its goals in the coming year. It should address the following topics:
  - Summary of financial results
  - Challenges encountered and achievements during the past year
  - The long-term strategy and how much of it the company will implement during the coming year
  - Milestones the company plans to meet during the coming year, which will demonstrate the company's ability to execute its plans
  - Upcoming challenges, and how the company plans to mitigate them
  - Any changes in governance and financial oversight
- *10-K extract.* Though not all of the information found in the annual Form 10-K is needed, any accounting information presented should be extracted directly from the 10-K, so there is no inconsistency between the two documents. Besides the financial statements, the annual report should certainly include extracts from the 10-K of the management discussion and analysis (MD&A) section, accounting policies, and segment results. Any comparative information should cover at least the last five years; some companies provide this information for ten years.
- *Statistical briefing.* A summary of key company metrics is commonly placed near the front of the report, with a more detailed analysis located at the back.
- *Contact information.* A contacts page should list the name and contact information for the IRO, the stock transfer agent, and corporate attorneys.

The preceding list covered only the *minimum* set of information to include in the annual report. For a more complete presentation, consider adding discussions of corporate objectives and strategy, industry conditions, and operating statistics (e.g., sales by product, and plant capacity). A part of the annual report that gives real value to readers is a question-and-answer section. During each year, the IRO should compile a list of questions that arose during conversations with the investment community. Since these questions are both current and foremost in the minds of readers, include at least the top ten questions and their corresponding answers in the annual report.

The annual report needs to be internally consistent. It should state the primary investment value that the company presents to its investors, and then follow up throughout the text with projections, strategies, and achievements that trace directly back to the underlying message.

Once the first annual report has been issued, the IRO should show continuity from one report to the next. This means that each annual report should revisit issues raised in the prior year's report, in order to review progress made against stated objectives. If targeted goals have not been attained, then state why this has not happened. Further, the same metrics should be reported from one annual report to the next, with only gradual changes in the information presented over a number of years. Readers will appreciate the long-term consistency of information being made available to them.

The IRO has a considerable amount of control over the contents of the annual report, but this does not usually include the introductory letter from the CEO. The chief executive should have control over this document, rather than signing off on a prewritten letter over which he had little control. Nonetheless, the introductory letter is one of the most heavily perused parts of the annual report, so some effort should be made to tie it into the remainder of the document. A good way to obtain this result without appearing overly intrusive is to give the CEO a prioritized list of the financial and operational highlights of the past year, as well as the chief points being raised within the annual report. Most CEOs find that this list helps them to structure the letter, which otherwise has a tendency to be excessively rambling and unfocused.

If the CEO is willing to let someone else write the introductory letter, then the IRO should take over this task. If so, then be sure to consult with the CEO for ideas, and certainly gain his approval of the final draft.

When assembling an annual report, be aware that its audience is primarily *current shareholders*. An IRO tends to focus the annual report on information that an analyst wants to see, even though analysts are not its primary audience. Since analysts are an extremely small proportion of the total number of people reading the annual report, it is better not to skew its contents in their direction—instead, create separate materials for analysts.

In those cases where a significant proportion of investors are located in foreign countries, consider issuing the annual report in multiple languages. This can be a considerable expense, which is only justified by a large user base capable of reading it.

A low-cost alternative to the annual report is called the *wrap report*. This is the annual Form 10-K, with a good-looking cover wrapped around it (hence the name), as well as some introductory materials, such as a letter from the chairman. It is frequently posted electronically on the company Web site, with no paper distribution at all. This an ideal way to edge into the process of having an annual report, without the considerable expense of a more formal document. An even-less-expensive version of the wrap report is one with a slightly reduced font size, which reduces the number of pages that must be printed. A variation is to create a short corporate overview document, and then mail it alongside the Form 10-K; this provides somewhat more information than a typical wrap report, while still keeping costs down.

A rarely used supplement to the annual report is the *quarterly report*. It is generally too expensive to formulate a comprehensive quarterly report, so this tends to be patterned after the 10-K wrap report instead. Also, to reduce costs, it is generally posted on the company Web site, rather than being mailed to investors. The main point when constructing a quarterly report is to ensure that its investment message and content have continuity with the corresponding information in the annual report.

It is also possible to create a *video annual report*, which is issued in addition to the regular annual report and is available on the Internet. This report can be an improvement on the regular annual report, because it may include video clips showing the company's products, manufacturing processes, and anything else that gives viewers a clearer understanding of what the company does. Also, investors can become more comfortable with the company officers presenting the information in the video. In addition, if investors elect to view the report, rather than taking delivery of the printed report, then this reduces the environmental cost of the report. The possible layout of a video annual report is as follows:

1. *Introduction.* The IRO discusses the layout of the presentation and describes additional information available on the company's Web site.
2. *Safe harbor notice.* The viewer must accept this notice before gaining access to additional video screens.
3. *Financial information.* The CFO presents key financial results and metrics.

4. *Question and answer.* The CEO answers the questions most commonly asked by investors.
5. *Product development.* The CEO describes new products and key manufacturing processes.
6. *Links.* The IRO describes how to obtain additional information about the company.

Creating a video annual report requires considerable time to practice for and record the video clips, as well as technical expertise to edit the video and serve the resulting files.

If a company elects to distribute its annual report by the *notice and access model*, it provides notice to its shareholders that they have a choice of receiving the report either by mail or online. The online version of the annual report can be a simple PDF document or a more elaborate HTML version that includes such features as Flash animation, hyperlinks, search capability, downloadable spreadsheets, and video clips. This approach can substantially reduce the cost of the annual report, especially when there are a very large number of shareholders. Thus, the notice and access model is most effective for large-cap companies, which have the largest number of investors.

 ## PRODUCT PIPELINE REPORT

The majority of companies decline to issue reports about the status of new products they are bringing to market on the grounds that this gives competitors too much information. However, investors are keenly interested in the status of products that are subject to regulatory approval, since an approval or rejection can have an enormous impact on a company's valuation. This is certainly the case in the pharmaceuticals industry, where a billion dollars of market capitalization can easily hinge on the outcome of a single phase of drug testing. In such cases, it makes sense to post a regularly updated product pipeline report on the company Web site.

A major pharmaceuticals firm issues a monthly product pipeline report that details the approval phase in which each of its products is currently located. This brief report gives the general status of each drug, without adding any commentary on likely prospects for approval in any given approval stage. Thus, their report is strictly limited to a factual presentation, and does not purport to express an opinion on final approval. Such a simple status report is not for everyone, but can be of value to investors when market capitalization is closely tied to new product approvals or introductions.

## COMPANY-PAID RESEARCH REPORTS

The IRO may occasionally pay an analyst to create a report about her company. This is perfectly acceptable, as long as the relationship between the company and the writer, as well as the amount of compensation being paid, is fully disclosed within the report. The amount of disclosure can go even further, delineating the extent of the writer's relations with the company; any professional credentials that make them qualified to write the report, and any other issues that might impair their objectivity in writing it.

Any amounts paid to a writer who creates a research report should be in cash, and paid in advance. By doing so, the writer will not be influenced by any remaining contingent payments that could increase based on how favorably the report describes the subject company. Also, paying in advance minimizes the risk that the IRO will withhold payment if the research report does not extol the company's virtues. It also helps to have a company policy for not attempting to influence the results of the writer, though in reality this is hard to enforce.

Clearly, finding the best writer is crucial to the creation of a thoroughly researched and well-written report. The perfect writer is one with industry experience, good writing skills, and the willingness to delve deeply into any information provided by the company or which is publicly available, in order to create a well-reasoned and insightful report.

The resulting report may be considered material nonpublic information. Accordingly, make sure that it is widely and equitably distributed, to avoid conflicting with SEC disclosure regulations.

## INDEPENDENT RESEARCH REPORTS

Though not directly sponsored or written by the investor relations department, the IRO should strongly consider issuing reprints of any favorable reports issued by independent analysts. Such reports have a high degree of credibility, given the expert nature of their authors, and so are given considerable credence by the investment community.

These reports are owned by the issuing analyst's firm, so the IRO must first obtain reprint permission. Also, add a disclaimer that the company does not necessarily agree or disagree with the points made in each research report, and that the reprint is strictly for informational purposes.

The buy side of the investment market is the usual target of a reprint mailing, including retail investors, brokers, and institutional investors. Also, sending a reprint to an industry or local publication may spark an inquiry to produce an article about the company.

## WELCOME KIT

Companies sometimes send welcome kits to new investors, especially those acquiring large blocks of company stock. The welcome kit is primarily an assemblage of the standard investor relations publications noted throughout this chapter, and serves to give new investors a solid grounding in the company's operations and potential as an investment.

A basic welcome kit includes a cover letter signed by the CEO, the latest annual report (and quarterly report, if available), and a reply card that asks why recipients bought the company's stock and who originally recommended that they buy it. If the recipient is an institutional investor (who has presumably acquired a very large block of stock), then supplement the welcome kit with annual reports for the last three years, as well as contact information for the senior management team.

A more comprehensive welcome kit could include the most recent product pipeline report, as well as a selection of research reports and media clippings about the company.

Given the cost of a welcome kit and the short duration of some investor holdings, the welcome kit might not always appear to be a cost-effective investor relations publication. However, if limited to those stockholders with significant holdings, it can contribute to somewhat longer-term stockholding periods and even somewhat larger stockholdings.

A larger company with a large investor base can bring some order to the distribution of welcome kits by outsourcing distribution to a distribution center. A smaller firm can assign this function to an administrative person.

## VIDEOS

A few IROs are now delving into the creation of company videos, which are typically posted on the company Web site. The visual impact of a video can supersede the message conveyed through words, and so can be a useful tool in a limited number of situations.

The simplest video with the lowest production cost is of the annual meeting. It requires a single camera that is positioned in a fixed location, and a single microphone on the podium. With a minor amount of editing, someone with minimal training can create an adequate video in short order. Unfortunately, videotaped annual meetings do not make for an exciting viewing experience.

The best use of a video is when the IRO wishes to convey the complexity of a production process, product, or facility. For example, a manufacturer of the new breed of lightweight business jets will certainly want to have a video of a jet in action that it can send to investors. Such products are so exciting that a video presentation will be more likely to sway a potential investor than a glossy brochure. Similarly, a video of an unusual building, such as one of the massive Boeing assembly facilities, conveys the enormous scope of an operation.

Unfortunately, companies rarely have sufficient in-house expertise to create the more complex videos needed to adequately document a product, process, or facility. Instead, it is customary to farm out the work to a professional video shop. Given the expense of these operations, the IRO would be well advised to limit the use of videos to only those applications having the greatest impact on investors.

##  OTHER PUBLICATIONS

There are a variety of supplemental publications that an IRO may find useful in reinforcing the investment message to key constituents. Here are some possible publications to consider:

- *Farewell letter.* A letter sent to investors who have recently sold their shares in the company. This letter is usually signed by the CEO, asks the recipient to keep the company in mind as a future investment, and includes a reply card in case the former investor has concerns about the company that are worth communicating back to the company.
- *Industry articles.* Reprints of informative articles about the industry in which the company operates. These are intended as background information, since they may not even mention the company specifically by name.
- *Internal investor relations handbook.* A short text that instructs internal managers regarding how to deal with inquiries from the investment community. This can include internal contact information for deferring questions to the IRO, disclosure rules, and answers to a set of standard questions.
- *Letters to shareholders.* Letters to shareholders are relatively uncommon but can be used to advise of major corporate events, such as acquisitions or

new product introductions. They can also be used to either amplify upon or contradict a news report, such as a story about a supposedly faulty company product. In addition, they may be necessary for clarifying or debunking a serious rumor, such as takeover discussions.

- ▪ *Product catalogs.* The marketing department likely creates a new product catalog at least annually. If so, send it to key investors and analysts, with a note pointing out which products in the catalog are upgrades or entirely new within the past year.
- ▪ *Speech summaries.* Either synopses or the complete text of major speeches made by senior managers to the investment community. For example, this may include the CEO's speech at the annual shareholders meeting, or a speech made by the CFO during a recent non-deal road show.
- ▪ *Trinkets.* A variety of gifts for analysts, brokers, and investors that remind them of the company. The best gifts are ones that will stay directly in front of the recipient for a long period of time, such as a calendar, mouse pad, or coffee mug.

Who should receive this information? The IRO should consider sending all or a selection of these items to the larger institutional and retail investors, as well as any analysts who follow the company.

## INFORMATION TRACKING SYSTEMS FOR PUBLICATIONS

Over time, an investor relations department will accumulate a large quantity of information for its publications. Given the need for consistency in the information presented, the IRO should institute several systems to ensure that the correct information is sent to the investment marketplace, and that the information is properly stored for easy retrieval.

One useful technique is document version control. Although most easily controlled through a workflow management system, the least expensive approach is to adopt a standard file labeling methodology to ensure that the latest document version is published. This can include the use of a version number on each document, or the incorporation of the current date into the file name. An alternative method is to add a routing sheet to the front of each document, with check boxes and date fields to be completed by each required reviewer. This last method is the low-cost alternative to a workflow management system, and works well as long as someone is monitoring the progress of each document through the reviewer checklist. Otherwise, a document will tend to stall in someone's e-mail box prior to completion.

Once documents have been issued as official publications, store them in a separate subdirectory. This segregates official publications from draft versions. Also, store them within an additional sub-subdirectory by publication type, so that similar documents are conveniently located in the same place. This makes it easier to determine what information was included in previous versions of the same publication. Finally, periodically ensure that this subdirectory is included within the most frequent corporate data backup routines in order to minimize the risk of lost documents.

The cost of new photographs can be considerable, so consider setting up a digital repository for all photos that have been used in the past. It is much less expensive to selectively reuse old photos for which all reprint fees have already been paid than to pay for new photos.

## LEGAL LIABILITY

When creating any publication, consider inserting in it a disclaimer regarding the intent of the document, the source of underlying materials, and any forward-looking statements (see Chapter 10). An example follows:

> The information contained in this document is neither an offer to sell nor a solicitation of an offer to buy any securities mentioned. This document is an information publication and is considered investor relations material. All information regarding [company name] is compiled from SEC (Securities and Exchange Commission) filings, press releases, conference calls, shareholder meetings, investment conferences, and analyst reports. This document may contain "forward-looking statements" as described in the Private Securities Litigation Reform Act of 1995.

## SUMMARY

The ongoing production and dissemination of a variety of publications is a major investor relations task. Though the traditional investor relations publication has been the annual report, it is no longer considered sufficient to issue an annual report and nothing else. Instead, the IRO should authorize a broad mix of publications that conveys to investors a detailed picture of all aspects of a company's financial and operating condition.

# CHAPTER SEVEN

# Investor Relations Web Site

T HE INVESTOR RELATIONS PORTION of a public company's Web site has gradually assumed an increasing level of importance, as investors use the Internet to access the bulk of their investment research information. Accordingly, the public company should pay a great deal of attention to the level of investor relations content provided in its Web site. This chapter provides guidelines for the construction of basic, intermediate, and advanced investor relations Web sites, while also addressing the layout of the site. As examples of Web site excellence, links are also provided to ten sites that incorporate many of the features recommended in this chapter.

## BASIC INVESTOR RELATIONS WEB SITE

The typical investor relations Web site contains the basic set of information required by investors, which includes:

- Stock prices and trading volume (including a history of all transactions, such as stock repurchases, stock splits, and dividend issuances)
- Securities and Exchange Commission (SEC) filings
- Investor relations contact information
- Corporate governance and ethics documents

Even providing this minimal level of information may be a burden if supported internally. The least expensive alternative is to reference the related financial information on either the Google Finance or Yahoo! Finance Web sites. These sites are located, respectively, at www.google.com/finance and yahoo.finance.com. However, sending either current or potential investors to an alternate site will not ensure that they will return to the company Web site to obtain more information about the company. Further, sending them to either of these finance sites will expose them to sites that do not have the same look and feel as the company's Web site, which does not leave an impression of a professionally run site. Finally, these sites regularly post information about the company's competitors, so that potential investors may end up using the Google and Yahoo! sites to invest in a competing company!

An alternative that keeps investors from being redirected outside of the company Web site is to import the requisite information from a third-party provider, who is responsible for updating it on an ongoing basis. An example is Quote Media (accessible at www.quotemedia.com), which compiles current and historical stock prices and trading volumes, charts, and press releases, and feeds it into the corporate Web site. This information can be configured to match the look and feel of the corporate site, and requires essentially no internal programming support. The cost of this service ranges from about $800 to $2,000 month, with the essential stock price and SEC information being available at the lower end of this price range.

The recommendations itemized here for a basic investor relations Web site call for a minimal amount of programming skill and should be achievable by any company. However, though the information provided is adequate, it does nothing to create an environment that investors will want to return to regularly, nor will it create a relationship with investors; these two goals are critical for creating a stable group of long-term investors. The following two sections address these issues.

## INTERMEDIATE INVESTOR RELATIONS WEB SITE

The goal of the intermediate-level investor relations Web site is to increase the "stickiness" of the site, so that visitors will stay there longer and return to it frequently. The improvement recommendations noted in this section require only a modest increase in programming over the requirements of a basic investor relations site. The investor relations officer (IRO) would be well advised to incorporate a mix of the following topics into such a site:

- *Frequently Asked Questions (FAQs)*. Investors usually ask the same questions many times over. For example, they may ask for contact information for the company's stock transfer agent, or whether the company has a dividend reinvestment program or stock purchase program. To accumulate an appropriate set of FAQs, write down the questions posed during conference calls, annual meetings, and investor meetings, and post them, with accompanying answers, on the Web site. Also, consider grouping them by topic. In addition, remember to update the list on an annual basis, since questions will change over time. Further, include a button at the bottom of the FAQs page, which users can click on to submit additional questions.
- *Glossary of terms*. Most industries employ a variety of special terms that may be entirely foreign to a prospective investor. If so, prepare and post a glossary of terms. This is a simple chore, and rarely requires updating.
- *Guide to understanding the financial statements*. Although this feature may seem elementary, it can be useful to include a guide to the layout and presentation of the financial statements. Individual investors especially appreciate this feature.
- *Management and board resumes*. The management team and board of directors may include individuals with impressive credentials. If so, presenting their abbreviated resumes on the Web site may give investors confidence in the ability of this group to lead the company and improve the price of their stock.
- *Board member contact information*. One way to make the members of the board of directors highly accessible to investors is to post their contact information on the Web site. However, this may result in well-known individuals being bombarded with messages. To keep board members from being overwhelmed, route their e-mail addresses posted on the Web site through an administrative assistant, who can screen the incoming mail.
- *Event calendar*. An event calendar should itemize the dates and locations of all upcoming events about which investors may have an interest, such as road shows, sponsored sports events, regulatory filing dates, the annual report publication date, and trade shows. Some companies also include dividend payment dates on the event calendar.
- *Annual meeting home page*. It is useful to congregate all information relating to the annual meeting on one page, rather than scattering it

throughout the site. By doing so, investors can easily locate all of the reports, third-party endorsements, and the information they need for voting purposes.

- *Industry overview.* Many investors have no idea about how a company's industry functions, so prepare and post information about its dynamics and overall growth prospects. This can be in the form of a downloadable white paper. If prepared in sufficient detail, such an overview could be of considerable use to an analyst, who may be sufficiently grateful to at least include the company in an industry analysis, and perhaps even a formal research report. A good example is provided by BP (see the Sample Web Sites section), which posts an overview of the energy markets.

- *Industry trade groups.* List the names and contact information for every industry trade group that the company is a member of. Investors will appreciate this information, since they may want to conduct research through these entities. However, since there is a risk that site visitors will immediately depart for the trade group sites and not return, attempt to have each trade group post on their sites a link back to the company's Web site.

- *List of analysts.* List the names and contact information for all analysts who track the company's performance. It is generally not considered advisable to also include analyst research reports on the Web site, on the grounds that the company may be perceived to be endorsing the analyst opinions as stated in the reports.

- *List of investors.* If the company has notable investors, such as prominent venture capital funds, then consider listing their names on the site. However, this should only be done with the permission of the investors, who may prefer anonymity.

- *Photo archive.* Though not a significant issue, the media will appreciate it if there is a repository of high-resolution photos on the site that they can download. This involves posting a low-resolution thumbnail version of a photo (usually of a manager, board member, or company facility), with a link back to a high-resolution photo that is accessible by clicking on the thumbnail photo.

- *Press release archives.* The typical company issues a multitude of press releases. If so, preserve them in an archive section of the Web site. However, these press releases will likely incorporate forward-looking statements that are now outdated, so include a warning that the information is being provided for historical purposes, but may now be outdated, and so should not be relied upon for investment purposes. Also, include in the summary listing of press releases a one-line summary of each release, so that users will not have to click on each press release link to ascertain the contents of each one.

- *Send a message.* Install an e-mail link on every page, so that visitors can send an e-mail to the investor relations staff. If possible, set up the e-mail system so that an automatic acknowledgment is sent in response to every e-mail. Also, have a procedure in place for responding to these messages, and track the amount of time that passes before each response is sent.
- *Site search feature.* Install a search option on every page of the site. Users should be able to enter search text, and have the system respond with a ranked listing of search results.
- *Software download links.* If any information presented on the Web site requires the use of special software, such as Adobe Acrobat for PDF files or Adobe Flash for a flash presentation, include links to the sites where they can download this software.
- *Speech and conference call transcripts.* If a senior officer of the company makes a speech or there is an investor conference call, prepare a transcript of it, and post it on the Web site. Since speeches are also likely to contain forward-looking statements, post their transcripts in the same archives section as the press releases, so that readers must access the same warning information noted in the previous bullet point for press releases before they can access the transcripts. Also, if a PowerPoint presentation is posted alongside a speech, be sure to strip out lead pages and unnecessary graphics from the files, thereby improving the download speed for these files.
- *Split files.* Many of the files posted on the investor relations site are lengthy, and so present a considerable download problem for those visitors using a slower Internet connection. The solution is to split large reports into sections, and have each section be separately downloadable. For example, the annual Form 10-K can be split into the financial statements in one file, and all other information in another file.
- *Site map.* With all of the additions to the site that are noted in this section, it may become difficult for visitors to navigate the site. To ease navigation, consider adding a site map that lists every page in the investor relations section of the company Web site.

## ADVANCED INVESTOR RELATIONS WEB SITE

The advanced investor relations site requires a considerable and ongoing investment in programming, but pays for this investment by establishing a relationship with each investor who registers on the site. The IRO with a sufficient programming budget should consider incorporating a selection of the following best practices into an advanced investor relations Web site:

- *Alternate language version.* If there are many foreign investors, or if the company plans to attract them, then create a foreign-language version of the site. Obviously, this requires a considerable investment, and so should be limited to a small number of languages. As examples, see the AT&T and Millipore Web sites (see the Sample Web Sites section).

- *Insider stock trades.* The stock trading activity of a company's managers and directors is usually a popular topic with investors, since this activity can indicate insiders' opinion of the value of the stock. Accordingly, offer a database of such trading activity, including the dates and share volumes of each transaction.

- *Interactive tools.* Investors like nothing more than to determine the current value of their stockholdings in the company (especially if the price is trending up!), so post an interactive tool on the site that allows investors to calculate the value of their current holdings, based on the most recent stock price.

- *Issue event reminders.* If there is a posting of upcoming events on the Web site, then offer a service to investors, where the company will send them a reminder e-mail a few days prior to the event. An excellent example of this service can be found on the Millipore Web site (see the Sample Web Sites section).

- *Pop-up survey.* A great way to determine the effectiveness of a Web page is to incorporate a pop-up survey that asks a viewer about the usability and presentation of information found on a specific page. Only use this feature selectively, since it can become annoying if it appears on every page.

- *Registration option.* The best single way to build a relationship with a Web site visitor is to encourage them to register to receive additional information from the company. At the point of registration, users could be asked for their contact information, age, number of shares owned, how long they've held the stock, how they found the Web site, and so on (also provide a privacy statement, itemizing how the company plans to use this information). This can be a difficult task, so encourage them with an incentive, such as a discount coupon to purchase a company product or a charitable donation on their behalf. Also, itemize on the registration page exactly what information the company will send to them, and how frequently it will be sent. The user can even select from a menu of different mailings, such as notifications of SEC filings, press releases, copies of investor presentations, or an audio CD containing the latest conference call or video presentation. Also, once users register, send them an automated confirming e-mail message that is signed by the company CEO, thanking them for their interest in the company. There are numerous examples of this option listed in the Sample Web Sites section.

- *RSS feed.* An RSS feed is a subscription to updates from a Web site, so that subscribers are automatically notified when updates are made. To use it, a site visitor clicks on the RSS button posted on the site, copies the associated link, and pastes it into his RSS reader software.

- *Send page link.* If an investor likes a Web page on the company's site, encourage them to send it to a friend by entering an e-mail address on the page. This also gives the company contact information for another person who may eventually become an investor.

- *Short Messaging Service stock price updates.* A small number of sites offer a short messaging service (SMS) to registered users that sends updates to the company stock price directly to their cell phones in the form of text messages. The Invensys Web site, which is referenced later in the Sample Web Sites section, contains this feature.

- *Tailored Web pages.* Give people who register on the site the option to create a customized Web page that clusters together only the information they want to see. This customized page can then be activated by a cookie, or by their signing into the site. Though difficult to implement, this feature represents the state of the art in establishing relationships with individual investors.

- *Unsubscribe option.* If a Web site actively encourages people to register to receive additional communications from the company, then there is also an obligation to allow them to unsubscribe. The unsubscribe option should be discretely included in every communication sent to anyone who has registered to receive information from the company.

- *Video feed.* The Web site can include a selection of video presentations by the management team, and even speeches by director candidates. Ideally, the video feed can also list a rolling transcript of the speech, for those users who do not have access to an audio link. There can also be an associated link to any PowerPoint slides used during the presentation. Given the complexity of such an integrated feed, it may be easier to have a third party host the feed, with a link to it on the company's Web site.

Of these items, the registration option is by far the most important. Nearly all of the most advanced Web sites contain this feature. The trend appears to be in the direction of only obtaining a visitor's e-mail address, with no additional information requested. Also, the most popular registration format is to allow visitors to select from a set of newsletters in determining what information shall be delivered to them.

One of the key aspects of an advanced site is to "push" information to registered users. When doing so, be very careful of the size of the files being sent. An excessively large file, which should be considered anything larger than one megabyte, may be rejected by the recipient's e-mail system. Further, these bounced messages will then be scheduled by the company's e-mail server for several additional send iterations, which will slow down the server's perform- ance. Consequently, it is better to post large files to the company Web site, and only send e-mails to recipients that contain links back to the files, which they may then choose to download.

 ## WEB SITE LAYOUT

No matter what level of content is included in the investor relations section of the Web site, it should follow a general format that eases site navigation and presents the most important information to investors at once. Here are some site layout options to consider:

- *Initial link.* From a company's home page, the traditional format of the link to the investor relations section is to include either "Investors" or "Investor Relations" in the header bar. When visitors click on the word or phrase, they will be sent to the home page of the investor relations section of the Web site.
- *Link summary.* The home page of the investor relations section should prominently display all links in either a header or side bar. Given the large potential number of links to be contained within this bar, it is generally easier to list it down the left side of the page, where it can be extended considerably. A typical layout of this information is as follows:
  - About the company
  - Structure and management (subheadings for corporate governance documents and management resumes)
  - Financial performance
  - Share information
  - Press releases
  - Presentations and Webcasts
  - Calendar of events

■ Investing in the company (subheadings for stock purchase plans and dividend reinvestment plans)
■ Investor relations contacts
■ E-mail alerts
■ Investor tools
■ Information request

■ *Stock quote information.* It is customary to include the most recently quoted stock price in a box that is placed in the same position on every page of the investor relations site, on the assumption that this is the single most important item of information that visitors want to see. In addition to the stock price, this box may include the name of the exchange where the stock is traded. It is usually located in the upper-right corner of every page.

■ *Fresh information on home page.* The investor relations home page should contain the most recent news, in order to attract visitors back to the site on a recurring basis. Thus, it is customary to see links on the home page to the latest conference call transcripts, press releases, and general industry news that may impact investors. In an effort to provide extremely fresh information, some sites even invite registered users to post questions to the company, to which the management team posts answers at regular intervals.

■ *Printing option.* Always offer a printable version of each page, since the structure of some Web pages makes them difficult to print. The printing option should be in the form of a printer icon, which is usually located near a corner of each Web page.

■ *Last updated notice.* Every page of the site should contain a notice at the bottom of the page that states when the page was last updated. Visitors will be more likely to review a page if it was recently updated.

##  HYPERLINK LIABILITY

The SEC issued an interpretive release in April 2000 in which it provided guidance regarding whether a hyperlink on a company's Web site to a third-party site creates an assumption that the company has adopted the information in the third-party site. The following issues tend to support that assumption:

■ *Context.* A hyperlink is contained within a portion of the company Web site that constitutes a document that satisfies the delivery requirements of the securities laws.

- *Differentiation.* The shift to a third-party site is not readily discernible to the user. This issue can be mitigated by inserting a screen that appears after a user clicks a hyperlink, stating that the user is now leaving the company's Web site.
- *Endorsement.* The company has specifically endorsed the statements in the third-party site.
- *Timing.* The company is in the process of registering its securities.

If, based on these criteria, it appears that a company has adopted the information in a third-party Web site, the SEC can hold the company accountable for statements made on that site. Consequently, it is extremely advisable to only include hyperlinks after review by corporate counsel.

 ## SAMPLE WEB SITES

The reader should supplement the information noted in this chapter with a perusal of the sites of companies having excellent investor relations Web sites. For this purpose, Exhibit 7.1 itemizes the names, Web site addresses, and prominent features of the investor relations sites of ten companies.

**Exhibit 7.1**  Sample Investor Relations Web Sites

| Company Name | Site Link | Site Features |
| --- | --- | --- |
| AT&T | att.com | Guide to determining stock cost basis, RSS feed, glossary of industry terms, available in 12 languages, supplementary operating data |
| Bottomline Technologies | bottomline.com | Sign up for four types of mailings, itemizes all analysts providing coverage, offers an investor kit |
| BP | bp.com | Search archives based on category and date, RSS feed, interactive charting tool, online investment courses, industry overview, summary of share ownership by type, region, and holdings |
| ExxonMobil | exxonmobil.com | Risk factors report, glossary of terms, shareholder issues section (conservation, human rights, political contributions) |
| IBM | ibm.com | Multiple podcast subscriptions, RSS feed, new investor package, glossary of industry terms, guide to reading an annual report, separate FAQs for institutional investors |

| Company Name | Site Link | Site Features |
|---|---|---|
| Invensys | invensys.com | Sends stock price information to a mobile device, summarizes all outstanding debt and related credit ratings, RSS feed |
| Merck | merck.com | Research pipeline report, RSS feed, podcast |
| Millipore | millipore.com | Presented in eight languages, will e-mail reminders of upcoming events, can compare stock performance against other companies or indexes |
| Vodafone | vodaphone.com | Thorough explanation of dividend strategy, can click on specific days on the stock chart to determine prices and volumes by day, can convert share value to euros, dollars, or yen |

## SUMMARY

There are two crucial elements involved in the design of the investor relations Web site. First, try not to redirect visitors outside of the site, since they may not return. Second, try to build a relationship with users through the use of extra content, constantly refreshed information, and a registration that entitles users to additional features. Although the first element can be dealt with through careful site design, the second element can be expensive to implement and maintain.

Further, be sure to track the site traffic with a Web analytics package, to see which features are being most heavily used by site visitors. If a specific feature enjoys high popularity, then move it onto the investor relations home page, or within one click of that page.

Finally, even the finest investor relations Web site will attract no visitors if no one knows about it. Accordingly, continually promote the site by describing it in the annual report, promotional materials, press releases, speeches, and company newsletters. Also, include the site link on company business cards. These continuing efforts will raise awareness of the site and drive more visitors to it.

# CHAPTER EIGHT

# Management Discussion and Analysis Section

THE MANAGEMENT DISCUSSION AND Analysis of Financial Condition and Results of Operations (MD&A) section of the financial statements is closely examined by investors because it contains management's perspective on a company's financial performance. This is an area in which the investor relations officer (IRO) should have a great deal of input, because it forms a core part of the information issued by a company. It appears in the annual 10-K and quarterly 10-Q filings, as well as registration statements for securities, and is commonly added to earnings releases.

## MD&A REPORTING REQUIREMENTS

The requirements for the contents of the MD&A section are outlined in Item 303 of Regulation S-K, Items 303(b) and (c) of Regulation S-B, Item 5 of Form 20-F, and paragraph 11 of General Instruction B of Form 40-F. Regulation S-K describes the form and content of financial statements filed by most larger public companies, while Regulation S-B sets forth the same requirements for small businesses. Form 20-F sets forth the filing requirements for the registration of securities by a foreign company, while Form 40-F describes the same requirements for Canadian companies. The requirements under Regulations S-K and S-B are paraphrased in the following paragraphs. The instructions for Forms 20-F and 40-F can be found at the "Descriptions of SEC Forms" link on the www.sec.gov home page of the Securities and Exchange Commission.

The primary instructions for the MD&A sections of larger public companies are contained within Item 303 of Regulation S-K. These requirements are divided into the following five sections:

1. *Liquidity.* Identify any trends or events that are likely to result in a material change in liquidity. If there is likely to be a material deficiency in liquidity, then indicate steps being taken or contemplated to correct the problem. Also, describe both internal and external sources of liquidity, and discuss any material unused sources of liquidity. Further, note any restrictions on the ability of subsidiaries to transfer funds to the parent company as dividends, loans, or advances, and the impact these restrictions have had, and are expected to have, on the company's liquidity. This discussion should be on both a short-term and long-term basis.

2. *Capital resources.* Note all material commitments for capital expenditures at the end of the latest fiscal period, the purpose of the expenditures, and the source of the funds needed to make the expenditures. Also, discuss any trends in capital resources, including expected changes in their mix and cost.

3. *Results of operations.* Discuss any unusual or infrequent events that materially impacted income from continuing operations, and the extent to which the income was changed. Further, describe any other elements of revenue and expense that assist the reader in understanding the results of operations. Also, describe any trends or uncertainties that will materially alter net sales or income from continuing operations. If there are material changes in net sales, then describe the extent to which the changes are caused by differences in prices, sales volume, or new products, respectively. Finally, for the last three fiscal years, describe the impact of inflation and changing prices on net sales and on income from continuing operations, though only if these changes are material.

4. *Off-balance-sheet arrangements.* Discuss any off-balance-sheet arrangements that will likely have a material effect on the company's financial condition. This discussion should include the business purpose of each such arrangement, as well as its importance to the company's liquidity, capital resources, and risk. Also, describe the amount of any company revenues, expenses, and cash flows resulting from such arrangements, the amounts of interests retained, and the amounts of securities issued and debt incurred

as a result of such arrangements. Note the extent of any material liabilities that are likely to be caused by such arrangements and the triggering events that will cause them. Further, note any events or uncertainties that could reduce the benefits derived by the company from such arrangements, and the steps taken by the company to deal with them.

5. *Tabular disclosure of contractual obligations.* Itemize in a tabular format, as of the latest fiscal year-end balance sheet date, the aggregated amounts of the following contractual obligations: long-term debt obligations, capital lease obligations, operating lease obligations, purchase obligations, and other long-term liabilities. The table shall separate these aggregated amounts into payments due in less than one year, in one to three years, in three to five years, and in more than five years. This disclosure may also include descriptions of any contractual obligations that change or accelerate obligations, as well as any other information that increases the reader's understanding of the obligations.

Item 303 also requires that the causes of material changes occurring from year to year in the financial statements be described sufficiently to provide an understanding of the reasons for the changes. This does not mean that a line-by-line analysis of the financial statements be provided, nor is it necessary to itemize the amounts of changes from year to year that the reader can readily compute from the financial statements. Item 303 specifically states that the discussion should not "merely repeat numerical data," shown in the financial statements (more on this issue shortly).

Item 303 also notes that discussions of liquidity and capital resources may be combined whenever the two topics are interrelated. Further, a discussion of segment information should be included when this will increase a reader's understanding of the business.

Items 303(b) and (c) of Regulation S-B also address MD&A, but only for smaller public companies. The amount of required disclosure for this class of company is reduced from the requirements for a large business, as just described for Item 303 of Regulation S-K. The key reporting requirements for smaller public companies are as follows:

- *Liquidity trends.* Discuss trends, events, or uncertainties that are likely to have a material impact on liquidity.
- *Liquidity sources.* Discuss both internal and external sources of liquidity.
- *Capital expenditures.* Note any material commitments for capital expenditures and how the company plans to obtain funding for these expenditures.

- *Revenue and income trends.* Itemize any trends, events, or uncertainties that may have a material impact on net revenues or income from continuing operations.
- *Nonoperational issues.* Describe any material elements of income or loss not caused by continuing operations.
- *Inter-period changes.* Address the causes of any material changes in financial statement line items from one reporting period to another.
- *Seasonality.* Note any seasonality that materially affects the results of operations.
- *Off-balance-sheet arrangements.* Discuss any off-balance-sheet arrangements that will likely have a material effect on the company's financial condition. This discussion should include the business purpose of each such arrangement, as well as its importance to the company's liquidity, capital resources, and risk. Also, describe the amount of any company revenues, expenses, and cash flows resulting from such arrangements, the amounts of interests retained, and the amounts of securities issued and debt incurred as a result of such arrangements. Also note the extent of any material liabilities that are likely to be caused by such arrangements, and the triggering events that will cause them. Further, note any events or uncertainties that could reduce the benefits derived by the company from such arrangements, and the steps taken by the company to deal with them.

Unfortunately, and despite the specificity of the SEC's requirements, a great many MD&A sections have degenerated into a bald analysis that shows percentage changes in various accounts over the previous period, with a minimum of additional discussion. An example follows:

> The margin of our consulting segment improved to $(261,000) in fiscal 2007 from $(475,000) in fiscal 2010. Of this $214,000 improvement, $131,000 was caused by an increase in revenues due to the continuation of a consulting services contract that began during the second half of 2010.

The example suffers from several flaws. Even though there is an improvement in margins, there is no commentary on why the segment still suffers from a loss. Also, there is no mention of what specific factors drive the segment's performance. In short, the two-sentence discussion of a company's entire operating division leaves the reader with very little information about how the segment really operates, and why it has achieved the itemized results.

## SEC GUIDANCE

The Securities and Exchange Commission (SEC) has become concerned about this trend toward minimization of the MD&A section, and so issued guidance on the topic in 2003. The full 28-page document is available at www.sec.gov/rules/interp/33-8350.htm. The SEC's overview of this guidance clearly reveals the general type of MD&A disclosure that it would like to see:

> We believe that management's most important responsibilities include communicating with investors in a clear and straightforward manner. MD&A is a critical component of that communication. The Commission has long sought through its rules, enforcement actions and interpretive processes to elicit MD&A that not only meets technical disclosure requirements but generally is informative and transparent.

The guidance document goes on to point out that its MD&A requirements are intended to satisfy three objectives, which are (1) to provide a narrative of a company's financial statements that enables investors to obtain management's view of the company, (2) to provide the context within which financial information should be analyzed, and (3) to provide information about the quality and variability of a company's earnings and cash flow.

The guidance document then provides a series of qualitative directives for the improvement of MD&A, which are as follows:

- *Overview.* Provide an executive-level overview at the beginning of each MD&A that provides context for the remaining information presented in the MD&A section. The overview could contain a discussion of industry-wide factors that may impact the company, how the company earns revenues and income, how it generates cash, key lines of business and products, and key opportunities and challenges.
- *Measurements.* Discuss key performance indicators (of both the financial and operational varieties) that management uses to run the company. If used, companies should provide an explanation of the calculation of each indicator, so that investors can compare its results to those of other companies.
- *Implications.* Note management's view of the implications of the information presented in the MD&A section. This should extend to an analysis of the specific reasons why an event has occurred. For example, if sales decline, then describe the underlying material reasons for the decline, such as a constriction in the supplies of a key product component. This level of description should also extend to changes in accounting estimates. For

example, if a change in estimate materially impacts reported profitability, then disclose the reason for and amount of the change attributable to the change in estimate. By doing so, readers will not incorrectly attribute the change to the company's operational performance. As another example, the incurrence of debt should be accompanied by a discussion of the circumstances necessitating the use of debt, how the funds are to be used, and how it fits into the company's business plan.

- *Presentation by level of importance.* Design the disclosure so that the most important information is displayed most prominently.
- *Immaterial and duplicative information.* Eliminate immaterial information that does not lead to a better understanding of a company's financial condition and liquidity. Similarly, avoid duplicative disclosure, since it overwhelms readers and interferes with the identification of important information. It is both acceptable and encouraged to group line items in the MD&A section in order to avoid duplicative disclosure.
- *Tabular presentation.* Consider using a tabular presentation of results in different periods, including percentage changes. This presentation would then be followed by a narrative discussion of the information contained within the table.

In particular, the SEC states multiple times in the guidance that it encourages the use of forward-looking information. For example,

we ... encourage companies to discuss prospective matters and include forward-looking information in circumstances where that information may not be required, but will provide useful material information for investors that promotes understanding.

## EXAMPLES OF ENHANCED MD&A DISCLOSURE

Given the SEC's guidance, it is apparent that a substantially different level of disclosure should be issued than that noted in the earlier example, which is repeated here:

The margin of our consulting segment improved to $(261,000) in fiscal 2010 from $(475,000) in fiscal 2009. Of this $214,000 improvement, $131,000 was caused by an increase in revenues due to the continuation of a consulting services contract that began during the second half of 2009.

A more appropriate level of MD&A disclosure reveals the underlying revenue and profitability drivers of the segment, as well as management's plans for how to achieve profitability:

> The operating results of our consulting segment are influenced primarily by the billable percentage of its employees and their average billing rate per hour. The segment's billable percentage increased from 67 percent in 2009 to 74 percent in 2010, while the average billing rate per hour increased to $102 from $93 during the same period. The increase in the average billing rate is indicative of the company's decision to employ more consultants with top-secret clearances, which command higher hourly rates. Thus, the margin of our consulting segment improved to $(261,000) in fiscal 2010 from $(475,000) in fiscal 2009. The continuing losses in this segment are caused by low billable percentages, which management is addressing by consolidating the work force and avoiding smaller consulting contracts for which billable percentages tend to be low.

This level of disclosure is in accordance with the spirit of the SEC guidance, which is to place the investor in the position of management in understanding how the business operates.

Another example is shown below, where disclosure (a) itemizes nothing more than the facts surrounding an increase in working capital, while disclosure (b) expands on the situation to reveal exactly why the changes occurred and how management has dealt with it. If investors were to read disclosure (a), they would have no idea why the receivables investment increased and might react negatively by selling their shares. However, the addendum in disclosure (b) shows that management has deliberately sold off inventory that would otherwise become obsolete, and has guarded against expected bad debt losses with a substantial reserve. Because of the extra information in disclosure (b), investors would rightly conclude that management has just made an excellent decision regarding the disposition of selected inventory items, and might even buy more shares to express their confidence in management.

(a) During the year ended December 31, 2010, our operating activities used $78,000 of cash. This reflected a $200,000 net profit and a $278,000 use of cash that was caused by an increase in accounts receivable.

(b) [in addition to the preceding disclosure] The increased investment in accounts receivable was the result of a loosening of the company's credit policy for selected products that were scheduled for replacement by new product lines in 2011. Management expects that the company will experience losses approximating 25 percent of sales on the incremental sales of expiring products, and has fully reserved this amount in the 2010 financial statements.

A final example is shown next, where disclosure (a) reveals that a company has drastically reduced its capital expenditures. This is in contravention to the standard industry practice (in the example) of heavy annual capital expenditures. A reasonable investor would assume that the spending reduction is caused by decreasing cash flow, and would likely sell shares. Only through the use of disclosure (b) does the company show that this change is not based on poor liquidity but, rather, on a strategic shift to a different investment strategy that may propel the company to above-average profitability in comparison to its peers. Once again, the extra level of disclosure is of assistance in clarifying financial information, which investors might otherwise find disturbing.

(a) Net cash used in our investing activities was $354,000 and $1,806,000 for the years ended December 31, 2010 and 2009, respectively.

(b) [in addition to the preceding disclosure] The reduced investment during 2010 reflected management's change in strategy to invest only in those manufacturing bottleneck operations where increased capacity will lead to direct, proven increases in throughput. As a result, we expect reduced levels of capital expenditures for the next two years.

## A CASE FOR FULL DISCLOSURE

What if the enhanced levels of MD&A disclosure advocated by the SEC result in the release of information that does not cast the best light on a company's operations? Is this bad? The alternative is for investors to ask questions during conference calls or annual meetings about topics that have not been adequately disclosed. In these cases, management must provide answers that may not be entirely scripted, resulting in answers that leave investors wondering if management is hiding information, or does not have a firm grasp on company operations. In short, it is always better to use full MD&A disclosure, since this is an excellent avenue for presenting a carefully constructed message to investors.

Typically, MD&A is written by the accounting staff and reviewed by the corporate attorney before being released to the public. This common scenario is a bad one for the IRO, because the accounting staff wants to spend the least possible amount of time writing the MD&A, and so will copy forward the information from the immediately preceding filing, with the smallest possible number of updates. Further, the attorney will advocate a minimum of presented information, on the grounds that there will be less released information for which the company can be sued. In short, the most common procedure for writing the MD&A results in the worst possible presentation of information from the perspective of investor relations.

To combat this situation, the IRO should appeal to the chief executive officer to adopt a more comprehensive approach to MD&A that results in a significantly greater degree of disclosure. If the combined weight of the arguments presented by the accounting and legal departments continue to prevail, then another alternative is to bring in the services of an independent investor relations agency to provide a third-party view of the correct level of disclosure. Yet another alternative is to conduct a benchmarking analysis of the levels of disclosure practiced by competing firms, or by those who are generally considered to exercise best practices in investor relations. If all of these options fail and the company continues to practice minimal MD&A disclosure, then record all investor and analyst questions posed during subsequent conference calls and annual meetings and note how these questions could have been answered through an expanded MD&A section. Armed with this additional information, the IRO may eventually win over the other parties to the more expansive viewpoint of constructing a more informative and useful MD&A section.

## SUMMARY

In summary, the MD&A section is a critical part of the information package presented by a company to its investors. Not only does the SEC require an expansive presentation of information in the MD&A, but this is also good business practice from the perspective of investor relations. Accordingly, the IRO should be deeply involved in the construction of every MD&A section included in any SEC filing.

# CHAPTER NINE

# Disclosure

NFORMATION ABOUT A COMPANY is considered material when it can sway investors to alter their holdings of company stock. When company employees release such information, the company must disclose it through a limited set of information channels that are acceptable to the SEC, so that everyone in the investment community has equal access to it. If this information involves a company's financial and operating results, then the SEC requires that it be disclosed in a precise format, known as *structured disclosure*, through an annual 10-K report, quarterly 10-Q report, Form 8-K, and the like, with the intent being to allow investors to compare similar information for multiple companies that are provided in the same format.

There is also *unstructured disclosure*, which is information that a company can disclose without using an SEC-mandated format. Examples of unstructured disclosure are annual reports, letters to shareholders, press releases, advertisements, speeches, conference calls, and phone conversations with investors and analysts.

What types of information must be disclosed, and in what format? Although the extremely detailed requirements for 10-K and 10-Q reporting are beyond the scope of this book, the next section provides guidelines for Form 8-K event reporting; this covers structured disclosure for a large number of events that a company will regularly encounter. A later section also notes the correct format for the disclosure of non-GAAP (Generally Accepted Accounting Principles) information. Also, we address the important Regulation FD (Fair Disclosure), which generally applies to unstructured disclosure, and governs the release of material information. Finally, we describe a disclosure policy and how to enforce it.

 ## FORM 8-K

A public company is required to file a Form 8-K to report a material, undisclosed event. The form must be filed within four business days of the event. If the event occurs on a weekend or holiday, then the four-day rule shall begin on the next business day thereafter. A moderately active company will find itself filing this form quite frequently; possibly more than all other forms combined.

The SEC defines a number of types of material events that must be reported in a Form 8-K; they are described in Exhibit 9.1. For the more common Form 8-K disclosures, examples are also provided.

**Exhibit 9.1**　Material Events Reported in a Form 8-K

**Section 1—Company's Business and Operations**

| | |
|---|---|
| Item 1.01 | *Entry into a material definitive agreement.* This is for a material definitive agreement not made in the ordinary course of business. Disclose the date of the agreement, the parties involved, and a brief description of the agreement. |
| | **Example:** On [date] we entered into an amendment to our senior secured credit facility with ABC Bank, which amends the borrowing base definition. Under the terms of the amendment, the percentage of receivables to be included in the borrowing base is changed from 70 percent to 80 percent. |
| Item 1.02 | *Termination of a material definitive agreement.* This is for the termination of a material definitive agreement not made in the ordinary course of business. Disclose the termination date, the parties involved, and a brief description of the agreement, as well as the circumstances surrounding the termination and any material early termination penalties incurred by the company. |
| | **Example:** On [date] the Company terminated its previously announcement Agreement and Plan of Merger, dated as of [date], with XYZ Company. The Company's board of directors did not believe that the merger could be finalized. |
| Item 1.03 | *Bankruptcy or receivership.* This is for a company's entry into bankruptcy or receivership. Identify the proceeding, the identity of the court, the date that jurisdiction was assumed, and the identity of the receiver. If a plan of |

reorganization or liquidation has been entered, then disclose the court, confirmation date, and the material features of the plan.

**Example:** On [date], ABC Company filed a voluntary petition for relief under chapter 11 of the United States bankruptcy code in the United States Bankruptcy Court, Southern District of New York (case number 01234). The Debtors will continue to operate the business as "debtors-in-possession" under the jurisdiction of the Court and in accordance with applicable provisions of the Bankruptcy Code and orders of the Court. The filing is attached hereto.

### Section 2—Financial Information

| Item 2.01 | *Completion of acquisition or disposition of assets.* For the purchase or sale of a significant amount of assets, disclose the transaction date, the other party, the amount of consideration involved, and the source of funds used for an acquisition. |
|---|---|

**Example:** On [date], stockholders of ABC Company ("ABC") approved and adopted the Agreement and Plan of Merger, dated as of [date] by and among XYZ Company ("XYZ") and ABC, which contemplated that XYZ will merge with and into ABC, with ABC surviving the merger as a wholly owned subsidiary of XYZ. On [date], the merger was consummated. Pursuant to the terms of the Merger Agreement, former ABC common stockholders are entitled to receive $1.15 in cash in exchange for each share of ABC common stock, outstanding immediately prior to the effective time of the merger.

| Item 2.02 | *Results of operations and financial condition.* Note the date of the release of any material, nonpublic information regarding the company's results of operations or financial condition, and attach the text of the release. |
|---|---|

**Example:** On [date], the Company announced its financial results for the quarter ended September 30, 20XX. The full text of the press release issued in connection with the announcement is furnished as an exhibit to this Form 8-K.

| Item 2.03 | *Creation of a direct financial obligation or an obligation under an off-balance-sheet arrangement of a company.* When the company enters into a material obligation, disclose the transaction date and the amount and terms of the obligation. |
|---|---|

**Example:** ABC Company ("ABC") will become obligated on material direct financial obligations pursuant to the Credit Agreement dated as of [date], among ABC and Big Bank ("Big"). Under the terms of the Credit Agreement, Big will make available to ABC up to a $100,000,000 term loan commitment and up to a $50,000,000 revolving loan commitment. Proceeds of the credit agreement may be used for general corporate purposes. The principal amount outstanding of all term loans and revolving loans is due and payable on [date]. Loans will bear interest at Big's base rate plus an applicable margin ranging from 0 percent to 0.2 percent, based on ABC's credit rating. Interest on base rate loans is payable on a quarterly basis on the last day of March, June, September, and December, and interest is payable at the end of the applicable interest period.

*(continued)*

## Exhibit 9.1  *(Continued)*

| | |
|---|---|
| Item 2.04 | *Triggering events that accelerate or increase a direct financial obligation or an obligation under an off-balance-sheet arrangement.* If a triggering event occurs, note the date of the event and provide a brief description of it, as well as the amount of the obligation. |

**Example:** On [date], the Company received notices from ABC Advisors, holder of the Company's convertible debentures, claiming that the Company was in default of the terms of the debentures for failure to maintain current financial statements in the registration statement relating to the sale of the Company's common stock issuable on conversion of one of those debentures, and as a result that ABC Advisors was exercising its right to accelerate payment of the full principal amount of the debentures. Approximately $25 million, including interest, is currently outstanding on the debentures.

| | |
|---|---|
| Item 2.05 | *Costs associated with exit or disposal activities.* If the company commits to an exit or disposal plan, note the date of the commitment, the course of action to be taken, and the expected completion date. For each major type of cost, also estimate the range of amounts expected to be incurred. |

**Example:** On [date], the Company committed to a restructuring plan that includes a reduction in force of approximately 500 positions. The restructuring plan is intended to improve operational efficiencies. The Company anticipates that it will complete the restructuring by [date]. In connection with the restructuring, the Company expects to incur total expenses relating to termination benefits of $21 million to $24 million, all of which represent cash expenditures. The Company expects to record the majority of these restructuring charges in the quarter ending December 31, 20XX.

| | |
|---|---|
| Item 2.06 | *Material impairments.* If the company concludes that one or more of its assets are impaired, then disclose the date of the decision, describe the asset, and note the circumstances leading to the conclusion. Also note the amount of the impairment. |

**Example:** During the quarter ended September 30, 20XX, as part of the Company's ongoing strategic review of the business, an impairment analysis was performed on the Aerospace segment goodwill and intangible assets. On [date] the Company concluded that noncash goodwill and intangible asset impairment charges of $10 million were required and such charges were recorded in the quarter ended September 30, 20XX.

### Section 3—Securities and Trading Markets

| | |
|---|---|
| Item 3.01 | *Notice of delisting or failure to satisfy a continued listing rule or standard; transfer of listing.* Disclose the date when the company received notice from a national exchange that a class of its common equity does not satisfy its continued listing, or that the exchange expects to delist it. Also note the rule being violated that led to the notification, and the action the company expects to take in response. If company has caused an exchange listing to be withdrawn, then describe the action taken and the date of the action. |

**Example:** ABC Company today announced it has received notice from NASDAQ that its common stock is subject to potential delisting from the NASDAQ Capital Market because the bid price of the Company's common stock closed below the minimum $1.00 per share requirement for 30 consecutive business days prior to [date]. The Company has been granted an initial 180 calendar days, or until [date], to regain compliance.

Item 3.02

*Unregistered sales of equity securities.* In the event of an unregistered security sale, state the date of sale, the type and amount of securities sold, the consideration paid, the type of exemption from registration being claimed, and any convertibility terms. This report only need be filed if the shares issued are more than 1 percent of the shares outstanding. For a smaller reporting company, the reporting threshold is 5 percent of the shares outstanding.

**Example:** On [date], accredited investors purchased an aggregate of 25,000,000 shares of common stock at $2.00 per share for an aggregate purchase price of $50,000,000 from ABC Company ("ABC"). The funds raised will be utilized by ABC for working capital and research purposes. The shares were offered and sold to the accredited investors in a private placement transaction made in reliance upon exemptions from registration pursuant to Section 4(2) under the Securities Act of 1933. Each of the Investors are accredited investors as defined in Rule 501 of Regulation D promulgated under the Securities Act of 1933.

Item 3.03

*Material modification to rights of security holders.* Disclose the date of modification, the type of security involved, and the effect of the modification on the rights of the security holders.

**Example:** On [date], ABC Company entered into an amendment to its Preferred Stock Rights Agreement dated [date] with XYZ Trust Company to amend the exercise price of a right to purchase one share of its Series A Preferred Stock to $25.00 per share, and to make certain conforming changes related to the change in exercise price.

**Section 4—Matters Related to Accountants and Financial Statements**

Item 4.01

*Changes in the company's certifying accountant.* If the company's auditor resigns or is dismissed, disclose whether the change was a resignation or dismissal, and whether the auditor's report for either of the past two years contained an adverse opinion or disclaimer of opinion, or was qualified. Also state whether the change was recommended or approved by the company's board of directors or its audit committee, and whether there were any disagreements with the auditor during the two most recent fiscal years that were not resolved to the satisfaction of the auditor.

**Example:** On [date], our client-auditor relationship with XYZ Auditor ("XYZ") ceased. As of that date, ABC Company (the "ABC") had no disagreements with XYZ on any matter of accounting principles or practices, financial statement disclosure, or auditing scope or procedure. We have provided XYZ with a copy

*(continued)*

**Exhibit 9.1** *(Continued)*

of the disclosures we are making in response to this Item 4.01. XYZ has furnished us with a letter dated [date], addressed to the Commission, and stating that it agrees with the statements made herein.

Item
4.02

*Nonreliance on previously issued financial statements or a related audit report or completed interim review.* If the company concludes that any previously issued financial statements cannot be relied upon because of an error, disclose the date of this decision, and describe the facts underlying the decision. There are multiple additional steps to be taken besides filing this Form 8-K.

**Example:** On [date], management of the Company, with concurrence of the Audit Committee of the Company's Board of Directors (the "Audit Committee"), concluded that the Company's previously issued financial statements for the three months ended March 31, 20XX (the "Financials"), incorrectly valued an allowance against deferred tax assets. As a result, the Financials should no longer be relied on. The Company intends to file amended financial statements in a Form 10-Q/A for the three month period ended March 31, 20XX, no later than May 31, 20XX. During the first quarter of 20XX, in accordance with Statement of Financial Accounting Standards No. 109, "Accounting for Income Taxes" ("FAS 109"), the Company recorded a valuation allowance of $125 million to reduce certain net deferred tax assets to their anticipated realizable value. The Company later realized it had incorrectly determined the valuation allowance against deferred tax assets. The Company and its auditors have reached a preliminary conclusion that an additional valuation allowance of $45 million should have been recorded at March 31, 20XX.

**Section 5—Corporate Governance and Management**

Item
5.01

*Changes in control of the company.* Identify the person acquiring control of the company and the date of the change, and describe the transaction resulting in the change of control. Also note the amount of consideration used to effect the change and the source of the person's funds to do so.

**Example:** On [date], Current Investor, the controlling shareholder of ABC Company ("ABC"), entered into a Securities Purchase and Sale Agreement with XYZ Company ("XYZ"). Pursuant to the Securities Purchase and Sale Agreement, Current Investor agreed to sell all of his shares of the Company's common stock to XYZ. Upon the closing of the Securities Purchase and Sale Agreement on [date] (the "Closing"), a change in control of the Company occurred. Pursuant to the Securities Purchase and Sale Agreement, XYZ has acquired 5,000,000 shares of the Company's common stock from Current Investor. XYZ paid $15,000,000 to acquire such shares. Funds for the acquisition were from the working capital of XYZ. XYZ now owns 80 percent of ABC's issued and outstanding shares.

Item
5.02

*Departure of directors or certain officers; election of directors; appointment of certain officers.* If a director resigns, is removed, or refuses to stand for reelection because of a disagreement with the company, note the date of the event, the director's committee positions held, and describe the disagreement. If the director has provided any written correspondence related to the disagreement, then this must be attached as an exhibit.

**Example:** Mr. Alfred Director resigned as a director of ABC Company ("ABC"), effective on [date]. Mr. Director was a member of ABC's audit committee and governance committee. He gave no reason for his resignation.

Item 5.03  *Amendments to articles of incorporation or bylaws; change in fiscal year.* For such amendments that were not previously disclosed in a proxy statement, disclose the amendment date and describe the change.

**Example:** On [date], ABC Company filed with the Secretary of State of the State of New York a Certificate of Amendment to its Certificate of Incorporation establishing the terms of a new class of Series A Preferred Stock.

Item 5.04  *Temporary suspension of trading under the company's employee benefit plans.* For such a suspension, note the reason for the blackout period, the plan transactions to be suspended, the class of equity securities affected, and the duration of the blackout period.

**Example:** On [date], the Audit Committee of the Board of Directors of ABC Company ("ABC") concluded that the Company's financial statements for one or more prior periods will likely need to be restated in conjunction with revising its sales return reserve calculations. Because of the potential restatement of this information and in order to ensure compliance with applicable securities laws, participants in the ABC Company 401(k) Plan (the "Plan") will be temporarily subject to a blackout period during which they will be precluded from acquiring beneficial ownership of additional interests in the Company's common stock fund under the 401(k) plan. During the blackout period, Plan participants will be unable to direct investments into the Company's stock fund under the Plan. The blackout period began at 7:00 a.m. Eastern time on [date] and is currently anticipated to end at 7:00 a.m. Eastern time on the day immediately following the day on which the restated financial statements are filed with the Securities and Exchange Commission.

Item 5.05  *Amendment to company's code of ethics, or waiver of a provision of the code of ethics.* Note the date of any change that applies to the company's CEO, CFO, or principal accounting officer; the name of the person to whom it was granted, and describe the nature of the waiver.

**Example:** On [date], the Board of Directors of the Company approved a Code of Business Conduct and Ethics, which covers all employees and directors of the Company. The new Code of Business Conduct and Ethics encompasses and supersedes the Code of Business Conduct and Ethics for the Company's Senior Officers, which has been posted on the Company's Web site.

Item 5.06  *Change in shell company status.* If a company is no longer a shell company, disclose the material terms of the transaction.

*(continued)*

## Exhibit 9.1 (Continued)

**Example:** The disclosure regarding the reverse merger in Item 2.01 is hereby incorporated by reference. Prior to the effective time of the reverse merger, ABC Company was a shell company.

### Section 6—Asset-Backed Securities (ABS)

Item 6.01 *ABS informational and computational materials.* Report any information and computational material filed in, or as an exhibit to, this report.

Item 6.02 *Change of servicer or trustee.* If a servicer or trustee has resigned or been removed, or if a new servicer has been appointed, state the event date and the circumstances of the change.

Item 6.03 *Change in credit enhancement or other external support.* If the company becomes aware of any material enhancement or support regarding one or more classes of asset-backed securities, then identify the parties to the agreement causing the change, and describe its date, terms, and conditions.

Item 6.04 *Failure to make a required distribution.* If a required distribution to holders of asset-based securities is not made, identify the failure and state the nature of the failure.

Item 6.05 *Securities Act updating disclosure.* If any material pool characteristic of the actual asset pool at the time of issuance differs by 5 percent or more from the description of the asset pool in the prospectus, then disclose the characteristics of the actual asset pool.

### Section 7—Regulation FD

Item 7.01 *Regulation FD disclosure.* Disclose under this item only information that the company elects to disclose pursuant to Regulation FD.

**Example:** On [date], ABC Company ("ABC") will make a presentation to potential lenders. A copy of the slides to be used in the presentation is furnished herewith as an exhibit.

### Section 8—Other Events

Item 8.01 *Other events.* Disclose under this category any events that the company considers to be of importance to its securities holders.

**Example:** On [date], ABC Company ("ABC") entered into a Settlement Agreement with the United States Department of Justice to settle all outstanding federal suits against ABC in connection with claims related to the Company's alleged off-label marketing and promotion of its ABC Product® to pediatricians (the "Settlement Agreement"). The settlement is neither an admission of liability by ABC nor a concession by the United States that its claims are not well founded. Pursuant to the Settlement Agreement, the Company will pay approximately $10 million to settle the matter between the parties. The Settlement Agreement provides that, upon full payment of the settlement fees, the United States releases ABC from the claims asserted by the United States. As of [date], ABC accrued a loss contingency of $10 million for this matter.

Please note that the various types of disclosure in the preceding table were presented in summary format *only*, and should not be relied on as the basis for a Form 8-K filing. Only use the advice of corporate counsel for such disclosures.

Clearly, a large number of events must be reported on a Form 8-K. In order to ensure that all events are properly reported, the IRO should keep corporate counsel fully informed of all company activities, possibly on a daily basis. It is always safest to ask for a legal opinion on items that may seem marginally applicable under the SEC's disclosure rules, rather than to not report an event and later learn that the company is in violation of those rules.

## DISCLOSURE OF NON-GAAP INFORMATION

The disclosure by a public company of non-GAAP information is governed by the SEC's Regulation G. Under this regulation, the SEC requires that a company issuing information about a non-GAAP financial measure accompany that presentation with the following information:

- A presentation of the most directly comparable financial measure, calculated and presented in accordance with GAAP
- A reconciliation of the differences between the non-GAAP financial measure with the most comparable financial measure as calculated and presented in accordance with GAAP

The SEC defines a non-GAAP financial measure as one that excludes amounts that are included in the most directly comparable GAAP measure, or that includes amounts that are excluded from the most directly comparable GAAP measure.

The regulation also prohibits a company from disclosing non-GAAP financial information that contains an untrue statement of a material fact or omits to state a material fact.

If a non-GAAP financial measure is made public by any oral means, the regulation holds that a company comply with the preceding reporting requirements, and list the resulting information on the company's Web site. Further, the person orally disclosing the information must make known the location of that information on the corporate Web site during the same presentation.

The reporting of non-GAAP information requires a layout similar to the format shown in the following example. In the example, the company explains the reason why it is including an adjusted EBITDA measurement in its 10-Q report, and then goes on to describe the components of the measurement and its limitations. The example ends with a table that begins with the adjusted EBITDA measurement, and which then adds or subtracts a variety of items to arrive at a GAAP net loss number.

Our reported net loss is strongly impacted by the amortization expense associated with our various acquisitions, goodwill impairment, and equity compensation paid to both employees and suppliers. We believe that adjusted EBITDA earnings are more representative of our actual operating performance than net earnings, because they more closely indicate the state of our cash flows than the net profit or loss. We define adjusted EBITDA as earnings before interest, taxes, depreciation, amortization, equity payments, and goodwill impairment.

Adjusted EBITDA is not a financial performance measurement under generally accepted accounting principles. Adjusted EBITDA has material limitations and should not be considered as an alternative to net income (loss), cash flows provided by operations, investing or financing activities, or other financial statement data presented in the consolidated financial statements as indicators of financial performance or liquidity. Items excluded from adjusted EBITDA are significant components in understanding our financial performance. Because adjusted EBITDA is not a measurement determined in accordance with GAAP and is subject to varying calculations, adjusted EBITDA as presented may not be comparable to other similarly titled measures of performance used by other companies.

Exhibit 9.2 reconciles our adjusted EBITDA to our net losses during 201X.

**Exhibit 9.2**   Reconciliation of Adjusted EBITDA to Net Losses

|  | Quarter Ended September 30, 201X | Nine Months Ended September 30, 201X |
| --- | --- | --- |
| Adjusted EBITDA | $(140,000) | $(1,420,000) |
| Depreciation and amortization | 681,000 | 2,017,000 |
| Equity compensation | 84,000 | 377,000 |
| Goodwill impairment | 0 | 618,000 |
| Interest expense | (16,000) | 157,000 |
| Taxes, income | 2,000 | 2,000 |
| Net loss | $(891,000) | $(4,591,000) |

Much of the content and format of this example can be recycled in successive quarters, so that only the table requires updating in later SEC filings. Thus, once the non-GAAP to GAAP reconciliation has been created, this becomes a relatively simple reporting structure to maintain.

A company should have a strong inclination to avoid non-GAAP measures in its SEC filings. The reason is not that reconciliation to GAAP is required, but rather, that it confuses the investment community when a variety of non-GAAP measures are mixed in with more common GAAP results. This is a particular concern when a company only uses a non-GAAP measure for a short period of time, since it implies that the company cannot focus on the key measures that are most indicative of its underlying business model. Consequently, there should be a policy that places considerable restrictions on the use of non-GAAP measures, such as:

> Non-GAAP measures shall *not* be included in any SEC filings unless they clearly provide better information about the company's results than GAAP measures, and can be reasonably expected to do so for a multiyear period. The use of non-GAAP measures must be approved in advance by all members of the disclosure committee. Stopping the use of an existing non-GAAP measure must also be approved in advance by all members of the disclosure committee.

Note the requirements for *unanimous* approval of non-GAAP measures by the disclosure committee. This group is typically composed of the CFO, corporate counsel, and IRO, so the use of non-GAAP measures must appeal to advisors having a broad range of perspectives on the investment community; thus, few non-GAAP measures will be approved for use, or disapproved from current use.

If a company intends to use non-GAAP information in a speech, conference call, or Web cast, it is usually easier from a control perspective to issue the non-GAAP reconciliation to GAAP in an 8-K filing, rather than on a page in the company's Web site. This avoids the risk that the Web page will never be created, or might be inadvertently deleted. The following policy addresses the issue:

> Whenever non-GAAP information is included in a speech, conference call, webcast, or other oral presentation, the non-GAAP to GAAP reconciliation shall be included in an 8-K report that is filed coincident with or immediately following the oral presentation.

The use of an 8-K filing permanently eliminates any risk to the company of having breached Regulation G.

It is unfortunately easy to include non-GAAP measures in oral presentations, unless all such presentations are written in advance and approved by the disclosure committee. This scenario calls for the following policy:

> All oral presentations to the investment community shall be written and submitted in advance to the disclosure committee. Oral presentations shall only be given following the approval of a majority of the disclosure committee.

Unanimous approval by the disclosure committee is not required for oral presentations in companies where there is a considerable volume of such presentations, on the grounds that the committee will be overwhelmed with review work. However, it is possible to obtain unanimous committee approval in those entities where interaction with the investment community is more sparse.

##  REGULATION FD

The SEC has issued Regulation FD, which stands for Fair Disclosure. In essence, the regulation states that a company must make public disclosure of any material nonpublic information that it gives to a broker-dealer, investment advisor, institutional investment manager, investment company, or a holder of the company's securities. The regulation does not apply when a company gives information in the following situations:

- The recipient is a person who owes a duty of trust or confidence to the company, such as an attorney, investment banker, or accountant.
- The recipient expressly agrees to maintain the disclosed information in confidence, such as by signing a nondisclosure agreement.
- The recipient is a credit rating agency, as long as the purpose of the disclosure is solely for developing a credit rating and the company's credit ratings are publicly available.
- The recipient is connected to a registered offering by the company, on the assumption that the documents related to the offering will provide sufficiently broad disclosure.

If the disclosure of material nonpublic information is intentional, then the company should simultaneously disclose the information to the public. A disclosure is considered intentional when the person making the disclosure "either knows, or is reckless in not knowing, that the information he or she is communicating is both material and nonpublic."

If the disclosure is not intentional, then the company must promptly disclose the information. The SEC considers "promptly" to mean "as soon as reasonably practical (but in no event after the later of 24 hours or the commencement of the next day's trading on the New York Stock Exchange) after a senior official of the [company] . . . learns that there has been a non-intentional disclosure by the [company] or person acting on behalf of the [company] of information that the senior official knows, or is reckless in not knowing, is both material and nonpublic."

The SEC considers an 8-K filing to always be an adequate public disclosure of information. An acceptable alternative to an 8-K filing is to disseminate the necessary information through another method of disclosure that is reasonably designed to provide broad, nonexclusionary distribution of the information to the public. A good example of such a method is to use a press release that is issued through a news wire service. Several of the wire services offer a combined release service, where they issue both a press release and an 8-K that contains text identical to the press release.

Posting information to the company Web site is *not* considered to be a sufficient level of disclosure. A company could bury key information far down in a subsidiary Web page, where it may take days for anyone to locate the information. Also, a Web site does not usually employ "push" technology, where information is actively disseminated to users (that is only available if users sign up for Really Simple Syndication, or RSS, feeds). Instead, the typical Web site is a passive technology, which users must browse in order to locate information. For these reasons, a Web site is not an appropriate or accepted way to disclose information.

## DISCLOSURE POLICY

Every public company should have a disclosure policy. If properly enforced, it channels a company's investor communications into a carefully defined disclosure path, so that it consistently handles disclosure issues in the same manner. This policy should include statements about the following items (examples are noted after each item):

- *The company's commitment to the policy.* "The company is committed to the provision of timely and credible information to the investment community that meets all regulatory requirements, and which results in realistic investor expectations about company performance."

▪ *Positions authorized to be spokespersons for the company.* "The chief executive officer, chief financial officer, and investor relations officer are authorized to be the company's spokespersons. They will represent the company in all meetings and other communications with the investment community. In order to do so effectively, they must be kept aware of all material events in the company, or affecting the company. All other employees should defer questions to these individuals."

▪ *Designate a disclosure committee, and its role.* "The disclosure committee's members shall include the corporate counsel, chief financial officer, and investor relations officer. This committee shall review and approve all corporate disclosures prior to their dissemination to the investment community."

▪ *Policy on reviewing analyst reports.* "The company will only review and give feedback on the factual content or underlying assumptions of analyst reports, and will not retain any draft reports or models provided by analysts. It will not comment on the conclusions reached in analyst reports, or state the extent to which company earnings will vary from analyst estimates."

▪ *Policy on how to comment on market rumors.* "Authorized spokespersons shall consistently respond to market rumors by stating that "It is not our policy to comment on market rumors or speculation." If a stock exchange on which the company's stock is listed requests a statement, then the disclosure committee shall make a recommendation to the chief executive officer."

▪ *Policy on the provision of guidance.* "The company shall provide guidance on a quarterly basis if earnings are likely to fall outside of the range of estimates that the company previously provided to the investment community. It shall provide this information through a press release, followed by an earnings conference call. In addition, the company will observe a quiet period during the two weeks preceding each quarterly earnings announcement." A variation on the duration of the quiet period would be, "The company will observe a quiet period prior to each quarterly earnings announcement that begins when earnings results have been finalized." This variation tends to result in longer quiet periods.

▪ *Policy review frequency.* "The disclosure committee shall review this policy at least annually and update it as needed."

The market rumor policy is specifically designed to impart no information to the marketplace, rather than categorically denying that there are no company events that might be causing rumors. The reason for this noncommittal language is that the company spokespersons may not be aware of significant company events that are causing a marketplace rumor. Though the disclosure policy is designed to channel material information to the spokespersons, the process does not always work as planned, so that the marketplace may obtain information before the spokespersons.

The disclosure policy is only effective if consistently applied, so the disclosure committee should actively enforce it throughout the company. Given the considerable responsibilities of the committee members, this means that a support staff may be needed to monitor disclosures on an ongoing basis and to warn the committee members of disclosure violations.

##  DISCLOSURE PROCEDURE

Use this procedure to handle the appropriate disclosure of material nonpublic information:

1. If an employee believes that he has revealed material nonpublic information to an outside party, the employee must fill out the Material Information Disclosure Form (see Exhibit 9.3).
2. In the first section of the form, there is no material disclosure if the party to whom the information was revealed is one of the four itemized parties. If this is the case, the employee need not submit the form.
3. If the employee disclosed information to an outside party *not* listed in the first section of the report, then briefly describe the nature of the disclosure in the second section of the form, as well as the name of the other party and the date and time of the disclosure.
4. Send the form by the quickest means to the investor relations officer *and* the company attorney, to ensure prompt handling.
5. The IRO and attorney jointly create either an 8-K disclosure or a press release that addresses the material nonpublic information itemized in the form, and either submit the 8-K to the SEC or submit the press release to a news wire service.
6. The IRO or attorney then attaches a copy of the filed 8-K or press release to the material information disclosure form, notes the date and time of submission, and signs the form.
7. The attorney notes the name of the employee who originally submitted the form, which may be used for later follow-up training.
8. The form is filed in a locked filing cabinet.

---

**ABC Company**
**Material Information Disclosure Form**

---

This form is designed to identify outside parties to whom material nonpublic information was disclosed, describe the disclosure, and guide subsequent remediation.

---

This section is intended to identify the type of party to whom disclosure was made. If the information recipient was any of the following four types, then no further action is necessary. If the recipient was not one of the following types, then identify the recipient, the date and time of disclosure, and the specific information revealed.

☐    Attorney, accountant, auditor, or investment banker working for the company

☐    Has signed a nondisclosure agreement with the company

☐    Is a credit rating agency, and the disclosure was intended to help develop a credit rating

☐    Is connected to a registered offering by the company

---

Name of receiving party:      *Matthew McPherson*

Date and time of disclosure:      *April 14, 9 a.m.*

Nature of the disclosure:
     *Mentioned to this broker that we are working on the new Alpha product line.*

Employee signature:      *James Arbuckle*

---

☑   8-K issued?                           ☑   Press release issued?

     Date and time:    *April 15, 11:54 a.m.*          Date and time:    *April 15, 1:20 p.m.*

     (attach a copy)                                (attach a copy)

Attorney signature:    *John Quigley, Esq.*         IRO signature:    *Mary Alberts*

---

Filing Requirement: Attorney retention

---

**Exhibit 9.3**   Material Information Disclosure Form

---

 **ENSURING COMPLIANCE WITH DISCLOSURE RULES**

It is extremely easy to inadvertently breach the requirements of Regulation FD. To avoid doing so, the IRO should implement a strict set of controls that includes mandatory training, nondisclosure agreements, and an aggressive disclosure policy.

The first step in the control process is a Regulation FD training class for anyone who deals with outside entities on a regular basis. The IRO should discuss with each participant the specifics of the regulation and then give a number of examples of correct and incorrect disclosures. Following this training, have the company's securities attorney interview the class participants to see if they respond correctly under the FD provisions. If not, then immediately impose a follow-up discussion to correct their knowledge of the regulation.

A single training class is not sufficient, since anyone's knowledge of a specific regulation will fade over time. At a minimum, distribute a training brochure once a year to all class participants. Better yet, require a short refresher training class once a year. A more technologically advanced alternative is to create an online training class and integrated quiz that participants can take at any time. The IRO should have access to their online test scores to ensure that they have taken the class.

When briefing employees about material information, the IRO should always include in the discussion a statement that they are not allowed to disclose this information to any outsider, and that they cannot trade on this information.

A seemingly more onerous additional step is to have all employees sign a document stating that they will not talk to outsiders about the company, or will not do so without first clearing their discussion with the IRO. Employees do not like to sign such an agreement, but it does emphasize the seriousness of disclosure violations. Use the same approach with outside entities, and require them to sign a nondisclosure agreement (NDA) whenever possible. This shifts the burden of disclosure to them, since the NDA prohibits them from disclosing the information to a third party.

As noted earlier in the disclosure policy, a company uses designated spokespersons to ensure that appropriate information is disseminated to the marketplace. However, other employees may sometimes make statements to the public, since a variety of public relations activities may bring the media in contact with any number of company employees. During these events, the IRO should be present to monitor the discussion. If the IRO cannot be available, then she should debrief employees after such meetings to see if any material information was disclosed.

A major disclosure problem is when an employee inadvertently lets slip some material, undisclosed information during a presentation. This can happen to the most careful person, even a well-trained spokesperson. The problem is especially insidious when making a new presentation, since the presenter is not thoroughly familiar with the materials and may resort to "off the cuff" comments instead of following the presentation materials. To avoid such inadvertent disclosure, it is best to script a large proportion of any presentation (essentially converting it into a speech). Further, the IRO should schedule at least one practice session prior to making a formal presentation, in order to give participants time to learn the materials. The author takes this a step further, preferring to practice every presentation a minimum of *four* times prior to the actual event, presenting formally from behind a lectern. Also, bring to all presentations a reminder list of items *not* to disclose, and review it just beforehand.

A company may be accused of privately disclosing material information to analysts. One way to avoid this accusation is to ban all meetings with analysts. However, since this does not contribute to friendly analyst relations, a better approach is for the IRO to maintain a log of all analyst contacts, including a brief description of the subject of each discussion. It can be difficult to maintain a comprehensive contact log if analysts are regularly talking to multiple people within a company, so the IRO should insist that all contacts be channeled through her.

Conversations with analysts can be trying, because they frequently want clarification of previously disclosed information. If the company provides clarification, this is called "differential disclosure," since no one else is receiving the new information; this is likely to be a Regulation FD violation. Thus, the IRO should develop a guideline for the types of information to issue during an analyst meeting—and, more importantly, the types of information *not* to issue. The general guideline is to only reveal background information about the company. The individual pieces of information revealed during such a discussion are not material, but analysts are free to assemble it into a coherent model from which they can develop performance estimates (known as the "mosaic" approach).

An excellent method for ensuring compliance with Regulation FD is to aggressively disclose everything. If the IRO is constantly churning out 8-K filings and press releases for every conceivable type of information, then it is unlikely that any employees will be at risk of revealing material information. This approach also has the effect of giving the company an excellent reputation in the investment community for full disclosure, and can decrease its stock price volatility in comparison to the stock of those competitors who do not release such a quantity of information.

## DISCLOSURE DURING AN INITIAL PUBLIC OFFERING

There is some misconception surrounding the types of information that can be released during an initial public offering (IPO). It is indeed necessary during the

IPO quiet period to not issue any information that can be construed as attempting to enhance the stock price, which tends to put the IRO in the unusual position of halting all information releases, rather than providing a constant stream of information to the investment community. In particular, the IRO cannot initiate any new activity that can be construed as selling company stock or conditioning the market to buy its stock at an increased price.

However, there are several types of information releases that are entirely acceptable to the SEC. A company can still advertise its products during an IPO, as well as make announcements of a factual nature regarding business and financial developments, distribute customary reports to stockholders, answer investor questions at stockholder meetings, and respond to unsolicited inquiries. When making any of these disclosures, the company cannot expand on currently available information unless it plans to make a formal, structured disclosure and add the new information to the prospectus being used for the IPO.

## SUMMARY

One of the largest problems for an IRO is dealing with disclosure rules. A company can get into serious difficulty with the SEC if it leaks material information to the investment community without also giving it widespread distribution through a few approved communication channels. Accordingly, the IRO must implement and rigorously adhere to a disclosure policy and related procedures to ensure that only approved material information is released, and that it is released in an approved format.

A rare benefit of the disclosure rules is that a company can potentially reduce the cost of its directors' and officers' liability insurance by having a written disclosure policy. The fee reduction will not be significant, but is worth exploring with the company's insurance underwriter.

# CHAPTER TEN

# Forward-Looking Statements

THE RELEASE OF INFORMATION to the investing public used to be fraught with peril, because legislation dating from the 1930s allowed investors to initiate class action lawsuits whenever a company's stock price dropped, due to alleged malfeasance by the company. In the face of the potentially massive awards arising from these lawsuits, companies were inclined not to reveal any information beyond those items required by law. The situation changed when new, protective legislation was passed in 1995. This chapter describes the legal environment that leads to class action lawsuits, the legislation that mitigates the problem, and what actions an IRO should take to be in compliance with this protective legislation.

## BASIS FOR CLASS ACTION LAWSUITS

Section 10(b) of The Securities Exchange Act of 1934 gives shareholders the right to sue a company in federal court to recover damages sustained from a securities fraud. Specifically, it states that "it shall be unlawful . . . to use or employ, in connection with the purchase or sale of any security registered on a national securities exchange or any security not so registered, any manipulative or deceptive advice . . . " The Securities and Exchange Commission (SEC) expanded on this law in its Rule 10b-5, part of which reads as follows:

It shall be unlawful for any person, directly or indirectly, by the use of any means or instrumentality of interstate commerce, or of the mails or of any facility of any national securities exchange,

(a) To employ any device, scheme, or artifice to defraud,
(b) To make any untrue statement of a material fact or to omit to state a material fact necessary in order to make the statements made, in the light of the circumstances under which they were made, not misleading, or
(c) To engage in any act, practice, or course of business which operates or would operate as a fraud or deceit upon any person, in connection with the purchase or sale of any security.

Based on this rule, shareholders have brought thousands of legal actions against companies for alleged securities fraud. The basic process flow for such an action is that a plaintiff files a complaint in a federal court, after which the defending company files a motion to dismiss, on the grounds that the alleged facts of the case are not sufficient to create a liability under Rule 10b-5. This is a critical junction in such cases, because if the court does not dismiss the case, the plaintiff then has the right to obtain documentary evidence (discovery) from the company, which can involve thousands of hours of work and potentially millions of dollars of legal fees. Given the cost of the discovery phase, many companies will reach a settlement with the plaintiff, even if the plaintiff's case is not a strong one.

Once a federal court allows a case to proceed, the plaintiff usually seeks class certification, so that the case becomes a securities fraud class action lawsuit. At this point, the company faces a potentially enormous liability if the case were to be decided against it, because now a verdict would cover all of its shareholders. At this point, companies frequently settle with plaintiffs rather than run the risk of an adverse judgment in court.

##  PRIVATE SECURITIES LITIGATION REFORM ACT

Clearly, the key point in a securities fraud lawsuit is the motion to dismiss, with plaintiff's attorneys desiring less demanding rules to govern the process and defendant's attorneys advocating more stringent rules. This debate came to a head in the Private Securities Litigation Reform Act of 1995 (PSLRA), in which more stringent rules were adopted. The objective of the lawmakers who created the PSLRA was to reduce the routine filing of lawsuits against public companies whenever there was a significant change in their stock price.

The PSLRA requires that plaintiffs identify three items in their filed complaints:

1. Provide each company statement that is alleged to have been misleading, the reasons why the statement is misleading, and all facts on which that belief is formed.
2. Itemize the facts giving rise to a strong inference that the defendant knew the challenged statement was false at the time it was made, or was reckless in not recognizing that the statement was false.
3. Prove that the defendant's acts or omissions have caused the plaintiff's loss.

These three requirements force plaintiffs to present a stronger up-front case, which defense attorneys have a better chance of arguing against in obtaining a dismissal of the case. Further, the PSLRA requires the court to dismiss the complaint if the first two requirements are not met.

The PSLRA also imposes several restrictions on who will be appointed as the lead plaintiff and the payment of that plaintiff, with the intent of eliminating "professional" plaintiffs who work with attorneys to file multiple lawsuits on an ongoing basis.

## FORWARD-LOOKING STATEMENTS

From the perspective of the IRO, the key protective aspect of the PSLRA is Section 102, "Safe Harbor for Forward-Looking Statements." Section 102 provides companies with a safe harbor from liability for forward-looking statements to the extent that such statements are identified as forward-looking statements, and are accompanied by *"meaningful cautionary statements* identifying important factors that could cause actual results to differ materially from those in the forward-looking statement." Further, if a company wishes to obtain protection for an oral statement under the provisions of the PSLRA, then it must include in the oral statement a "statement that additional information concerning factors that could cause actual results to differ materially from those in the forward-looking statement is contained in a readily available written document" (such as a document filed with the SEC), and that "the information contained in that written document is a cautionary document." However, a company making such statements will still be liable if the plaintiff can prove that the written or oral statements were made with actual knowledge that the information being provided was false or misleading.

In the preceding paragraph, the words "meaningful cautionary statements" were italicized to highlight their importance. The inclusion of these words in the PSLRA implies that a company cannot simply use boilerplate cautionary statements, but must instead either specify risks that apply to the forward-looking statements being made or refer to a complete set of identified risks, such as are found in a company's annual 10-K filing with the SEC. No matter which approach is used, the IRO should carefully consider the key risks that could impact forward-looking statements and ensure that those risks are itemized, either in supporting documents or alongside the forward-looking statements.

Given the importance of the protections offered in the PSLRA for forward-looking statements, it is important to understand which statements can be considered forward-looking. A forward-looking statement is defined in the PSLRA as follows:

The term "forward-looking statement" means:

A statement containing a projection of revenues, income (including income loss), earnings (including earnings loss) per share, capital expenditures, dividends, capital structure, or other financial items;

A statement of the plans or objectives of management for future operations, including plans or objectives relating to the products or services of the issuer;

A statement of future economic performance, including any such statement contained in a discussion and analysis of financial condition by the management or in the results of operations included pursuant to the rules and regulations of the Commission;

Any statement of the assumptions underlying or relating to any statement described in subparagraph (A), (B), or (C);

Any report issued by an outside reviewer retained by an issuer, to the extent that the report assesses a forward-looking statement made by the issuer; and

A statement containing a projection or estimate of such other items as may be specified by rule or regulation of the Commission.

The preceding definition itemizes what information *is* considered to be a forward-looking statement. It is equally important to understand what types of information are *not* covered by the safe harbor provisions of the PSLRA. Section 102 of the PSLRA includes a lengthy list of exclusions, such as roll-up transactions, going-private transactions, tender offers, initial public offerings, investment company registration statements, and financial statements prepared in accordance with GAAP.

In order to be in compliance with the protections offered by Section 102, the IRO must include a statement in all corporate communications that identifies statements made as being forward looking, and adds cautionary statements identifying those factors that could cause actual results to differ from projections. What follows are three sample statements that can be used for different forms of investor relations communications.

## Safe Harbor Statement for a Conference Call

As we begin our review of the company's quarterly results, let me remind you that some of the statements made during this call may disclose certain subjects that contain forward-looking statements, as that term is described in the Private Securities Litigation Reform Act of 1995. These statements are based on management's current expectations and involve risk and uncertainty and may cause results to differ materially from those set forth in the statement. The forward-looking statements may include statements regarding product development, product potential, or financial performance, and no forward-looking statement can be guaranteed, and actual results may differ materially from those projected. Forward-looking statements in this call should be evaluated together with the many uncertainties that affect the company's business, particularly those mentioned in the risk factors and cautionary statements set forth in the company's Form 10-K for the year ending December 31, 201X, and in its periodic reports of Form 10-Q and 8-K, which the company incorporates by reference and which are posted on our Web site.

## Safe Harbor Statement for an Oral Presentation

This presentation contains forward-looking statements within the meaning of the Private Securities Litigation Reform Act of 1995, and are subject to the safe harbors created thereby. Actual results could differ materially from those projected in the forward-looking statements as a result of risk factors discussed in the company's reports that are on file with the SEC.

## Safe Harbor Statement for a Written Document

In accordance with the Safe Harbor provisions of the Private Securities Litigation Reform Act of 1995, the company notes that some statements in this press release look forward in time, and involve risks and uncertainties that may affect the company's actual results of operations. The following important factors, among others that are discussed in company filings with the SEC, could cause actual results to differ materially from those set forth in the forward-looking statements:

- Competition may cause us to lose projects or result in decreased revenues.
- We may be unable to hire qualified technical personnel.
- Acquisitions involve significant risks, including difficulties in operational integration, management diversion from normal daily operations of the business, and the potential loss of key employees of acquired companies.

## LEGAL LIABILITY FOR PAST STATEMENTS

Is there any legal liability associated with forward-looking statements that were made in the past, and which have not been subsequently updated? The PSLRA specifically states that "nothing in this section shall impose upon any person a duty to update a forward-looking statement." Despite the protection offered by this section of the PSLRA, the IRO should update forward-looking statements, simply because it is a good investor relations practice to keep investors informed of any material changes in a company's operations. All forward-looking statements should be reviewed by an attorney before being released to safeguard against possible language traps that would open the door to future lawsuits.

## SUMMARY

In summary, the Private Securities Litigation Reform Act allows the IRO to issue selected forward-looking information with safe harbor protection from litigation. To ensure protection under the PSLRA, the IRO must verify that meaningful cautionary statements are made in every public disclosure, and that they are identified as forward-looking statements. It is useful to have a documented procedure in place to ensure that the correct safe harbor language is used in each corporate communication, including a mandatory review by an attorney.

CHAPTER ELEVEN

# Providing Guidance

MOST LARGER PUBLIC COMPANIES provide some form of earnings guidance to the investment community. It is an important part of how the sell side and buy side determine valuation, and so is a key responsibility of the IRO. In this chapter, we will cover whether a company should issue guidance, what form guidance should take, the frequency and timing of guidance, and how to create a guidance policy.

 ## WHETHER TO PROVIDE GUIDANCE

Before getting into a discussion about the form and frequency of guidance to provide, we must first consider whether a company should provide any guidance at all.

Without guidance, analysts and investors have no idea how a company will perform in the future, and so must make their own estimates of the situation. These estimates may vary considerably from each other. The result is a heightened amount of stock price volatility, since everyone is assuming a different future earnings level.

Stock price volatility is not a desirable state of affairs for a company. It tends to attract short sellers, who make money from rapid changes in the stock price (see Chapter 15). It also drives away institutional investors, who prefer stocks whose prices move within a narrow range. Since institutional investors are driven away, there is less demand for a company's stock and its price will decline. This results in a higher cost of capital for the company since it must issue more shares in order to obtain a specific amount of cash. Thus, there are serious consequences to not providing guidance.

Also, a company may have no analyst following, which is the norm for microcap entities. If so, there is no one who can independently provide earnings predictions to the buy side, which leaves the marketplace completely devoid of information if a company refuses to provide guidance. This situation is most likely to result in excessive stock price volatility. Thus, in order to avoid volatility, the absence of analysts makes it even more necessary to provide guidance.

Though these issues are compelling, there is a situation where it still makes sense to avoid issuing guidance—specifically, when management does not have a clear picture of future results. This is most likely to occur when a company is generating a large part of its operating results from a series of acquisitions, is experiencing large swings in its material costs, or is entering new markets. In all of these cases, operating results may vary so significantly that it would be doing a disservice to the investment marketplace to issue guidance that could rapidly be proved erroneous. Under this scenario, it is better to state the situation and promise that guidance will be provided at some point in the future, once results become more predictable.

An alternative to a promise to provide guidance in the future is to provide it now, but within a very wide guidance range. This is a particularly appropriate scenario for a company that is already providing guidance, and does not want to send an excessively negative message to the market by terminating its guidance entirely due to various uncertainties. Instead, explain the situation, prepare scenarios, and describe the assumptions used in the most recent guidance. This still gives analysts some information to work with, as opposed to a sudden absence of guidance.

It is also possible that a company's forecasting systems are so inadequate that it is routinely exceeding or falling short of its guidance by significant amounts. In this case, the investment community will assume that the management team is incapable of forecasting its own business. If so, it may be better to forgo guidance until the company can install better forecasting systems that result in predictable guidance.

A downside of guidance is that a management team may have a propensity to focus too much attention on "making the numbers" that it has projected. Such behavior is not useful, since it diverts management's attention from the detailed operational conduct of the business. It also increases the risk of financial statement reporting fraud when operational results have fallen short, because management will be tempted to adjust the numbers to attain the forecast. This is a particular concern when guidance is so aggressive that it is difficult to attain (see the "Aggressiveness of Guidance" section later in this chapter).

In summary, guidance is useful for most companies, in order to smooth stock price volatility. However, it can be misleading and counterproductive when a company is uncertain of its own results, or if it persists in issuing aggressive guidance.

##  FORM OF GUIDANCE ISSUED

If the decision is to provide guidance, then the next issue to resolve is the form of guidance to be issued. This section notes a variety of alternatives.

The most common type of guidance issued is for either a range or specific point, and usually includes all key factors that would be of interest to an investor, such as revenue, margins, net income, and earnings per share. The range of expected results issued should be relatively narrow for the near future, and should expand as projections go further into the future, thereby allowing for greater uncertainty. An example follows:

> We are raising our guidance for the fiscal year ended December 31, 2010. We now expect 2010 sales to range between $120 and $135 million, resulting in net profits of between $14 and $17 million, and diluted earnings per share ranging from $1.43 to $1.49. For the year 2011, we are expecting sales to range between $130 and $160 million, resulting in net profits of between $16 and $21 million, and diluted earnings per share ranging from $1.48 to $1.60.

An alternative is to provide guidance using percentages. By doing so, analysts can construct their own models of a company's performance and plug in the latest guidance to arrive at their own conclusions about the company's likely performance. This type of guidance should include some sensitivity analysis, where the guidance states how a given percentage change in revenue will impact the gross margin and net profit. Some companies even itemize the business assumptions underlying their models. An example follows:

> Our projected revenue growth is 7 to 10 percent. Based on our estimated increase of 5 percent in cost of goods sold, we are projecting

gross margins in the range of 50 percent to 55 percent, with the low end of the range based on 7 percent revenue growth and the high end based on 10 percent revenue growth.

If a company is not willing to provide this level of guidance, then a lesser alternative is to discuss anywhere from a one- to five-year projection, the long-term strategy, or the business cycle within which the company operates, and how that cycle impacts its results. These alternative choices are deemed insufficient by analysts, since such broad categorizations of results are of little use to them when trying to construct an earnings forecast. Several examples follow:

We expect continued revenue growth of 60 to 80 percent for the next three years, as we continue a rapid expansion through our franchising model. Due to expansion costs, we expect net profits and earnings per share to grow during that period at a reduced rate of 15 to 25 percent.

Our long-term strategy is to expand our successful franchising model throughout the North American region, with a target store-opening rate of 150 per year.

The airline industry's fortunes are closely tied to the price of oil, since we must pass through the majority of oil price increases to our customers. During the past year, the price of oil increased 20 percent, resulting in an 18 percent increase in ticket prices and a decline in our passenger volume of 11 percent.

An alternative to the various types of formal guidance already shown is to release a broad range of nonmaterial information to analysts. They can then use this information to create their own models of a company's operations and likely operating results. This is called the "mosaic" approach, because they must assemble disparate information into a composite picture of the company. This is a useful approach for a company because it can avoid any specific guidance, but is painful for analysts, who must work much harder to create their earnings models.

Finally, once the decision is made to release a certain type of information to the marketplace, be prepared to continue issuing it on a long-term basis. Otherwise, the market can react quite negatively when information is discontinued, on the suspicion that the company is hiding information that no longer casts it in the best light. For example, a medical products company changed its guidance from a discussion of growth rates that included acquisitions to a discussion that solely focused on organic growth. When the altered (and substantially reduced) guidance was released, the company's stock price declined by 25 percent in a single day and did not recover. Thus, if the IRO feels that information formerly included in guidance is now irrelevant, then be sure to explain the reason for the discontinuance in detail, in order to avoid a significant price decline.

In short, guidance can range from a narrow range of prospective results to broad discussions of company and industry prospects. The most common form of guidance, by far, is the inclusion of ranges of specific dollar values in the guidance, as shown in the first example in this section.

##  FREQUENCY AND TIMING OF GUIDANCE

If guidance is given, then update it in a timely manner. This usually involves the consistent use of a forecast updating schedule, with quarterly guidance being the most common, usually right after the quarterly Form 10-Q is released. Analysts depend on quarterly guidance, so they can revise their own estimates of company performance. If a company elects to forgo quarterly guidance in favor of some longer period, it is possible that some analysts will find it too difficult to provide estimates regarding company performance and will drop their coverage. If this happens, stock price volatility may increase due to uncertainty about how the company is performing. Thus, frequent guidance updates are needed to avoid excessive stock price movement.

Those companies only providing annual guidance claim that the practice tends to provide longer-term valuations that are less susceptible to short-term variation. If a company intends to follow this path, it should at least consider providing updates whenever it expects a material change in results.

There are situations in which the IRO would be justified in issuing guidance even more frequently than on a quarterly basis. For example, if a company has an analyst following and a large proportion of those analysts are projecting excessively high or low short-term results, it may be necessary to give unscheduled and immediate guidance. By doing so, analysts can alter their projections at once, thereby keeping the company's stock price from tracking in accordance with the incorrect estimates.

Another scenario is when a company is in hypergrowth mode, which can happen when it is conducting an industry roll-up through a string of acquisitions, or when it first issues a fabulously successful new product. In either case, investors may bid up its stock price to extremely high levels. When the price/earnings ratio becomes too high, the stock price is likely to fluctuate continually, as the market reacts to any news it can scrounge up about the company.

In this case, the market requires a constant flow of information, which the IRO can provide by issuing guidance more frequently than normal.

Some companies routinely issue small amounts of additional information in advance of their regular quarterly guidance, in what is called a *preannouncement*. This extra level of communication states the date of the regular earnings call and points out that guidance will be updated during that call. Stating in advance that new guidance will be issued shortly tends to forestall analysts from making their own estimates prior to the call.

The preannouncement is not just a notification of an earnings call. It can also be used to disseminate new, material information to the market. By using the preannouncement to issue new information, this results in shorter periods during which a company runs the risk of inadvertently issuing material, nonpublic information. Thus, many companies use a quarterly preannouncement, timed to be well before the earnings call, to create a constant flow of new information to the market.

If a preannouncement is used to issue material information that the market might react strongly to, it is helpful to set up a special conference call immediately after the preannouncement to explain the new information. This is especially important if the preannouncement reveals a material decline in the operating results that were projected in the last guidance.

Finally, if a company does not revise its guidance, then the investment community will assume that the information contained within the last guidance is still current. If management becomes aware that changed circumstances have made the current guidance misleading, then it should consider issuing new guidance in advance of the normal guidance release schedule. This scenario normally applies only if the level of change is very substantial. Also, when formulating the new replacement guidance to be issued, it is better to wait somewhat longer to verify the latest operational results, in order to have a higher confidence level in the new guidance—it would not do to issue replacement guidance that must itself be replaced in short order! This is an area in which the IRO must exercise judgment in determining whether to issue unscheduled guidance, and how long to wait before doing so.

## AGGRESSIVENESS OF GUIDANCE

Under no circumstances should the IRO issue aggressive guidance, where the targeted results will be extremely difficult for a company to achieve. This may result in a short-term ramp-up in the stock price, but will inevitably yield a price crash when the company eventually cannot achieve its own guidance. If an IRO persists in repeatedly issuing aggressive guidance that her company cannot sustain, then the result will be persistent price gyrations, unusually high price volatility, and the arrival of short sellers.

A much better alternative is to always provide guidance that is solidly within the management team's comfort zone. If managers in a company know they can attain the guidance levels, then they will be less fixated on reaching the target, which reduces the risk of fraudulent reporting. Also, by providing reasonably conservative guidance, analysts will find a company to be more trustworthy and reliable, and will be more likely to provide coverage.

However, this does not mean that the IRO should always issue excessively low guidance. If a company routinely exceeds its guidance by a substantial margin, analysts will come to expect it in the future. Thus, if it were to only meet its own guidance, analysts might treat this as poor performance, and issue negative projections. Accordingly, the best level of guidance is to issue *slightly* conservative numbers.

Finally, there will inevitably be cases when the IRO finds it necessary to revise guidance downward. When this happens, assume that there is an underlying problem causing the downgrade, and that this problem will take a considerable amount of time to resolve. By incorporating the long-term resolution assumption into the revised guidance, a company will give itself an extra-conservative cushion of downgraded performance. This will yield extra time for the company to fix its problem, and allows it to avoid another guidance shortfall in the near term.

In short, it is far better to adopt a slightly conservative stance when issuing guidance, so that a company can comfortably achieve its numbers without giving the appearance of drastically underreporting guidance.

 **GUIDANCE POLICY**

Given the range of options regarding the format, frequency, and timing of guidance, it makes sense to formalize a company's preferred approach with a guidance policy. The policy should state the general type of information to be released, when guidance shall be provided, and whether current guidance will be updated when existing guidance is obsolete. Finally, the policy should require the inclusion of meaningful cautionary statements (see Chapter 10) to avoid liability for issuing guidance. A sample policy follows:

The company will provide guidance to the investment community, which shall encompass information regarding revenue, gross margins, net income, and earnings per share. Also, the company may selectively provide guidance regarding new products and markets.

The company will endeavor to update guidance when, in management's opinion, the current guidance has become materially misleading. At a minimum, new guidance shall be issued on a quarterly basis, immediately after the release of the Form 10-Q.

All guidance must be clearly identified as forward-looking statements, and be accompanied by meaningful cautionary statements that actual results could differ materially from the guidance.

The policy can also end with a statement that the IRO is responsible for policy management, if there is an in-house IRO.

 ## SUMMARY

Guidance is a critical part of the IRO's responsibilities and should be used whenever corporate results can be forecasted with some degree of accuracy. It is typically issued on a quarterly basis, immediately after the latest quarterly results have been released.

The main area in which guidance tends to become a problem is when it is too aggressive. Instead, the IRO should strongly recommend a long-term policy of providing slightly conservative guidance, which the company can reliably attain. In addition, guidance should consistently include the same types of information over a long period of time. By doing so, there is less risk of stock price fluctuation and fraudulent financial reporting.

CHAPTER TWELVE

# Dealing with the Sell Side

T HE INVESTMENT MARKET IS divided into two halves—the sell side and the buy side. The sell side is the middlemen who assist companies in locating funding, or who assist in selling company shares to investors. Sell-side entities include investment bankers and brokerage firms, and they employ analysts, stock traders, investment bankers, and institutional salespeople. The buy side is any entity managing capital funds, such as pension funds, mutual funds, or individual investors. A company can work through the sell side to reach the buy side, or work with the buy side directly. In this chapter, we'll cover how to deal with the sell side of the market, and address the buy side in the next chapter.

The bulk of the discussion in this chapter addresses analyst relations, because a favorable opinion by a well-known analyst has a multiplier effect throughout the buy side. The opinion will be broadcast widely through the business press and industry publications, which are monitored by fund managers. Brokers will also use this information to recommend stocks to their clients. Consequently, for companies with medium to large capitalizations, analyst relations is a crucial element of the IRO's toolkit.

 ## ANALYST'S PERSPECTIVE

The analyst is sometimes perceived as a partially mythical creature who can instantly accelerate or crash a company's stock price, who is constantly demanding more information than the management team is prepared to give, and who becomes decidedly cantankerous when the company's actual results do not attain expected levels. Some level of analyst coverage is necessary, since the withdrawal of coverage has led to an inordinate proportion of companies being delisted from stock exchanges due to declines in their stock prices. Consequently, it is useful to understand the pressures faced by analysts and the environment in which they operate so that the IRO can better support their needs.

The first factor to consider is that sell-side firms now budget for fewer analysts than in the boom years of the 1990s. Since the number of public companies has not declined, this means that analysts have withdrawn their coverage from some companies, usually those with smaller capitalizations. Small-cap companies suffer the most from the decline in analysts because an analyst's recommendation must maximize commissions for the employing sell-side firm, and companies with small capitalizations have an insufficient float to generate much commission volume.

Second, consider the types of companies that an analyst is willing to cover. A large sell-side firm with a massive sales staff is only likely to authorize coverage for larger public firms, since it needs to sell massive volumes of stock in order to earn sufficient commission volume. Conversely, an analyst employed by a smaller firm will be more willing to look at smaller companies that are not being provided coverage by larger firms. Thus, a company initially trying to attract analysts should ignore the larger sell-side firms and instead concentrate its efforts on smaller firms that are more likely to be receptive.

A third key factor to consider is the method by which analysts are paid. An analyst is paid to correctly predict the direction in which a company's stock price will move. If correct, the analyst's firm will earn trading commissions on the purchase of the company's stock—thus, predictions that drive large trading volume are the key to its success. Conversely, analysts suffer reduced compensation or are fired if they incorrectly predict stock price movements. This explains why analysts are nonplussed when management reports unexpected earnings levels—analysts can lose their jobs over the resulting stock price decline. Thus, it is critically important to be conservative in providing guidance, as well as open and responsive in issuing changes to guidance. Analysts appreciate the notice, so that they can change their estimates in a timely manner.

Fourth, be aware of how the analyst issues recommendations. The sales staff of the analyst's firm typically holds an early morning meeting each day, known as the *morning call*, before the markets open. During that meeting, analysts will present any companies they cover for which they have a "buy" recommendation, and the sales staff can question them about their views, recent research, and earnings estimates. It is also possible that the brokerage's client buy-side analysts and portfolio managers will access the morning call. The sales staff will push their clients to buy the stock of any companies for which a "buy" recommendation has been issued. If the analyst only has a "hold" recommendation, then the company will not be discussed during this meeting, so the sales staff will have no reason to encourage their clients to buy the stock.

Sell-side firms also try to pull in acquisition work or stock placement assistance by dangling the prospect of analyst coverage in front of a company. Since most companies will occasionally engage in either or both of these activities, it makes sense to obtain assistance from a firm that can also provide analyst coverage. Better yet, parcel out this business to multiple firms, so that coverage will be given by several analysts. However, such coverage can be short-lived if a company does not continue to dole out business to the same sell-side firms, so this is not a reliable source of coverage. Also, Section 501 of the Sarbanes-Oxley Act of 2002 states that employees of a broker/dealer who are:

> . . . involved with investment banking activities may not, directly or indirectly, retaliate against or threaten to retaliate against any securities analyst employed by that broker or dealer or its affiliates as a result of an adverse, negative, or otherwise unfavorable research report that may adversely affect the present or prospective investment banking relationship of the broker or dealer with the issuer that is the subject of the research report.

Further, a research analyst cannot be supervised or controlled by a firm's investment banking department, nor accompany investment bankers on road shows, nor be compensated based on the firm's investment banking activities. Thus, obtaining analyst coverage as part of a broader services deal may be a two-edged sword, since there is no guarantee that the coverage will be favorable.

Finally, analysts are unwilling to anger a company's management with negative ratings, since this could lead to their being excluded from access to the company. Accordingly, they use a broad range of recommendation types that keep them from having to clearly label a company with either a buy, hold, or sell rating. Instead, the "buy" category is also divided into (in increasing order of fervor) Moderate Buy, Long-Term Buy, Outperform, and Strong Buy. Many analysts will assign a rating of Moderate Buy, or some similar term, to a company's stock in order to ameliorate a management team when their company's earnings performance is mediocre, without taking the more drastic steps of assigning a Hold or Sell rating. In reality, a company whose stock is assigned a Moderate Buy rating may never be brought to the attention of the analyst firm's sales staff.

These observations lead to some conclusions regarding how to work with an analyst. First, do not repeatedly make outrageously high earnings claims, because this will result in wildly gyrating stock prices when earnings estimates are not met, and again when management makes stratospheric claims yet again. Under these circumstances, analysts will be at risk of not estimating earnings properly, and will likely drop their coverage of the company. Second, protect every analyst's job by issuing consistently conservative guidance that is based on clearly understandable assumptions. In addition, adopt and publicize a business plan that results in a quarterly earnings pattern consistent with the plan, and give analysts access to corporate officers. Analysts will then feel that the company is providing them with sufficient information to anticipate and understand the reasons for changes in actual earnings. This approach may even result in coverage by additional analysts, because they know that any earnings estimates and recommendations they issue will very likely be correct. Thus, conservative guidance, consistently applied, is the key to the long-term happiness of an analyst.

## FINDING THE RIGHT ANALYST

An analyst usually specializes in a single industry, and then on only a few companies within that industry. It takes a considerable amount of effort to thoroughly understand an industry, so analysts rarely depart from their chosen industries to provide coverage of companies in other areas. Also, they generally provide coverage to companies whose market capitalizations fall within a predetermined range. Thus, the pool of analysts who might be interested in providing coverage for a specific company is relatively limited. However, if they already cover a company's industry, they may be willing to provide coverage, since this represents a minimal amount of additional work for them. Consider using the following approaches to finding these analysts:

- Determine who provides coverage for comparable companies. Some public companies list on their Web sites the names and contact information of the analysts who cover them. This is especially common for smaller companies who only have limited coverage. Larger firms being covered by dozens of analysts rarely list analyst contact information.

- Hire an investor relations firm that has established contacts with the analyst community and that can provide a short list of the most likely analyst candidates.

If there is a pool of possible analysts, then pursue the ones that are asked to speak by industry organizations. If an analyst is asked to speak at an industry's annual conference, that is a good sign that the organizing entity thinks the analyst can provide valuable insights to participants. Also look for analysts who appear to spend considerable time meeting with customers; they place a greater emphasis on customer requirements, and less time touting their favorite companies. Finally, the best analysts issue research reports that focus on the underpinnings of industries and how they operate, and how companies and their offerings slot into the structure of the industry. This indicates comprehensive knowledge that investors appreciate, which is why these analysts attract strong followings in the investment community.

Once a pool of likely analysts has been developed, the next step is to contact them. The best approach is to provide them with a stream of useful information, such as industry data that they may not already have. By doing so, analysts are more likely to at least include a company in their industrywide research reports. Also, providing this service creates a sense of obligation, so that analysts are at least more likely to agree to an initial meeting in which the company can present an overview of its operations. This initial meeting is covered in the next section.

##  DEALING WITH ANALYSTS

The following discussion assumes that a company is large enough to attract the attention of analysts. It is extremely difficult to obtain analyst coverage if a company's market cap is less than $100 million to $200 million. If a company's market cap is too small, the IRO should not waste time trying to attract analysts who are unlikely to be interested, and instead should shift attention to specific types of brokers who are amenable to micro-cap situations, as discussed later in this chapter.

When planning for a meeting with analysts, always send them an advance packet of preparatory information. This packet should include a fact book about the company's strategy, performance, products, and customer references. The analyst must complete a considerable amount of analysis before issuing a recommendation, so issuing them the fact book will allow them to complete an initial set of questions, which they will then pose during the meeting. Thus, sending advance information allows the analyst to maximize his or her meeting time.

When preparing for an analyst meeting, it is extremely important to anticipate all questions that might be asked. If a manager were to appear befuddled by a question, the querying analyst might be concerned about the manager's ability to run the business, and so would decline to provide coverage of the stock. To avoid this problem, maintain a list of questions that have been asked during meetings with other analysts, and supplement the list with questions asked during investor conference calls or other investor meetings. In addition, brainstorm the types of questions that might be asked in response to current or prospective changes in the business. If other comparable companies are hosting conference calls prior to the analyst meeting, then listen to those calls to see if analysts are asking any new questions that have not been heard before. With these questions in hand, construct a standard set of answers and have a dress rehearsal with the managers who will attend the analyst meeting.

An analyst meeting should be between the analyst, the IRO, the CEO, and the CFO. Other managers may be added from time to time, but this is the core group. The analyst is primarily interested in the CEO's views, since this is the one person responsible for all operations, and who can provide the best information about the company's strategic direction. However, if the CEO has poor presentation skills or does not exhibit a high level of interest in the company and its products, then it may be better to substitute a senior-level executive who exhibits these traits.

An analyst expects to be provided with a considerable amount of information about the company. During the meeting, the IRO should address the types of products and services that the company sells, which ones provide the bulk of the company's revenues, and the geographic areas and markets in which the products and services are sold. This sales discussion should also include the overall size of the company's markets, the future of those markets, its share of those markets, the market growth rate, and management's expectation for its eventual market share. Analysts are very interested in competitors, so be prepared to discuss primary competitors, their sales volume and market share, and their strengths and weaknesses. If there have been acquisitions in the past or are likely to be in the near future, then also be prepared to discuss the criteria the company uses to select acquirees and how it integrates acquirees into the rest of the organization. In addition, be prepared to talk about growth goals, how the company plans to meet them, and the company's recent track record for meeting those goals. Finally, analysts concentrate heavily on how various risks will impact a company's prospects, so cover the key risks faced by the company and how the company is prepared to protect itself from them.

In addition, analysts are very interested in intangible issues, such as the ability of the management team to run the company. For this reason, they will likely probe management's commitment to long-term planning, profit planning, and control systems, all of which are cornerstones of long-term management success. In addition, they will probably want to meet with the managers of the product development and marketing departments to ascertain their skills in these two key areas. Given the likelihood of this level of questioning, the IRO should ensure that anyone who may come in contact with an analyst is coached in the legalities of disclosing information. Further, the IRO should attend any meeting between an analyst and an employee to ensure that disclosure rules are followed, and to make note of any inadvertent disclosures that must then be released to the public in an 8-K filing.

A key element of an analyst meeting that has a major bearing on the analyst's target price for the company's stock is the discussion of comparable companies. Unless persuaded otherwise, most analysts will base their target stock prices on the prices of the stocks of comparable companies in the same industry. For example, if the stock prices of comparable companies result in market capitalizations that are two times revenues, then analysts will assume the same ratio for all companies in the industry. The analyst may not even bring up this issue, assuming that the usual industry comparisons will be used. If the IRO feels that the company is more readily comparable to other companies, perhaps outside of the industry, then this is a good time to discuss which companies are better "comps" and why the analyst should use them as such. In short, define a group of comps for the company, or else analysts will independently do so, likely resulting in lower target prices being included in analyst reports.

The preceding description of topics shows that there is a massive amount of information to impart to an analyst. This does not mean that the information should be stuffed into a lengthy set of PowerPoint slides. The analyst is more interested in a chat with the management team, not a mind-numbing display of bullet points. Consequently, only use slides to the minimum extent possible, using them more to lay out the general points of the agenda than to impart large volumes of information.

After having completed a presentation to an analyst, always leave behind a financial and operational summary of the presentation. The intent of this summary document is to be a reminder to the analyst of the company's salient points, with additional contact information in case the analyst wishes to pursue additional research.

A single analyst briefing, no matter how spectacular, will not guarantee coverage. Instead, the management team should commit to a long-term relationship that involves the provision of ongoing access, building trust, and showing over time that the company can achieve long-term success. A key part of this relationship is making sure that an analyst gets plenty of responsive customer references, since they can glean a great deal of information from the company's customer base. This can even include having analysts meet with early adopters of the company's latest products, so that they can obtain first-hand knowledge of the company's sales prospects. The analyst also appreciates it when the CEO listens to and discusses his advice, which shows that management is willing to make changes in order to better position itself.

If an analyst then decides to provide coverage of the company, part of her research will include in-depth discussions with the company's customers, suppliers, and employees to verify that the information presented by the company is correct. These discussions will also include a search for undisclosed issues that may impact the company's financial performance. Though this may appear to be an undue degree of prying, the management team must become used to this detailed level of review on an ongoing basis. Indeed, the IRO can assist analysts with this review work by providing contact information to them.

Once the analyst has completed a detailed review of the company, she creates a research report that includes an earnings estimate, a recommendation, and a price target for the stock. The analyst will periodically update the report as new information about the company or its industry appears, if that information will result in a material change in the earnings estimate and price target.

The analyst may ask the company to review the research report for factual errors. If the IRO agrees to this review, first send a copy of the original document to the company's legal department, so that an unaltered version is available in the event of a later lawsuit, alleging that the company made significant changes to the document in order to improve the appearance of future growth. Also, create a redlined version of all changes to the analyst's report and send this version to the legal staff. Further, do not comment on any conclusions reached by the analyst, since this could be construed as jointly taking ownership of the analyst's recommendations. Many companies refuse to review analyst reports, on the grounds that they could be legally liable for tacitly agreeing to the information and conclusions contained in them.

Given the amount of information required by an analyst in order to create a quality research report, it is clear that the management team must set aside a significant amount of time to meet their needs. If there are too many analysts requesting management resources, it may be necessary to require inquiring analysts to meet certain minimum criteria before being allowed access to key employees. Examples of qualifying criteria are having exceptional industry experience before becoming an analyst, having previously published reports on the industry, credentials as a Chartered Financial Analyst (issued by the CFA Institute), or a significant number of years of experience as an analyst. However, exclude analysts judiciously—any analyst may eventually become highly influential, and could have a major impact on a company's stock price. If a company finds that it simply has no time to deal with analysts at all, then it should establish a minimum level of access that is available to all interested parties and require that all analysts adhere to that standard.

After an analyst issues a recommendation, the IRO should review it in detail. Analysts are among the most knowledgeable independent observers of a company and its industry, so their commentaries are worthy of considerable review and discussion within the management team. In particular, note any commentary regarding how an analyst has arrived at a particular estimate of revenue or profit, especially the assumptions used to arrive at those numbers. By understanding analyst assumptions, it is possible to predict their behavior when the company's metrics change in the future. Also, if an analyst points out in a report a perceived flaw in the company's strategy or operating assumptions, the flaw may be indicative of a general marketplace perception that is keeping the company's stock from achieving its full valuation. If so, treat these perceived flaws as opportunities for strategic changes, or perhaps as grounds for additional education of the marketplace to mitigate the perceived impact of the flaw.

It may be tempting to post the complete text of a favorable analyst report on the company Web site. However, this is not advisable, because it gives the appearance of endorsing the report, which could be used in a shareholder lawsuit as evidence that the company is attempting to defraud investors by making excessively aggressive statements about its future performance. Also, if a company were to post a favorable analyst report, what happens if the analyst later issues a negative report? Is the company then obligated to post the replacement report? Instead, just list analyst contact information on the company Web site, and let site visitors contact the analysts for more information.

## NEGATIVE ANALYST REPORT

The reason for attracting the attention of analysts is to obtain favorable research reports, which will presumably result in an increase in the price of a company's stock. However, favorable reports do not last forever. At some point, the stock price will reach an analyst's target level, after which the analyst will likely change from a buy recommendation to a hold or sell recommendation. Also, some analysts may occasionally act on incorrect information or incorrectly interpret information that results in a negative report. Further, junior analysts with little industry experience are more likely to issue earnings estimates that vary significantly from what a company expects to achieve. Finally, an analyst who provide coverage of an entire sector may conclude that economic conditions will lead to a decline in profitability for all of the companies in that sector, and so downgrades all of them; there is nothing that an individual company can do about this if their stock will be downgraded simply because of the industry in which it operates.

Management should expect these negative reports from time to time, and should not be flustered or react angrily to them. Instead, the best approach is to not comment on the reports at all, and instead provide a steady flow of information to the investing public, which helps analysts arrive at high-quality earnings estimates that will eventually result in renewed buy recommendations. The most aggressive action an IRO should ever consider is contacting an analyst's research director to discuss perceived factual errors in a research report that might have negatively impacted the recommendation. A key point is that analysts will publish earnings estimates no matter what information they have available, so it is always in the company's best interests to give them more information, rather than less.

The worst reaction to a negative analyst report is a public rant (which usually seems to occur during a quarterly conference call), which merely gives analysts an unflattering view of the management team. Also, it is not wise to cut off an analyst from access to company information or mailing lists, just because she issued a negative report. By doing so, the analyst now has even less information to use for future reports, which may result in increasingly inaccurate recommendations.

## DEALING WITH BROKERS

There are more than 660,000 brokers registered with the Financial Industry Regulatory Authority (FINRA). Maintaining contact with each of these brokers over a long period of time is not always cost-effective, given the relatively small volume of share purchases that each one may generate. Given this problem, the best way to maintain broker relations is to determine which ones are considered opinion leaders by their peers and ply these key individuals with a continuing stream of information about the company. If the opinion leaders are

**Exhibit 12.1**   Sample Layout of a Broker Presentation

| Step | Duration | Content |
|------|----------|---------|
| 1. | 1 minute | Overview of company business and its goals. This contains minimal company history, with more emphasis on giving a snapshot of the business today. |
| 2. | 2 minutes | Financial overview, including the revenue run rate, organic growth, acquisition history, cash flow, and profitability. |
| 3. | 3 minutes | Business opportunity, including the markets where the company is a player, opportunities, and the company's competitive advantages. |
| 4. | 3 minutes | Growth strategy, both for organic growth and by acquisition. |
| 5. | 2 minutes | Critical path, showing key milestones and the status of progress toward each one. |
| 6. | 1 minute | Management track record |
|    | **12 minutes** | |

convinced, they will pass along their opinions to their broker networks, which, in turn, can create a significant amount of share purchase volume.

An excellent approach for meeting brokers is to sponsor a gathering at a public venue shortly after the markets close. Alternatively, consider sponsoring a luncheon at a brokerage firm (where participation rates are usually very high), or at a popular local restaurant. In either case, the company pays for all food and drinks provided. The presentation should be short, certainly no more than 30 minutes, and should give brokers an overview of the company's operations and prospects. The emphasis in this type of presentation is much less on numerical performance and more on a company's story. An example of the layout of a broker presentation that lasts 12 minutes is shown in Exhibit 12.1.

Have written materials available for any brokers interested in additional information. Unlike analyst meetings, which are one-on-one, broker meetings usually include many participants, who are free to informally arrive or leave during presentations. The better brokers who will be of the most assistance in creating new stock sales may be difficult to identify or chat with, since they are so busy that they are likely to arrive late and leave early.

If a company has a low level of market capitalization (a "micro-cap"), it will have a difficult time attracting brokers, because most of them are told which stocks to pitch to their clients, and those stocks almost always involve companies with larger capitalizations. To avoid this problem, do not waste time contacting brokers with conservative clients (usually those approaching retirement age), since these clients are unlikely to put their money into a higher-risk investment. Also, only deal with brokers having at least ten years of experience with the same firm, since these individuals are more likely to have been given some leeway in making stock recommendations. These more senior brokers are also more likely to have high-net-worth individuals as clients, who are more likely to make investments in micro-cap companies if there is a significant level of perceived reward.

Another alternative for locating brokers willing to recommend micro-cap stocks is to call local brokerage firms after trading hours and ask the branch manager if any of their brokers specialize in companies with lower market capitalizations. Another option is to hire an investor relations firm that already knows these brokers, and who can arrange introductions with the IRO.

Brokers do not need as detailed a set of information as would be required by analysts. Instead, they require information about three key issues, which they will pass along to their clients:

1. The stock should be actively traded, so their clients can easily buy and sell without any liquidity problems.
2. A company should have a solid performance record, in the form of multiple quarters of gradually increasing profitability.
3. A company should have excellent visibility in the marketplace, in the form of active public relations and investor relations programs.

If these three factors are in place, a company has the capability to attract the attention of a large number of brokers.

Brokers are especially appreciative if the company creates for them a prepackaged set of sales pitches and supporting information that they can use to pitch the company to their clients. There can be several variations on the sales pitch, which the company can create based on conversations with key brokers. In addition to the sales pitches, consider issuing reprints of articles about the company, which brokers can pass along to their clients.

## PUMP AND DUMP

Smaller public companies, especially those in the over-the-counter (OTC) market, are subject to the *pump and dump* scam. This tactic is used by shady individuals to artificially boost the price of a company's stock with an overhyped public relations campaign that increases demand for the stock. Once the company's stock price rises on this news, the perpetrators dump their shares on the market, resulting in quick profits for them and a steep stock price decline for the company. This practice can have a long-term negative impact on a company's stock price, even if it had nothing to do with the scheme, because investors have long memories, and will likely shun the stock for years to come.

If a broker approaches a company's managers with any proposal that sounds even remotely like a pump and dump scheme, be sure to check out their background at www.nasd.com. This site is run by the Financial Industry Regulatory Authority (FINRA). There is a page link on the FINRA home page called "BrokerCheck," which contains information about the professional background, license status, and disciplinary history of more than 5,000 registered firms and 660,000 brokers.

Unfortunately, pump and dump schemes are increasingly found on the Internet, where anyone can buy company stock, send out positive messages about the company's prospects, and then promptly sell the shares when the stock price peaks. There is little a company can do about this type of scheme. At best, try to have the company's stock traded on a formal exchange, such as the American Stock Exchange, where there is orderly trading and much better information available about listed companies.

## DEALING WITH INVESTMENT BANKERS

An investment banker locates money on behalf of a company. The usual process is that the company and investment banker mutually create a multiyear forecasting model of the company's likely growth rate, cash flow, and valuation (based on the valuations of comparable public companies). The investment banker then sends a summary of the model and the company's operations and strategy to a large number of fund managers to obtain an initial expression of interest. If some interest is expressed, the investment banker helps the company's management team create a presentation that ranges in length from 30 to 45 minutes, and coaches them through several iterations of the presentation. Once ready, the management team goes on a road show to pitch its case to the fund managers who expressed initial interest. Usually, this means making multiple presentations per day in such cities as Atlanta, Boston, Charlotte, Chicago, Dallas, Des Moines, Kansas City, New York, and Pittsburgh, where many of the funds are located. The investment banker then contacts the fund managers to see who is interested in making an investment and under what terms, and then closes the deal. The investment banker is usually paid based on a sliding scale of the amount of funds raised.

When picking an investment banker, base the decision on their experience with the company's industry, because only certain fund managers will invest in that industry, and the investment banker must have relationships with those managers. Also, a company will very likely require additional funding at some point in the future, so it makes sense to select an investment banker who can be a trusted advisor and confidant.

 ## DEALING WITH SELL-SIDE SPECIALISTS

There are investor relations specialists who will represent a public company to brokers and analysts. They have extensive contacts with the sell side, and will make many contacts on behalf of a company. They do not engage in analyst or broker meetings, nor do they fulfill any public relations functions. Their stock in trade is strictly their sell-side contacts. These specialists are most frequently retained by smaller OTC companies with small floats and low stock prices, in hopes of achieving rapid stock price increases. Though the desired price increase may very well occur, the increase will likely be a short term one if it exceeds the underlying fundamentals of the company.

Many sell-side specialists agree to be paid in stock, since smaller public firms are not always able to pay in cash. This gives the specialists a strong incentive to increase the price of the stock, since it increases their own compensation. However, given the thin trading volumes of the companies they represent, specialists can have difficulty liquidating their stock holdings.

If a company chooses to deal with sell-side specialists, it should supplement its investment in this activity with other public and investor relations activities and operational improvements so that the resulting stock price increases are not short-lived, but rather, can form the foundation for long-term value for investors.

 ## SUMMARY

The sell side of the investment market is of great use to the IRO, because it can not only attract capital for the company but also contribute greatly to increases in its stock price. For example, several studies have shown that the greater the number of analysts following a company (which implies greater publicity for the company), the higher the price-earnings multiple of the stock. Because of its importance, the IRO must deal with the sell side in an appropriate manner, which involves the consistent provision of conservative guidance to the marketplace that is supported by easily understandable assumptions.

Besides providing information to the sell side, it is also possible to create a reverse flow of information back to the company. Some analysts will provide information about how their rating systems work and under what circumstances they will upgrade or downgrade their stock ratings. This is extremely useful for anticipating when the announcement of new information by the company will trigger a change in analyst recommendations. Also, brokers and investment bankers can provide feedback from their buy-side clients regarding concerns about the company's strategic direction or perceived risks. In addition, it may be possible to discuss potential strategic scenarios with analysts to see how they respond, or to find out what they consider to be key issues within the company's markets. However, the sell-side will not hand out this information unless asked, so the IRO must be proactive in continually plumbing contacts for feedback.

CHAPTER THIRTEEN

# Dealing with the Buy Side

A S NOTED IN THE preceding chapter, the investment market is divided into two halves—the sell side and the buy side. The sell side comprises the middlemen who assist companies in locating funding, while the buy side is any entity managing capital funds, such as pension funds, mutual funds, endowments, or individual investors. The buy side executes orders to buy or sell stock through the sell side. Examples of these entities are Fidelity, Vanguard, and T. Rowe Price. The buy side is the ultimate target of public companies and the sell side, since it controls the investable funds that companies want. In this chapter, we cover the types of investors to be found throughout the buy side, such as institutional, individual, and foreign investors, as well as investment clubs. We also describe how to present the company to investors as an investment prospect, and how to handle a private investment in public equity transaction.

## TYPES OF INVESTORS

There are several types of investors, each one with different reasons for buying, holding, and selling stock. The first type focuses on high growth rates; if a company can maintain a high rate of revenue or earnings growth, then it will continue to buy its stock, but will also dump the stock at the first report of a slowdown in growth. The *growth investor* focuses on trend lines of revenue growth, earnings growth, and the price/earnings ratio, and looks especially favorably upon companies growing faster than their industries.

Another investor type focuses on the value play. *Value investors* will only buy when a stock is trading at multiples well below the industry average, and will sell at a point when they think the stock is fully valued. Value investors tend to focus on the ratio of share price to book value, as well as cash flow. These investors retain stock longer than growth investors because it may take a considerable amount of time for the stock to reach its predetermined price point. Value investors may snap up a large proportion of stock if the stock price has cratered, and can be very effective in keeping the price from heading even lower.

The key financial focus of growth and value investors is fundamentally different. Growth investors are primarily concerned with the income statement, while value investors spend more time examining the balance sheet. The income statement contains the growth information most vital to growth investors, while the asset values on the balance sheet are what value investors want to examine. The IRO should be aware of these differences when dealing with either type of investor, and focus the conversation accordingly.

There is a crossover investor who is interested in both value and growth. These are known as *GARP investors*, for "growth at a reasonable price." GARP investors will search for bargain-prices shares as would a value investor, but also pay attention to the potential growth of the underlying business. They will typically sell their holdings when the company has achieved parity with the stock price multiples of its peer group.

A fourth investor type focuses on assured returns, and so will buy stock when the company offers dividends and disappear if dividends are cut. These *income investors* want to know how long the dividend has been at its current level, the company's history of altering it, and its ability to continue paying dividends.

Technical analysts, also called *chartists*, focus on stock momentum. These investors forecast stock prices based on their historical behavior, rather than on a company's future prospects, and are generally short-term investors.

Finally, *theme investors* are primarily concerned with general trends in a single industry or in the economy as a whole. For example, increasing levels of oil usage worldwide may drive them to buy the stock of companies throughout the oil exploration industry, or in the supporting oilfield services industry. These investors tend to invest in multiple companies that will be impacted by the same underlying theme, with moderate attention to the fundamentals of each company.

Within these categories, investors frequently restrict their activities to specific industries that they expect will achieve outsized returns. They may also focus on companies within a specific range of market capitalizations, which they feel will perform better under certain economic circumstances.

Though the IRO may try to pigeonhole all investors into the various categories just noted, a significant proportion of investors may not be holding the company's stock for any reason at all. In many cases, they have inherited the stock, and have no plans or expectations for it. These stockholders are unlikely to sell their existing holdings or to acquire new stock. Instead, they will passively retain their stock positions no matter what actions the IRO takes unless significant life events or news events move them to take action.

There are points in a company's life cycle when types of investors will buy and sell its stock, resulting in a continually varying mix of investors. The IRO may consider many of these investors to be transient and therefore undesirable, as they continually shift in and out of company stock holdings. Nonetheless, a public company is likely to experience all of these types of investors at some point during its life.

As a company changes over time, it will become more or less attractive to each of the investor types just noted. The IRO should modify the company's investor presentations to most closely coincide with its actual results and future prospects, which will naturally reduce the proportion of one type of investor, while encouraging investments by other types of investors. For example, the decision to issue dividends obviously attracts income investors, and may also turn away growth investors, who would prefer to see the cash reinvested in the business in order to spur more growth. These changes in the company presentation have such a large impact on the composition of the investor base that the IRO should discuss them at length with the management team and board of directors before implementing them.

Once the decision is made to alter the corporate presentation, there should be a thorough overhaul of all information issued by the company to the investment community. For example, if the decision is to focus the company as a growth investment, then every shred of information it presents should exude the growth theme. In the rare case where a company is actually undervalued and growing fast, it can take the more onerous path of creating separate presentations for growth and value investors, but it can be difficult to keep the stories separate.

## DEALING WITH INSTITUTIONAL INVESTORS

A professional investor is usually the manager of a fund, such as a pension fund or mutual fund, and is commonly described as an institutional investor. An analyst working for or serving the needs of a fund is considered a buy-side analyst.

Before contacting institutional investors about buying company stock, the IRO must first determine their investment strategies to see if the company meets their criteria. For example, about 30 percent of all institutional stock portfolios invest in stock indexes, where the amount and mix of shares held are automatically determined by the index. If a company is listed on an index, then institutional investors will buy it. If not, then they have no interest. Also, being listed on or de-listed from an index can have some interesting effects on a company's stock price. For example, a company may move up from one index to another, based on improvements in its financial performance. When this happens, investors in the old index funds will sell a larger proportion of the company's shares than investors in the new index funds will buy, on the grounds that the company is now weighted toward the bottom of the new index, whereas it used to be weighted near the top of the old index (since indexes are based on market capitalization). This preponderance of stock sales over stock purchases can result in a drop in a company's stock price. This is a good example of how stock pricing can vary, irrespective of the performance of the underlying company.

Also, institutional investors do not usually invest in micro-cap companies, because their stock is so thinly traded. When there is minimal trading, a fund manager will have great difficulty acquiring a large volume of shares, and similarly will have difficulty later in selling those shares without initiating a stock price decline. Also, if a company's stock is not listed on an exchange, then a fund manager will not consider it to be a viable investment. In these situations, the IRO should not expend any effort to contact institutional investors, because they will not purchase company stock under any circumstances.

An investment fund's rules may prohibit it from buying stock below a certain price point (usually $5), or from purchasing more than a certain percentage of a company's outstanding shares. It is useful to determine if these rules exist, to see if a potential investor will be constrained from making a significant (or any) investment.

The discussion thus far has been on those institutions *not* to pursue for an investment. Conversely, there are several ways to locate those funds that would be acceptable investors. First, contact an investor relations consultant who has contacts among the fund managers, and who knows the preferred investment types of those managers. Also, review the Web sites maintained by the various funds, where they frequently outline their investment strategies. In addition, continually review the industry news to see who is quoted in feature articles.

In many cases, a company manager will discuss how the company grew following an investment by a specific institution.

Another option is to look for institutions that invest in peer companies having similar investment characteristics, such as being in the same industry, or having a similar growth rate in revenue, profits, or cash flow. It is also possible that these peer companies may not be in the same industry. Once this peer group is established, comb the institution Web sites to determine which ones are investing in the peer group. Then contact their investment managers to point out the similarities between the company and the companies in which they currently invest, and to ask for a familiarization meeting.

Whichever search method is used, the key point is to target fund managers, investment advisors, or buy-side analysts who either invest or recommend investments based on general guidelines within which they can choose the stocks of individual companies. If these people are locked into only very specific investments by their fund investment policies, then there is no point in contacting them.

It may also be worthwhile to engage in conversations with institutional investors who are already investing in the company to see if they are willing to invest more. To research this, review the trend line of purchases by existing institutional investors to see who is accumulating a larger position, as well as the size of their investments in peer companies. If their proportional investments in other companies are larger, they may well be amenable to doing the same for the company.

If institutional investors are interested in investing in a company, one of their first actions is to delve into what is said in an analyst's report about that company, without paying much attention to the actual rating given. They understand that the rating is, to some extent, assigned based on the analyst's unwillingness to offend management, and so may not exactly reflect the contents of the report. Consequently, be thoroughly familiar with the contents of analyst reports and be prepared to answer questions from institutional investors who are equally familiar with the same reports.

The IRO needs to understand how institutional investors expect to be treated. First, they expect a tailored one-on-one meeting, where management makes a private presentation to them and sets aside sufficient time to answer all of their questions. Second, they will expect management to conduct a quarterly conference call, so that they can receive the latest information about the company's operational and financial results, and have an opportunity to pose questions to management. Third, do not bury them with annual reports and promotional materials, since they are already wading through enormous amounts of material sent to them by other companies. Instead, prepare a summarized version of key information from public filings, and send it to them in the format they prefer. This may seem like a great deal of work, but retaining an institutional investor is important, so paying special attention to their needs is appreciated.

Professor Sarah Mavrinac of the University of Western Ontario conducted a survey of institutional investors to see which intangible factors they include in their valuations of target companies (http://www.ivey.uwo.ca/publications/Impact/vol4_3mavrinac.htm). In order of priority, they are:

1. Execution of corporate strategy
2. Management credibility
3. Quality of corporate strategy
4. Innovativeness
5. Ability to attract employees
6. Market share
7. Management experience
8. Quality of compensation policies
9. Research leadership
10. Quality of processes

When meeting with institutional investors, the IRO should assume that they will structure their questions to address at least some of the points noted by Professor Mavrinac, and should prepare accordingly.

Though most IROs would love to have a few prominent funds invest in their company's stock, be aware that there are repercussions to having such investors. The main problem is that they accumulate so many shares that the trading environment becomes illiquid, with few remaining shares available for trading. Also, when institutions sell their stock holdings, the volumes sold are so large that there is a significant chance of a stock price decline.

 ## TRAVEL REQUIREMENTS FOR MEETINGS WITH INSTITUTIONAL INVESTORS

Institutional investors tend to be clustered close to each other, near or in such major cities as Atlanta, Boston, Charlotte, Chicago, Dallas, Des Moines, Detroit, Kansas City, New York, and Pittsburgh. They frequently correspond with each other, and so are not only aware of each other's investments but will also recommend that the IRO contact whichever investors in the area may also be interested in an investment.

Because of these investor clusters, it is most efficient to schedule trips to a city where the company's management team can meet with as many interested institutional investors as possible within a few days. The schedule shown in Exhibit 13.1 is a sample travel schedule for trips to Dallas and New York, with slots for meetings.

Exhibit 13.1 reveals that it makes sense to cluster investor meetings into close proximity, which minimizes travel time between meetings. For example,

**Exhibit 13.1**  Institutional Investor Meeting Schedule

|        | Friday – 4th | Weekend | Monday – 7th |
|--------|--------------|---------|--------------|
| 8:00   | Representative Capital – Scott Franklin 8000 N. Central Expressway Ste. ABC, Dallas (214) 819-4928 | | |
| 9:00   | (continued) | | Restricted Stock Investors – Thomas Aquinas 110 Hudson Street, Ste. ABC Jersey City (201) 985-8300 |
| 10:00  | Sunshine Capital – Walter Davis 8040 N. Central Expressway Ste. ABC, Dallas (214) 804-0629 | | (continued) |
| 11:00  | (continued) | | |
| 12:00  | | | Seminole Capital – Jason Short 640 Lexington Avenue, Ste. ABC New York (646) 229-7448 |
| 1:00   | | | (continued) |
| 2:00   | Creston Capital – Robert Mancini 105 Meacham Blvd., Forth Worth (817) 559-9487 | | |
| 3:00   | (continued) | | |
| 4:00   | Plainview Capital – Mitchell Gainer 265 Meacham Blvd., Forth Worth (817) 562-9034 | | Big Bend Equity – Helen Dust 111 River St., Hoboken (201) 748-1234 |
| 5:00   | (continued) | | (continued) |
| 6:00   | | | |

the Dallas meetings are a few blocks away from each other during the morning meetings, and shift to another city in the afternoon. This is extremely important for institutional investor meetings, because they tend to run longer than the budgeted time, which leaves little room for travel to the next meeting. Also, where possible, budget a reasonable block of time during mid-day to discuss the morning's meetings and adjust presentations as needed. Also, if the morning meetings run well over, this provides "catch up" time, so that they do not interfere with the afternoon meetings.

Also note that the exhibit includes phone numbers for each investor; the management team uses these numbers to warn meeting participants if they are running late or if they need directions.

Finally, if there is ever a meeting that justifies the use of a dedicated limousine service, this is it. The management team does not want the additional hassle of dealing with driving directions and potentially getting lost in a strange city. A limousine driver knows the area and can transport the group to its next meeting with minimal delay.

## DEALING WITH INDIVIDUAL INVESTORS

In an ideal world, individual investors (or *retail investors*) are the best kind of investor, because they tend to be more loyal than institutional investors, holding their stock for much longer periods of time. These "sticky" investors are prized because their steadfast refusal to sell stock keeps the stock price and volume of sales from gyrating excessively.

The best possible kind of individual investor is the high-net-worth investor, since a few contacts by the IRO may result in significant stock purchases. To locate these individuals, consider retaining an investor relations consultant who has a contact list. Alternatively, use the network of existing high-net-worth investors to determine who they use as advisors and reach out to these advisors to spread information about the company through their other contacts. Once high-net-worth investors become interested in the company, be prepared to assist them in obtaining additional information, because they are unlikely to have much research support.

Another source of new investors is the owners of the company's products. If a company is in the consumer products business and has a reputation for high quality, then it is a good bet that consumers will be sufficiently enamored of the company to buy and hold its stock. To attract these investors, put information about the company's public status on product packaging.

Conversely, consider turning current investors into product consumers by offering discounts on company products to investors. The main risk with this approach is ensuring that products continue to have a high level of quality. If the company begins to have product problems, then the investors originally attracted by the product line may leave in droves.

It may also be possible to target investors in competing firms. If so, the IRO must prove to these investors why purchasing the company's stock represents a superior investment over that of the competitor. This can be a difficult sales proposition if the competitor is the dominant player in the market, since these firms tend to generate the best investor returns. Another difficulty with this approach is that the targeted investors may feel that their current portfolio mix represents a sufficient weighting in the company's market, so they will only invest in the company if they also sell their holdings in the competing firm.

Another way to attract investors is through the brokers of existing investors. If the current group of investors bought the company's shares based on a broker recommendation, then building a direct relationship with that broker may very well result in the acquisition of new investors through the same broker. This requires a long-term commitment to excellent broker relations, including the retention of key brokers on all mailing lists, as well as invitations to them to participate in periodic investor conference calls. If a company drops its efforts in this key area, then expect those investors brought in by brokers to eventually sell their shares.

It is also possible to buy subscriber lists from publications and trade associations, if the IRO feels that a relatively high proportion of those subscribers might be interested in the company. The company sends a bulk mailing about the company to anyone on these lists, with a reply card that then qualifies each respondent for additional mailings. An expanded version of this approach is to include on the reply card a questionnaire that asks respondents for the names of their brokers, favorite publications, and investment clubs, so the IRO will have leads for further marketing efforts. The IRO should purge the list periodically, preferably before the mailing of expensive year-end reports.

Using a mailing list can be an expensive option because the IRO must blindly send out mailers to people whose only qualification is that they landed on a subscriber list; this generally results in a low investment rate and requires a high cost in issuing mailings. Thus, a cost-benefit analysis of this option will likely reveal that it is not viable.

If a company has a low capitalization, then the IRO will have an especially difficult time locating investors. Usually, only high net worth individuals are willing to invest in micro cap stocks. These people are typically looking for outsized growth rates in excess of 20 percent for revenue, income, or cash flow. They need high returns, because the transaction costs of buying and selling micro-cap shares are higher than for larger cap stocks, and they must be reimbursed for the added risk. For example, a key transaction cost for a micro-cap stock is the impact that a large buy or sell order has on the market price, which can shift significantly as a result of the order. There is also a time delay in obtaining or selling stock (since there may be few shares available for trading), during which time the stock price may shift unfavorably for the investor. These costs can make it several times more expensive to deal in micro-cap stocks than in stock having a large float.

Although it is important to pursue new investors in all geographic locations, it can make sense to pay special attention to those located near company facilities. Investors in these areas may feel an affiliation with the company, and so are more likely to back management's position during a proxy fight, as well as to retain the stock even when its price is underperforming. For the same reason, it makes sense to encourage employees to acquire the stock.

Clearly, there are many ways to locate prospective investors. The real problem is doing so in a cost-effective manner. The IRO should try all of the options noted here at least once and then narrow down the search methodology over time, based on which methods return the largest number of stock sales for the least effort.

There is also the issue of maintaining relations with existing investors. The two most obvious methods are through the annual shareholder meeting and the annual report. Investors have the option of attending the annual meeting or accessing a video of it, and will receive the annual report as is their right as shareholders. The IRO can budget extra funds for these two items, to advertise the shareholder meeting, to expand the amount of information imparted during the meeting, and to expand the content of the annual report. In addition, the investor relations staff can also arrange for conference calls with retail investors, which can either be a variation on the standard quarterly earnings call or a more prolonged question and answer session.

## DEALING WITH INVESTMENT CLUBS

Investment clubs can be an excellent source of investors. They tend to buy and sell in relatively large volumes, so making a presentation to a single investment club can potentially result in a large stock purchase. Also, because their investment decisions are made by consensus, they tend to retain acquired stock longer than would an individual investor who is more prone to make a spot decision to sell. According to the National Association of Investors, its investment club members tend to hold stocks for at least four years. For these reasons, the IRO should consider scheduling periodic presentations to investment clubs.

To locate investment clubs, consider advertising in the *Better Investing* magazine of the National Association of Investors (located at www.better-investing.org), or buying its mailing list. The association has more than 131,000 members who are organized into about 13,000 investment clubs.

To obtain a presentation invitation from an investment club, first put it on the company's mailing list to receive a fact sheet about the company, as well as periodic updates on its performance and key events.

##  DEALING WITH FOREIGN INVESTORS

Management may decide to pursue foreign investors, perhaps because the targeted set of domestic investors appears to be tapped out, or simply because the company has received investment inquiries from foreigners. If so, consider creating a version of the company Web site in the language of the country where the IRO plans to market the company's prospects. Also, it is easier to sell to foreign investors if the company is already doing business in their countries, because they will have greater familiarity with the company, and therefore a greater propensity to invest in it.

If the target area includes Europe, the best cities in which to make investor presentations are London, Edinburgh, Geneva, Zurich, Frankfurt, Paris, and Amsterdam. These cities house the bulk of the institutional investors in Europe. The greatest concentration of potential investors is located in London, while there are major private banking partnerships in Geneva. Amsterdam is the home of several large pension funds. For an extended road trip, consider adding Dublin, Milan, Munich, and Stockholm. To arrange these trips, it is extremely useful to engage the services of one or more investment banking firms having extensive contacts throughout Europe.

European investors are primarily interested in large caps and growth stocks. German and Swiss investors are especially focused on large-cap stocks. There is less interest in small-cap stocks. Within these categories, European investors are most interested in companies paying low dividends and displaying volatile returns, as well as a significant proportion of foreign sales.

It is generally better to avoid the summer months (especially August) when conducting a European road show, due to the absence of so many people on vacation. In particular, avoid the weeks around Wimbledon and the British Open, when other managers travel to Europe and combine road shows with visits to these events. Each country may have different holidays, so consult their national calendars to determine which days are designated national holidays.

There is currently little investment in American companies by Far East investors. If the IRO wishes to explore this area, then the major investment centers to visit are Hong Kong, Singapore, and Tokyo.

Another possibility is the sovereign wealth funds operated by the wealthier Middle East countries. These include the Abu Dhabi Investment Authority, Kuwait Investment Authority, and Qatar Investment Authority. However, these entities primarily invest from London, so a separate trip to the Middle East might not be necessary.

To acquire a significant base of foreign investors, the senior management team must commit to recurring visits. Ideally, it should engage in a foreign tour for at least a week, once a year. If the team cannot visit this frequently, then the IRO at least should have a continuing presence, while the remainder of the team should commit to periodic conference calls that are targeted at foreign investors.

Finally, if presenting in England, be aware that some financial terms are decidedly different there than in the United States. For example, British shareholders own *shares* in a company (not stock), while a British company considers its inventory to be *stock*. Further, a British investor is inquiring about a company's sales when asking about *turnover*. In addition, British investors consider a company listed on a stock exchange to be a *quoted company*. To be safe, avoid all acronyms and American jargon, and stick with plain English.

## INVESTOR PRESENTATION

It is customary to give presentations to groups of individual investors. Given the millions of potential investors available, this means that a company should have a perpetual schedule of investor meetings; some large public companies schedule as many as 200 investor meetings per year. Only institutional investors warrant one-on-one meetings, because they can potentially invest in a large proportion of a company's stock.

Prior to scheduling an investor meeting, see if there are any competing meetings in town that might draw away attendees from the meeting. To find out this information, contact local brokers to see if they have been notified of other events. In addition, call the local chapters of the national business associations to see if they are scheduling local meetings.

The goal of the investor presentation is to be short and to the point. Ideally, such a presentation should last no more than 15 minutes and use an absolute maximum of 30 slides. The presenter should pay particular attention to the first few minutes of the presentation, since people are most likely to remember it. This calls for a number of practice iterations. In addition, it is almost impossible to speak too slowly; the presenter should practice enough to achieve a measured pace that he can continue throughout the presentation.

The key elements of the presentation are to first make a brief statement about the company's primary strengths and competitive factors, as well as the core concept that makes it a good investment. Second, describe its strategy as succinctly as possible. Third, describe the company itself: what it makes, how it distributes to customers, the size of its markets, and why the company chooses to be in those markets. If the company is not currently profitable, then describe its path to becoming so. If significant to the business, it may also be worthwhile to mention the barriers to entering the company's business and how the company maintains those barriers. Finish with a description of the company's financial structure, and then open the meeting for questions. The focus of the presentation is on giving investors a taste of the company, so that they learn enough in a short period of time to decide if they should request additional information that could lead to an investment.

Also, consider the items that should not be included in an investor presentation. First, do not skew the focus toward an enthusiastic presentation of the company's products and services. Investors are interested in buying the investment opportunity that the company represents, not its products. Second, do not bury attendees with an overwhelming amount of information. The presentation should give them a clear notion of the company and the investment opportunity it represents—and that is all. If they want more information, they can ask for it. Third, do not present cluttered or unclear visuals. A PowerPoint slide should present a small amount of information as clearly as possible. Excessive information, small fonts, and unrelated graphics only confuse the investor.

And a final thought—never, ever cancel a scheduled presentation, even if there is an excellent reason for doing so. Following a cancellation, investors will think that something has happened at the company that management wants to hide, and will have a predilection to abandon the stock, or perhaps even sell stock short.

## MANAGING A PRIVATE INVESTMENT IN PUBLIC EQUITY

A private investment in public equity (PIPE) occurs when either a private investor or institution purchases a public company's stock directly from the company. This purchase is usually priced anywhere from 5 percent to 25 percent below the current market price of the stock, or is sold with warrants that effectively lower the price being paid. The company is usually obligated to register the shares with the SEC shortly after the placement is completed. PIPE transactions are among the easiest ways for a company to acquire equity, since they avoid the expense and time required for a public placement.

When a PIPE transaction is being contemplated, the IRO is placed in the unusual position of *not* initially publicizing it, because the market knows that PIPE transactions will be completed at a discount, which, in turn, could drive down the price of the company's stock. Instead, the IRO's primary focus is on working with the investment bankers retained to locate investors for the PIPE to create marketing materials for prospective investors. The IRO may also assist in preparing presentation materials for the associated road show where prospective investors meet the management team.

Once the PIPE has been completed, the IRO must reveal the event to the investing public with a Form 8-K filing. At that point, the IRO should be prepared to answer any investor questions regarding why the new investors were allowed to purchase the company's stock at a discount. Also, if warrants were issued as part of the PIPE, the IRO should be ready to discuss the number of additional shares that will potentially be issued, and how this will impact earnings per share. In addition, the IRO should fully explain how the funds are to be used, with a particular emphasis on how critical the new funds will be to achieving the company's goals. It is extremely helpful if the new investors are well known, since this indicates that experienced investors agree with management's use of the funds. If investors agree with the company's decision to complete a PIPE, then the stock price may increase. However, if they don't believe that the PIPE will eventually increase earnings per share, be ready for a stock price decline as some of the original investors sell their holdings.

## ACCREDITED INVESTOR

When a company is looking to sell its stock to investors, it must be mindful of the Securities Act of 1933, which requires that the stock be registered with the SEC. To avoid the time-consuming and expensive registration process, the SEC allows in its Regulation D the option of selling stock to accredited investors. Shares sold to accredited investors are restricted from sale for at least one year from the date of sale. To be an accredited investor, an individual must satisfy one of the following standards: (a) have a combined net worth with his or her spouse in excess of $1,000,000; (b) have individual income for the past two years and a reasonable expectation of income for the current year in excess of $200,000, (c) have joint income with the spouse in excess of $300,000 for the past two years and a reasonable expectation of such income for the current year; or (d) be a director or executive officer of the company.  Accredited investors also include banks, savings and loan associations, brokers, dealers, insurance companies, and other institutions.

Accredited investors can form an important part of a company's plans to sell stock, given the reduced cost of these sales. A large proportion of the buy side is composed of accredited investors, so keep in mind the value of these investors when considering who should be included in an outreach campaign.

 ## DIVIDEND REINVESTMENT

There may be no need for a specific equity raising campaign if a company has only modest funding requirements and already issues a discount. In this case, consider offering existing shareholders a waiver, under which they can reinvest their dividends in more stock. This does not mean that a company receives *new* cash, but rather, that it avoids disbursing cash that would otherwise have been allocated to a dividend payout. This constitutes virtually free fundraising, since there is no road show and no underwriter.

A side benefit of the dividend reinvestment plan is a tendency for reduced shareholder turnover, since shareholders are essentially buying stock directly from the company with no transaction fees.

 ## DIRECT STOCK PURCHASE PLANS

An enhancement of the dividend reinvestment plan just noted is to also offer shareholders the opportunity to buy directly from the company, and at a slight discount from the market price. These investments should be at the company's discretion, so that the company can choose when it will accept additional investments. The company can incorporate a number of features into such a direct stock purchase plan:

■ *Discount amount.* Alter the discount from the market price at its discretion.
■ *Funding amount.* Decide the amount of new investments to accept.
■ *Funding sources.* Select the investors from whom to accept funds.
■ *Minimum price.* Set a minimum price below which it will not sell stock.
■ *Price setting.* Set an averaging period over which the market price is determined.

If a company has these provisions in place, it can periodically decide whether to raise funds, set a discount amount, and calculate the minimum price below which it will not accept investments. It then notifies interested investors of the funding opportunity, and issues shares based on the average market price on the receipt date. The company can then shut down the plan as soon as its funding needs are fulfilled or market prices drop below the predetermined minimum price.

## SUMMARY

A number of buy-side investors are discussed in this chapter. Before initiating a campaign to contact them, the IRO should conduct an evaluation of potential investors to determine how investor relations activities are to be prioritized for each one, and what types of communications are to be used. A crucial part of this analysis is determining which types of investors are underserved and which ones are the most likely to retain company stock over the long term. This analysis may result in more efforts to retain select types of investors, as well as reduced efforts in areas where the company may have an excessively high proportion of investors. The ideal goal is to shift from a small number of owners with massive holdings to a larger shareholder base with each shareholder retaining proportionally fewer shares. As an example, it is generally not a good idea to have a very high percentage of institutional investors, since they can sell large blocks of company stock at one time, driving down the share price.

No matter what type of investor the IRO targets, it is useful to bring in the CEO to meet with larger prospective investors, as well as to ask for their assistance in closing a stock sale. In addition, the IRO should assist larger investors in locating sufficiently large blocks of stock to acquire. It is only by providing this kind of ongoing, personal support to the buy side that the IRO can expect to assemble a group of qualified investors who will be more likely to retain their holdings for a long time.

# CHAPTER FOURTEEN

# Dealing with Credit Rating Agencies

T HE CREDIT RATING ASSIGNED to a company's debt by a credit rating agency is taken more seriously than the range of buy, sell, or hold ratings assigned by an analyst. The reason is that Regulation FD (Fair Disclosure) exempts credit rating agencies from its requirements, because these agencies must have ongoing access to nonpublic information. Because of their deeper knowledge of a company's finances and operations, ratings issued by credit rating agencies are accorded considerable weight by the investment community. Thus, it is extremely useful to build a relationship with a credit rating agency.

## CREDIT RATING AGENCY RELATIONSHIP

If a publicly held company issues debt, it can elect to have that debt rated by either Moody's, Standard & Poor's, Fitch, or Dominion Bond Rating Service. These are the four credit rating agencies that the SEC allows to issue debt ratings. A debt rating results in a credit score that indicates the perceived risk of default on the underlying debt, which, in turn, impacts the price of the debt on the open market. Having a credit score is essentially mandatory, since most funds are prohibited by their internal investment rules from buying debt that does not have a specific level of credit rating assigned to it.

A company should expect to deal with a credit rating agency through a primary analyst who has considerable credit rating experience and is usually ranked at the director level. The primary analyst is supported by a senior analyst having direct experience in the company's industry. The primary analyst is responsible for formulating a rating, and for the ongoing monitoring of that rating.

The investor relations officer (IRO) is not the key individual representing the company to a credit rating agency. Instead, either the CFO or treasurer usually handles that chore. If there is a chief risk officer or similar position, then this person will also have discussions with the analyst team. It is also entirely likely that the managers of the company's operating divisions will be asked to participate in some meetings with the analyst team, or to assist them with tours of key company facilities. The IRO is generally limited to ensuring that the primary analyst is included in any mailing lists of new information that the company provides to investors on a regular basis.

In order to develop a credit rating, the analyst team uses the financial statements that a company has previously filed with the SEC, but also needs detailed information about its budgets, internal operating reports, risk management strategies, and financial and operating policies. To this end, it will ask the management team to complete an initial questionnaire that usually requires five years of historical financial data, five years of forecasted financial results, a summary of the business and its objectives, a comparison of its market share and growth prospects to those of its peer companies, and the biographies of the senior management team. The focus of this analysis is forward-looking, since the analyst team is most concerned with the company's future performance. Consequently, short-range and medium-range projections of a company's financial viability are considered more important than its historical performance.

A key part of the analysis will be a question-and-answer session with the management team. The CFO will be expected to make a presentation about the company, after which the analysts will ask about any areas of weakness that could impact the nature of their eventual credit rating. The general thrust of their questioning is to compare the company's current financial situation to its strategic intentions, to see if its financial structure can support where management wants to take the company.

The analysts will use their agency's standardized rating methodology to assign a credit rating to the specific company debt for which they are being hired. It is difficult to estimate in advance what the rating may be, since the relative weighting of factors in the methodology will vary based on individual circumstances. Generally speaking, the analysts will ascribe about 50 percent of the rating to the company's business profile and future prospects and 50 percent to its current financial profile.

No matter what the personal relationship with the company might be, credit rating agencies pride themselves on making an impartial judgment when setting or changing a rating. However, the rating given will certainly benefit from an open relationship between the two parties, since the IRO can relate the company's story and supporting information in considerable detail, including the reasons why specific actions are being taken.

If an agency issues a low credit rating or downgrades an existing rating, the best reaction by the IRO is to not publicly challenge it. There is no upside to a company complaining bitterly about the perceived injustice of a low rating, since it is very unlikely that the issuing agency will change its rating. The only result of such action is that the company has drawn attention to a negative opinion issued by a qualified third party, which may very well reduce investor confidence in the debt price. However, a company may certainly appeal the rating, usually by presenting new information to the agency. Appeals are very rare—affecting only about 0.5 percent of all ratings changes.

If a company wants to improve its credit rating, then it must take specific steps to make its financial structure more conservative, such as by issuing more stock and using the proceeds to pay down debt. The IRO can become involved in this process by assisting in the development of the plan to achieve the higher credit rating, and in communicating this information to the credit rating agency.

Once a credit rating agency has issued a rating, the IRO should keep the primary analyst on the company's investor relations mailing list. In addition, the agency will want at least an annual review with senior management, which the IRO should attend.

## SUMMARY

Though the IRO takes the lead in representing the company with many external constituencies, this is not the case with credit rating agencies. That role is reserved for the company's senior financial managers. Instead, the IRO can keep the credit agency's representatives informed of ongoing updates to its financial position by including them on various investor mailing lists, and should also attend meetings with them in order to provide tangential information for their credit analysis work.

# CHAPTER FIFTEEN

# Dealing with Short Sellers and Activist Investors

THE GOAL OF A short seller is to profit from the decline in a company's stock price. Since the investor relations officer is trying to increase the price of a company's stock, the short seller appears to be public enemy number one, and is usually treated as such. Activist investors try to alter a company's strategic direction or mode of operation. In this chapter, we explore how short sellers and activist investors operate and how to most effectively deal with them.

## HOW SHORT SELLERS OPERATE

A short seller is someone who expects a company's stock price to decline in the near term and who acts on this presentiment by selling borrowed stock with the expectation of earning a profit by buying back the stock at a lower price on a later date.

The basic short-selling process involves a three-step trading strategy. First, the short seller borrows the targeted company's stock, usually from a broker. Second, the short seller sells the shares on the open market. Third, the short seller waits for the stock price to (hopefully) decline, and then repurchases the shares (known as *short covering*) and returns them to the lender. A variation is *naked short selling*, where the short seller sells shares without first borrowing them, and which may lead to an excessive amount of downward pricing pressure on a stock. Naked short selling is generally illegal, with a few exceptions. The SEC regulations governing naked short selling are not closely enforced, so it likely still occurs. It is most likely when there is some difficulty in borrowing shares.

Short covering can increase the stock price, especially when many short sellers are repurchasing stock at the same time. Assuming that the share repurchase price was less than the initial sale price, the short seller pockets the difference as a profit.

Short selling is an extremely risky activity, since there is a potential for unlimited losses if the stock price goes up instead of down. For example, if an investor sells stock when the price is $10, the maximum possible profit on a short sell is $10 (and only if the price craters to $0); however, if the stock price jumps to $50, the investor must buy back at the higher price, resulting in a loss of $40. Given this high level of risk, investors will rarely sell short unless they feel strongly that a stock's price has topped out.

Because of the high level of risk, short sellers like to slam a company's prospects as publicly as possible, thereby influencing other investors to sell their shares, which, in turn, lowers the stock price. A favorite forum for short sellers is the Internet investment message board, on which they can anonymously post messages that anyone visiting the site can read. They may also post messages using multiple aliases, so that an innocent visitor to a message board may think that a large number of investors are all selling their holdings in a targeted stock. When a major short selling attack is going on, short sellers can effectively take over message boards with an extremely high volume of message traffic. Major investment message boards are located on the Motley Fool, Yahoo!, and Raging Bull Web sites.

If short sellers find that a negative publicity campaign does not work and the stock rises instead, then the customary reaction is to reduce losses by quickly buying shares to cover their short positions. If there are many short sellers, this sudden buying frenzy will drive up the stock price even more, thereby forcing any remaining holdout short sellers to buy even more shares to cover their positions. This "short squeeze" phenomenon is especially common with stocks whose prices are highly volatile.

One special scenario is the monitoring of the restricted stockholdings of company investors by short sellers. Restricted stock can be sold after one year under SEC Rule 144. Since the timing of restriction cancellations and the amounts of restricted stockholdings are public knowledge, it is an easy matter for short sellers to anticipate the sale of large stock holdings, which should reduce the price of the stock when they are dumped on the market. The classic short selling strategy in this situation is to sell shares at a higher price just prior to the restricted stock becoming available for sale, and then buying offsetting shares after the now unrestricted stock has been sold, when prices are presumably lower.

## HOW TO HANDLE SHORT SELLERS

A common reaction by a CEO who sees short selling activity is to attempt to force them out of their short positions by publicly issuing guidance of better-than-expected results. This type of publicity may increase the stock price in the very short term, creating a short squeeze that drives away short sellers. However, the more aggressive guidance also makes it more difficult to meet investor expectations, which thereby attracts even more short sellers as the CEO gradually paints the company into a *performance corner*. It eventually becomes impossible to meet the company's own increased guidance, so that reported earnings are bound to fall below the enhanced expectations of investors. The result is a stock price decline, allowing short sellers to reap profits that were very nearly guaranteed by the CEO's own actions to drive them away.

There are several effective methods for dealing with short sellers. First and most important, do not issue aggressive earnings guidance—ever. By issuing aggressive guidance, investor expectations are raised to heights that are difficult to sustain, resulting in increased stock price volatility and the arrival of short sellers. Instead, issue only conservative guidance that the company can comfortably meet on a long-term basis. This approach flattens stock price volatility, which keeps short sellers away.

It also pays to be proactive in dealing with short sellers by monitoring the larger message boards for sudden increases in activity concerning the company. These activity surges usually coincide with actual short sales, which are reported by the stock exchanges, and which are conveniently posted on www.shortsqueeze.com. Thus, an efficient approach to monitoring short sales is to review the shortsqueeze.com site each day to track short-selling volume, and then start reviewing the message boards as soon as there is a jump in reported short-selling volume. Another source of information is well-connected investors, who may hear rumors before anyone in the company. By maintaining good relations with these investors, they will be more likely to forward any information they hear. In either case, the IRO may elect to counteract the rumors by issuing statements that address the allegations being made.

At the first sign of trouble at a company, short sellers tend to circle like sharks, assuming that more bad news will follow. To avoid this issue, it is better to fully disclose every aspect of a bad news item at once, rather than dribbling it out over a long period of time. By doing so, the stock will probably suffer a single, sharp price drop to a new level that is not attractive to short sellers. Otherwise, short sellers will feast on each successive negative piece of news to reach the market, allowing them to reap profits from continuing declines in the stock price.

Short sellers may pose questions during conference calls, partially to probe for information that strengthens their case, and partially to lead management into an argument that will cast the company in a negative light. If such questions arise, state the counterargument in a simple and straightforward manner, and move on to the next question as rapidly as possible. It rarely makes sense to give a short seller credence by making an interminable response that seems to give weight to the question. Under no circumstances should the question-and-answer exchange grow heated.

Though unusual, it may be possible to open a line of communication with short sellers to hear the reasons why they are selling short. This is not usually necessary, since short sellers are likely to sprinkle their opinions all over the investment message boards, where the IRO can easily access them. When this information is available, consider including a statement in the next press release or conference call that offers a countervailing argument. This statement should be based on a heavy proportion of facts, rather than opinions. Under no circumstances should the statement mention any short-selling activity. Instead, take the position that the company is merely presenting additional information to the marketplace, which it can interpret in any way it chooses.

Finally, the IRO can create a list of preset responses to a variety of worst-case scenarios that can be quickly rolled out through press releases. For example, there may be boilerplate responses to a product recall, patent litigation, loss of a customer, or the departure of a key executive. By having canned responses available, the management team will spend far less time mulling over the appropriate response, resulting in the appearance of a management team that responds quickly and well to a crisis. This obviously competent response to crises tends to result in less stock volatility, and so keeps short sellers at bay.

## MONITORING SHORT SELLERS

It is not especially difficult to monitor short-selling activity on an ongoing basis. As noted earlier, go to the shortsqueeze.com site to determine the number of shares currently being sold short. Then divide this number by the average daily volume of shares traded to arrive at the short interest ratio. This ratio shows the proportion of short selling to total trading activity. When tracked on a trend line, any spikes will reveal sudden increases in short-selling activity. The ratio can also be used to determine the number of days of average trading that it will take before short sellers can cover their positions. For example, if the ratio is 3.5, then it will take short sellers $3\frac{1}{2}$ days to cover their positions. As this ratio rises, it becomes increasingly difficult for short sellers to cover their positions in a timely manner through stock purchases; this will eventually result in their scaling back from aggressive short positions in order to contain their risk.

## DEALING WITH ACTIVIST INVESTORS

An activist investor may attempt to have its nominees elected to the board of directors, or push unwanted measures onto the annual shareholder ballot, or publicly demand other changes to the company's operations or governance. Activists may simply want companies in which they invest to have a high level of ethical or environmental behavior, but their intent may extend into a discussion of strategic alternatives, or even to attain control over the company. Activist investors usually target larger firms, with a declining level of involvement with mid-cap and small-cap companies.

To prepare for activist investors, a company should have in place a shareholder response team that comprises senior management, the IRO, corporate counsel, at least one member of the board of directors, and its proxy solicitation firm. It may also be useful to retain an investor relations consultant who specializes in this area. The leader of this group should be the IRO, who calls it into action when a shareholder communication arrives that warrants their attention. For lesser emergencies, the IRO can likely handle the situation alone or with guidance from corporate counsel. Determining the degree of response is on a sliding scale, based on the nature of the issue, the size of the shareholder, and how long it has owned shares in the company.

The initial contact from an activist investor is likely to come by telephone or letter. If so, a procedure should be in place to route such communications to the IRO. There is a lesser possibility that an activist investor will make first contact during a road show or investor conference; if so, the management team should have considered in advance how it will generically respond to any public inquiry, with the intent of delaying a definite response until the shareholder response team can meet and derive a more definitive response.

Once communication commences with an activist shareholder, try to keep a direct dialog with the shareholder. The worst scenarios are for the shareholder to sue the company (which absorbs management time and legal fees) or engage in a public battle with the company, which absorbs management time and also reduces the investment community's view of the company.

Rather than being a passive entity, the shareholder response team can take a more active role. It can review the company's operations and strategic profile on a recurring basis, looking for weaknesses that an activist shareholder might capitalize on. After all, activist investors are more likely to pursue vulnerable targets. Typical issues to look for are the presence of large amounts of unused cash, questionable operations in developing countries, and poor financial performance. The team can also periodically talk to a selection of investors about the company's long-range direction and more recent performance. This is useful not only for gaining the support of these investors in the event of a battle with an activist investor, but also to learn more about shareholder concerns. Another possibility is to open a channel of communication with an activist as soon as the IRO becomes aware of an investment by the investor, rather than waiting to receive a communication.

There is certainly nothing wrong with listening to these shareholders in order to avoid the appearance of corporate arrogance and to alter some management practices if they have a reasonable point; however, a company should not accede to their demands to the extent that shareholders are running the company—that is the job of management.

To some extent, there is little an IRO can do to prevent shareholder activists from acquiring its stock. However, the IRO should certainly investigate the level of shareholder activism of any institution before arranging a meeting to pitch the company's prospects—it would hardly do to encourage these institutions to invest in the company.

## SUMMARY

The advice in this chapter has focused on monitoring investor activity, being prepared with a corporate response team, addressing concerns in a calm and measured manner, and providing conservative earnings guidance. A simpler approach to short sellers is to not even consider them a problem, and to ignore them. After all, they can be viewed as providing a public service, since they reduce stock volatility by keeping stock prices from going too high; also, they keep prices from dropping too low when they close out their positions with stock purchases, which tend to increase stock prices. Thus, both active and passive approaches to short sellers can be appropriate. Only an aggressive attitude plays fully into their hands.

Activist shareholders cannot be allowed to run a company through an ongoing series of demands. A shareholder response team should review their issues and deal with them as appropriate, but management runs the company, not the shareholders.

# CHAPTER SIXTEEN

# Dealing with the Board of Directors

THE IRO IS THE primary link between investors and the board of directors. In that role, she should attend all regularly scheduled board meetings and present a variety of information and advice to the board, as outlined in this chapter.

## IRO AND THE BOARD OF DIRECTORS

The board of directors is responsible to stockholders, so it should regularly talk to the investor relations officer to hear what investors think from the person assigned to communicate with them.

At the most minimal level, the IRO should present a brief packet of information to the board in order to establish a presence with board members. At this level, the chief communications goal is merely to gain an acknowledgment that there is an investor relations function that is moderately active. This approach works best in companies where investor relations has not yet established its reputation as a valued function. The IRO can then use future board presentations to gradually expand the scope of information provided and show a continuing level of progress in a variety of areas.

The IRO can establish a much more personal level of rapport with the board by scheduling meetings with new board members to acquaint them with

**Exhibit 16.1** Board Report—Investor Relations Metrics

| Measurement | Subject Company | Peer A | Peer B | Peer C |
|---|---|---|---|---|
| **Share information** | | | | |
| Stock price | $5.50 | $11.00 | $2.35 | $6.85 |
| Daily trading volume | 52,000 | 81,000 | 24,000 | 60,000 |
| Shares outstanding | 15M | 20M | 11M | 21M |
| Float | 15M | 20M | 9M | 18M |
| Market capitalization | $233M | $420M | $102M | $321M |
| **Valuation** | | | | |
| Price/earnings multiple | 20.3x | 26.2x | 18.1x | 19.0x |
| Market cap/revenue multiple | 4.0 | 5.0 | 3.5 | 4.0 |
| **Financial Results** | | | | |
| Revenue | $58M | $84M | $29M | $80M |
| Gross margin % | 40% | 47% | 38% | 42% |
| EBITDA margin % | 11% | 15% | 8% | 10% |
| Net profit margin % | 7% | 10% | 4% | 8% |

investor relations activities. This allows the IRO to give a detailed "canned" presentation without wasting the time of the longer-term board members. Also, this gives a new board member the extra time to ask more questions about investor relations than would be the case during a formal board meeting, when time is closely scheduled.

Once the IRO has established a working relationship with the board, she should develop a standard reporting package that itemizes a specific set of key investor relations metrics, stock price performance compared to a peer group or a stock index, activity for recent stockholder meetings, stockholder composition, and analyst coverage. For example, the Investor Relations Metrics report shown in Exhibit 16.1 reveals a company's key investor relations information in comparison to those of a peer group. It is essential to add the comparative peer group information, because board members will otherwise have no way of rating the relevance of the information presented.

The Stock Price Performance report in Exhibit 16.2 shows the percentage change in a company's stock price over several time periods, and in relation to the changes in several stock indexes. This report gives the board comparative information about the investment community's perception of a company's

**Exhibit 16.2** Board Report—Stock Price Performance

|  | Year-to-Date | One Year | Three Years | Five Years |
|---|---|---|---|---|
| Subject Company | −10.5% | 8.3% | 7.4% | 6.0% |
| Dow Jones U.S. Small Cap Value Index | 4.2% | 8.0% | 9.2% | 7.1% |
| S&P Small Cap 600 | 5.8% | 6.5% | 8.2% | 8.4% |

ability to perform in relation to comparable companies. In the example, the subject company's stock price has generally underperformed the comparable indices.

The IRO can give the appearance of a great deal of activity by constantly meeting with current or prospective stockholders during a series of road show meetings. However, the board needs to know if these meetings are effective. The Activity for Stockholder Meetings report in Exhibit 16.3 gives the board this information by itemizing how many shares were bought as a result of a specific meeting.

The Stockholder Composition report shows who owns how much of a company and the extent to which that situation has changed over the past few months. The report is sorted by institutional, retail, and insider investors, with subtotals. In the example in Exhibit 16.4, the report clearly shows that institutional investors are taking a commanding ownership position in the company. This can be a problem, since institutions can cause dramatic price volatility when they eventually sell off their large stock positions. In this case, the board would likely direct the IRO to boost the proportion of stock held by

**Exhibit 16.3** Board Report—Activity for Stockholder Meetings

| Meeting Date | Institution | Attendees | Net Stock Change |
|---|---|---|---|
| 6/10/2010 | Atlanta Hedge Investments | Adam Schembeckler | +150,000 |
| 6/22/2010 | Boston First Investments | Bruce Hensen | 0 |
| 7/05/2010 | Charleston Investments | Christopher Holland | +1,080,000 |
| 7/14/2010 | Denver Management Funds | Danna Taylor | +240,000 |
| 8/21/2010 | Easthampton Fund | Earnest Masterson | +720,000 |
| 8/29/2010 | Fall River Investment Fund | Frank Davies | 0 |
| 9/05/2010 | Gloucester Securities | Gordon Banks | +370,000 |

**Exhibit 16.4**  Board Report—Stockholder Composition

| Investor | % of Float | No. of Shares | Year-to-Date Change | Investment Style |
|---|---|---|---|---|
| **Institutional** | | | | |
| Jacobson Capital | 25% | 6,000,000 | +1,500,000 | Hedge Fund |
| Northern Liberty Investors | 12% | 2,880,000 | +100,000 | Index |
| Boston Investment Counsel | 11% | 2,640,000 | +2,400,000 | Growth |
| All others | 14% | 3,360,000 | +2,150,000 | |

retail investors, probably resulting in the scheduling of a number of road shows to meet with this type of investor.

The Stockholder Composition report can be expanded with additional information. For example, the IRO can add a column showing where each investor is located. This can be useful for identifying geographical concentrations of investors. Another possibility is to note the amount of historical turnover in each institutional investor's portfolio. This provides an indicator of how soon an investor may be expected to alter its position in company stock.

It may also be useful to include in the Stockholder Composition report an extra category called Fast Money. The term *fast money* represents those investors who are most likely to quickly jump in and out of investments in the company's stock, and who therefore have no intention of retaining a long-term investment. Fast-money investors can be responsible for rapid price swings and sudden jumps in trading volume. The Fast Money category includes unidentified or nonfiling hedge funds, risk arbitragers, shares held by investment bankers, and trading desk inventory.

There may be some interest by the board in learning more about individual investors. The IRO can prepare an overview of the larger investors, describing their basic investment approach and any other relevant information pertaining to the company. For example:

> *Boston Investment Counsel.* Currently holds 11 percent of the float. The firm has been a holder of company stock since 2005, and has continually added to its position since then, with no position reductions. The firm looks for companies with a low P/E ratio and high growth potential. The majority of its investments are passively managed. It has no history of being an activist investor with the company or any of its other investments.

**Exhibit 16.5**   Board Report—Analyst Coverage

| Buy Recommendations | Neutral Recommendations |
|---|---|
| I.P. Farrar Investments | Wells Fargo Equity Securities |
| J.P. Morgan | Morgan Stanley |
| Kinder Folsom Securities | Prudential Securities |
| Longerhorn Investment Funds | |
| Raymond James | Sell Recommendations |
| | Goldman Sachs |

An Analyst Coverage report, such as the one shown in Exhibit 16.5, itemizes those analysts who have issued buy, neutral, and sell recommendations for a company's stock. The IRO should supplement this information with a discussion of key points from analyst reports that have inclined analysts to issue recommendations below a "buy." This can be a fruitful discussion, since it targets the specific problem areas that the investment community has with a company.

It is not sufficient to simply distribute these reports. In addition, the IRO should offer an interpretation of the information. This can include the reasons stockholders have given for retaining or selling their shares, feedback from both the sell side and buy side, analyst estimates compared to guidance, and the IRO's opinions regarding significant stock price shifts. The board may also be interested in the backgrounds and investment philosophies of major new investors. The interpretation can even be as simple as adding text to a chart of stock price movements, noting when certain events occurred, and what happened to the stock price immediately after those events. Also, the IRO should blend into the presentation any relevant macro information about the market as a whole that may be impacting the company's stock price.

The IRO should also present the annual investor relations plan of activities and related budget, and describe any progress made toward achieving the plan. Where possible, this part of the report should address which investor relations activities have had the greatest impact in terms of stockholder retention or stock purchases.

Finally, the IRO may add her opinion regarding any upcoming board decisions that relate to investor relations, such as the amount or timing of dividend declarations, or the use of stock purchase plans or dividend reinvestment plans. In some instances, a board might take action on these items without considering the action's impact on the investment community. The IRO can provide valuable advice in this area, which may alter the board's decisions.

It may also be useful to periodically bring in investor relations consultants to answer board questions or to engage in projects commissioned by the board. This could include an audit of investor relations activities or a survey of major investors. By doing so, the board gains an independent perspective on its company's investor relations activities.

 ## INVESTOR RELATIONS BOARD PACKET

An alternative to sending a formal investor relations packet to the board is to post it to a secure Web site that is designed for board-only access, and from which they can download any reports they need. Such an environment can be custom-designed and added to a company's Web site.

An alternative is to pay a periodic fee for access to a third-party system, such as Thomson's BoardLink$^{TM}$. This is a highly secure Web site to which the board has access for a variety of secure messaging, voting, and document repository functions. The IRO can post reports to it and board members can download the reports from it at their leisure. It also contains a research section that gives board members direct and independent access to analyst estimates and recommendations, stock ownership information, market news, and peer group financial analysis. BoardLink's research functionality is particularly useful for those board members who want to independently verify the information being reported to them by the IRO.

 ## SUMMARY

The bulk of this chapter has focused on the various types of reports that the IRO can present to the board. However, the true value of this information is the accompanying interpretative comments and recommendations provided by the IRO. Consequently, the IRO should treat the initial packet of information as merely the supporting materials upon which to create an insightful presentation to the board of directors.

# CHAPTER SEVENTEEN

# Major Stock Exchanges

B EING LISTED ON A major stock exchange is a significant goal for any IRO. Many fund managers are only allowed to invest in exchange-listed companies, so being listed on a major exchange dramatically increases the pool of potential investors. Also, because there is a readier market to buy and sell stock, the bid–ask spread is considerably reduced in comparison to the over-the-counter bulletin board market; this greatly reduces investor transaction costs. Thus, obtaining a stock exchange listing and maintaining that listing are key goals.

This chapter discusses the listing process, as well as the listing requirements, fees, advantages and disadvantages of the three major stock exchanges—the American Stock Exchange (Amex), NASDAQ, and New York Stock Exchange (NYSE). The original listing fees and annual listing fees for these exchanges are consolidated for comparison purposes in the Comparing the Stock Exchanges section.

 ## LISTING PROCESS

The listing process is similar for all three exchanges. The first step is for a company to file a listing application with the exchange of its choice, along with a filing fee. The introductory application includes an itemization of the amounts and types of stock that the company wishes to list on the exchange, the size and composition of its shareholder base, and identification of its directors and officers. The exchange then follows up with more detailed questions, which generally inquire about any outstanding lawsuits, the availability of financing arrangements, recent SEC comment letters, recent private placements, investor relations consulting agreements, and research reports and investor newsletters about the company. The exchanges are also very particular about having a company conform its bylaws to their requirements, particularly in regard to the structure and composition of its audit, nominating, and compensation committees.

The exchange then reviews the application to ensure that the applicant is in compliance with the exchange's listing qualifications. The review is typically two-stage, with a staff person conducting the initial review and summarizing the application for a supervisor, who will then pass judgment on the application. If there are issues, then the exchange sends a comment letter to the company, describing what must be changed before it will approve the company for listing. The exchange also reserves a ticker symbol for the company at this time. The applicant then sends back a response letter, detailing the actions it has taken to comply with the exchange's requirements. There may be several iterations of questions and answers between the exchange and the company, which usually requires multiple months to complete.

If the exchange approves the applicant for listing, then the company and the exchange mutually agree upon an initial trading date. Depending on the exchange, the company's CEO may be invited to ring the opening bell on the initial trading date. Also, for the American and New York Stock Exchanges, the company will select a specialist who is responsible for making a market in its stock.

##  AMERICAN STOCK EXCHANGE

The Amex targets smaller companies with modest market capitalizations. It is easily the most aggressive of the three exchanges in attracting new listings. Its staff regularly scans new stock registrations that are filed with the SEC, and contacts registrants about listing with them. Amex also sends staff out to prospects to discuss the advantages of listing. Thus, a micro-cap company is far more likely to be petitioned by the Amex than by any other exchange.

The Amex provides a number of services to each listing company:

- ▪ *Specialist.* The key Amex benefit is an assigned trading specialist. The specialist is obliged, to the extent reasonably practical, to purchase and sell a listed company's securities for its own account in order to help maintain an orderly market, with minimal price changes between transactions. Listed companies have direct access to their specialist, who can tell them about the market activity in their shares.

- *Liaison.* The Amex assigns a liaison, called an Amex Issuer Services Director (ISD), to every listed company. The ISD assists each company in obtaining services provided by the Amex.
- *Amex Online Web site.* This Web site allows listed companies to conduct peer analysis comparisons and historical charting, locate analyst ratings, research contact information for analysts and investment management firms, and view a complete calendar of earnings releases and conference calls.
- *Strategy seminars.* The Amex makes available a pair of strategy seminars each year to listed companies. These seminars focus on topics in investor relations, investment banking, corporate governance, equity trading, and regulatory issues.
- *CEO dinners.* The Amex coordinates a series of CEO dinners throughout the country that allow CEOs to network with their counterparts in other Amex-listed companies.
- *Investor relations audit.* The Amex conducts a review of a listed company's communication materials, develops an investor fact sheet, and provides buy-side and sell-side contacts.

The Amex's listing requirements are designed to attract smaller companies with relatively small floats. A company can qualify under any one of the four standards shown in Exhibit 17.1 in order to be accepted for listing on the Amex.

**Exhibit 17.1**  American Stock Exchange Initial Listing Guidelines

| Requirements | Standard 1 | Standard 2 | Standard 3 | Standard 4 |
|---|---|---|---|---|
| Pretax income | $750,000 | | | |
| Market capitalization | | | $50 million | $75 million or |
| Total assets | | | | $75 million and |
| Total revenue | | | | $75 million |
| Market value of public float | $3 million | $15 million | $15 million | $20 million |
| Minimum price | $3 | $3 | $2 | $3 |
| Operating history | | 2 years | | |
| Stockholders' equity | $4 million | $4 million | $4 million | |

**Exhibit 17.2**    American Stock Exchange Stock Distribution Guidelines

| | |
|---|---|
| Public stockholders | Option A: 800 |
| | Option B: 400 |
| | Option C: 400 |
| Public float (shares)* | Option A: 500,000 |
| | Option B: 1,000,000 |
| | Option C: 500,000 |
| Average daily volume | Option C: 2,000 |

*Public float is all shares not held directly or indirectly by any officer or director of a listed company, or by any other person who is the beneficial owner of more than 10 percent of the total shares outstanding.

Exhibit 17.2 lists stock distribution guidelines that are intended to ensure that a sufficiently broad array of investors own a company's stock.

A close reading of these listing guidelines reveals that the Amex is extremely amenable to listing almost any company, and it has created many variations on its acceptance criteria in order to attract the largest possible number of companies. For example, only Standard 1 even requires reported income; in all other cases, the Amex does not require evidence of profitability. Also, three of the Standards do not require an operating history, so short-lived entities can very quickly become listed. Standard 4 was specially designed for telecommunications companies, which rarely report profits, but which have considerable revenue and assets. The only area in which the Amex has significant requirements across all Standards is the market value of a company's public float. Thus, as long as a company has a sufficient volume of tradable stock, the Amex is interested in listing it.

Of some interest, the official Amex guidelines are literally *guidelines*. The Amex has been known to waive some listing requirements, so it is best to make inquiries, rather than to simply assume that certain initial listing standards are unattainable.

On an ongoing basis, a listed company must maintain a $1 million market value of public float. In addition, it must maintain $2 million in stockholders' equity if it has had losses in two of the most recent three years, or $4 million if it has had losses in three of the most recent four years, or $6 million if it has had losses in the five most recent fiscal years. If a company cannot satisfy these equity requirements, it can still remain on the Amex if it has a market capitalization of at least $50 million or total assets and revenue of $50 million each. The Amex does not have an ongoing minimum stock price requirement.

In short, the Amex is ideal for listing by smaller companies. Its main competition is the NASDAQ's Capital Market, which similarly caters to smaller entities.

## OVERVIEW OF THE NASDAQ

The NASDAQ acronym stands for the National Association of Securities Dealers Automated Quotation. In brief, it is the largest electronic stock market in the United States. Being entirely electronic, it executes orders faster and at lower cost than most other stock exchanges. However, there is no assigned specialist who makes a market in a company's stock. This can result in somewhat greater stock volatility, as well as a larger relative spread (see the Comparing the Stock Exchanges section).

The NASDAQ operates the Market Intelligence Desk (MID), which monitors the activity of a listed company's stock. The IRO can contact the MID for updates about recent stock activity. This contact is through an MID director, who is a predetermined point of contact for each company. In isolated instances, the MID may contact the IRO by phone or e-mail if there is unusual market activity.

The MID director arranges for additional services to its listing companies. These include a full-service corporate insurance broker, a research report service, and investor relations services. However, in most cases, a listed company will incur extra fees for these services.

## NASDAQ CAPITAL MARKET

The NASDAQ operates a stock exchange for smaller companies, called the NASDAQ Capital Market. This exchange competes with the American Stock Exchange.

A company can qualify under any one of the three standards shown in Exhibit 17.3 in order to be accepted for listing on the NASDAQ Capital Market. On an ongoing basis, a company must exceed one of the three standards shown in Exhibit 17.4 to continue to be listed on the exchange.

As was the case with the Amex, the NASDAQ Capital Market substantially reduces its continued listing requirements from the initial listing requirements, so that it is relatively easy to remain on the exchange.

**Exhibit 17.3**　NASDAQ Capital Market Initial Listing Standards

| Requirements | Standard 1 | Standard 2 | Standard 3 |
|---|---|---|---|
| Stockholders' equity | $5 million | $4 million | $4 million |
| Market value of publicly held shares | $15 million | $15 million | $5 million |
| Operating history | 2 years | | |
| Market value of listed securities | | $50 million | |
| Net income from continuing operations (in the latest fiscal year or in two of the last three fiscal years) | | | $750,000 |
| Publicly held shares | 1 million | 1 million | 1 million |
| Bid price | $4 | $4 | $4 |
| Round lot shareholders | 300 | 300 | 300 |
| Market makers | 3 | 3 | 3 |

**Exhibit 17.4**　NASDAQ Capital Market Continued Listing Standards

| Requirements | Standard 1 | Standard 2 | Standard 3 |
|---|---|---|---|
| Stockholders' equity | $2.5 million | | |
| Market value of listed securities | | $35 million | |
| Net income from continuing operations (in the latest fiscal year or in two of the last three fiscal years) | | | $500,000 |
| Publicly held shares | 500,000 | 500,000 | 500,000 |
| Market value of publicly held securities | $1 million | $1 million | $1 million |
| Bid price | $1 | $1 | $1 |
| Round lot shareholders | 300 | 300 | 300 |
| Market makers | 2 | 2 | 2 |

## NASDAQ GLOBAL MARKET

The NASDAQ operates a stock exchange for larger companies, called the NASDAQ Global Market. This exchange competes with the New York Stock Exchange.

A company can qualify under any one of the three standards shown in Exhibit 17.5 in order to be accepted for listing on the NASDAQ Global Market.

**Exhibit 17.5**  NASDAQ Global Market Initial Listing Standards

| Requirements | Standard 1 | Standard 2 | Standard 3 |
|---|---|---|---|
| Pretax earnings | Aggregate $11 million in past three years, and $2.2 million in each of the past two fiscal years, and $0+ in past three years | | |
| Cash flows | | Aggregate $27.5 million in past three years, and $0+ in each of the prior three fiscal years | |
| Market capitalization (average over prior 12 months) | | $550 million | $850 million |
| Revenue (previous fiscal year) | | $110 million | $90 million |
| Bid price | $5 | $5 | $5 |
| Market makers | 3 | 3 | 3 |

In addition, an applicant must have either 450 round lot stockholders or a total of 2,200 stockholders, and 1,250,000 publicly held shares.

On an ongoing basis, a company must exceed one of the two standards shown in Exhibit 17.6 to continue to be listed on the exchange.

**Exhibit 17.6**  NASDAQ Global Market Continued Listing Standards

| Requirements | Standard 1 | Standard 2 |
|---|---|---|
| Stockholders' equity | $10 million | |
| Market value or Total assets/total revenue | | $50 million or $50 million/$50 million |
| Publicly held shares | 750,000 | 1.1 million |
| Market value of publicly held shares | $5 million | $15 million |
| Bid price | $1 | $1 |
| Round lot stockholders | 400 | 400 |
| Market makers | 2 | 4 |

##  NEW YORK STOCK EXCHANGE

The NYSE specifically caters to the largest and wealthiest public companies in the world. It is considered prestigious to be listed on the NYSE. To keep this club exclusive, the NYSE has the toughest initial and continued listing standards of any exchange. Besides prestige, the main advantage of an NYSE listing is that some fund managers are only allowed to invest in NYSE-listed companies, so the pool of potential investors is quite large.

The NYSE hosts a number of virtual investor forums, which are Web conferences designed to provide investors with direct access to executives from companies listed on the NYSE. It also hosts industry-specific conferences, which the executives of NYSE-listed companies can attend.

The NYSE also assigns a client service team to each listed company, which fulfills the same role as the Amex's issuer services director and the NASDAQ's market intelligence desk director. Also, as was the case with the Amex, a newly listed company selects a specialist who is responsible for making a market in the company's stock.

The NYSE's listing requirements are designed to attract larger companies with significant market capitalizations and operating results. It requires minimum standards in two areas, which are stock distribution and financial results. Its stock distribution requirements are as follows:

- 400 round-lot stockholders *or*
- 2,200 total stockholders and average monthly trading volume for the last six months of 100,000 shares *or*
- 500 total stockholders and average monthly trading volume for the last 12 months of 1,000,000 shares

An additional stock distribution requirement is to have 1.1 million public shares outstanding, with a market value of $100 million.

The NYSE also has multiple variations on its initial listing requirements relating to financial results:

- Aggregate pretax earnings over the past three years of $10 million, and a minimum of $2 million in each of the two most recent years *or*
- Aggregate operating cash flow of $25 million over the last three years (only applicable for companies with at least a $500 million market cap and $100 million revenues during the most recent 12 months) *or*
- Revenues for the most recent fiscal year of at least $75 million, and a market capitalization of at least $750 million

**Exhibit 17.7**   New York Stock Exchange Continued Listing Standards

| Requirements | Earnings Standard | Cash Flow Standard | Pure Valuation Standard |
|---|---|---|---|
| Average closing price over a 30-day trading period | $1 | $1 | $1 |
| Average market capitalization over a 30-day trading period | $75 million and | $250 million and | $375 million and |
| Total stockholders' equity | $75 million or | | |
| Average market capitalization over a 30-day trading period | $25 million | | |
| Total revenues for most recent 12 months | | $20 million | |
| Total revenues for the most recent fiscal year | | | $15 million |

On an ongoing basis, a listed company must maintain performance under one of three standards, which are outlined in Exhibit 17.7. This is a simplified version of the complex NYSE standards—see the www.nyse.com site for a complete set of continued listing standards.

 ## COMPARING THE STOCK EXCHANGES

There are significant differences in the fees charged by the various stock exchanges. Exhibit 17.8 shows the initial listing fees for the exchanges, showing the lowest and highest possible prices. For companies having in excess of 50 million shares, the maximum fees will apply.

The Amex has positioned itself to be slightly less expensive than the NASDAQ Capital Market, though the pricing difference is minor. Similarly,

**Exhibit 17.8**   Comparison of Stock Exchange Initial Listing Fees

| Shares | Amex | NASDAQ Capital Market | NASDAQ Global Market | NYSE |
|---|---|---|---|---|
| Up to 5 million | $45,000 | $50,000 | $100,000 | $150,000 |
| 50+ million | 70,000 | 75,000 | 150,000 | 250,000 |

**Exhibit 17.9** Comparison of Stock Exchange Annual Listing Fees

| Shares | Amex | NASDAQ Capital Market | NASDAQ Global Market | NYSE |
|---|---|---|---|---|
| Up to 5 million | $16,500 | $27,500 | $30,000 | $38,000 |
| 50 million | 32,500 | 27,500 | 45,000 | 46,500 |
| Maximum | 34,000 | 27,500 | 95,000 | 500,000 |

the NASDAQ Global Market has positioned its prices to be clearly below those of the NYSE. However, for companies with the resources to list on the NYSE, its higher fees are probably not a significant factor.

In addition, each exchange charges an annual listing fee, which is shown in Exhibit 17.9. Again, rather than showing the full range of prices, the table reveals the lowest and highest possible prices. The maximum annual listing fee for the NYSE is misleading, since it only applies to a very high share volume. Accordingly, an additional row is included for 50 million shares, to give some indication of pricing for a mid-range share volume.

The differences between the annual fees charged by the Amex and the NASDAQ Capital Market are insignificant. If a very large company lists on the NYSE, then its annual fees can substantially exceed those it would incur if it listed on the NASDAQ Global Market.

The number of required round lot stockholders does not vary significantly amongst the exchanges, with the usual requirement varying between 300 and 500 round lot stockholders. Once a company has been trading on an exchange for a few months, it usually exceeds these figures by a substantial amount.

All of the exchanges allow a company to be listed even if it does not report pretax income, by alternatively requiring a higher float, cash flow, or market capitalization. These alternative requirements are easier to meet on the Amex and NASDAQ Capital Market, and more difficult on the NASDAQ Global Market and NYSE.

The continued listing requirements are much lower than the initial listing requirements for all of the exchanges. For example, the Amex has no minimum stock bid price for a continued listing, while the NASDAQ Capital Market's bid price requirement drops from an initial listing requirement of $4 to $1, and the NASDAQ Global Market's requirement drops from $5 to $1.

The Amex has issued a study claiming that the average relative spread of its listed stocks is somewhat lower than the same spread on the NASDAQ. The relative spread is the difference between a stock's quoted bid and ask price relative to the stock price, with a small relative spread indicating a high degree of stock liquidity. Being an internally generated study, it is impossible to say if the Amex's findings are accurate. However, an item of note is that the study also reveals a relative spread for over-the-counter stocks of nearly triple the Amex and NASDAQ spreads. This shows a high level of illiquidity in the over-the-counter market, which is an excellent reason for a company to step up to a major stock exchange listing as soon as possible.

Of more importance is that Amex directors do not sell products or services to their assigned companies, whereas NASDAQ directors' compensation is partially based on their ability to sell products and services to their assigned companies. A company may not experience any real difference in costs because of these differences, but there is certainly more selling pressure in the NASDAQ environment.

All of the exchanges require compliance with a variety of governance standards, such as a majority of independent directors, audit committees, and codes of conduct. There are no significant differences between the governance standards required by the various exchanges.

## SUMMARY

Being listed on a stock exchange is a key goal of any IRO. The usual track is for a company to initially list on either the Amex or NASDAQ Capital Market, and then move up to either the NYSE or the NASDAQ Global Market when it increases in size. By moving up to a higher-end exchange, a public company becomes eligible for trading by more funds. This increases a stock's trading volume, hopefully reduces its volatility, and may positively influence its price because of increased demand.

# CHAPTER EIGHTEEN

# Monitoring the Market

T HE INVESTOR RELATIONS OFFICER must constantly monitor the investment community to determine its perception of the company. There are a number of monitoring tools available, which are outlined in this chapter.

##  MONITORING THROUGH INTERNET SERVICES

Several services are available that monitor a broad range of news groups and public areas on behalf of a company. When they spot a reference to the company, they extract the relevant reference and e-mail it to the IRO, and usually also provide a hyperlink back to the source location or a central database in which the information is stored.

One such service is Business Wire's NewsTrak Clips. It monitors over 25,000 online news sources, 1,800 television news programs (from their close-captioned text), more than 100,000 message boards, and 5,000,000+ blogs. Another service is PR Newswire's eWatch, which has a similar monitoring scope.

Both services vary from a standard search engine, in that they search for specific key words repeatedly on a daily basis. A search engine may not return to a news source for several weeks, which would not give fresh information to an IRO. Also, they automatically forward their fully compiled results to the IRO on a daily basis, whereas the IRO would have to continually run a search each day under her own initiative on a search engine. Finally, the clippings are stored in a password-protected, searchable database.

## MONITORING THROUGH INDIVIDUALS

A small number of investors are extremely well connected within the investment community, and so may have insightful comments about actions being taken by a company. If these people are readily identifiable, contact them regularly to learn about any rumors concerning the company or that may impact it.

The best approach is a personal meeting or a phone call, where the IRO or a staff person asks investors questions, but also reserves a great deal of time to listen to their comments about the company, and how the investment community views it. These investors likely have the largest number of market contacts, so it is best to keep the discussion relatively free-form in order to address any revelations they may have, rather than using a detailed questionnaire to control the flow of the discussion.

If any investor contacts the company directly with market information or suggestions, then build the relationship by sending a personal note of thanks, which also requests further information. If the information provided is unusually insightful, then the IRO should immediately call the person, with the same message.

It may also be useful to stay in touch with small-lot stockholders, not because of their access to market rumors, but because they represent a significant number of relatively stable investors. Any information the IRO can glean from this group that will assist in retaining smaller investors is worth the effort. One way to do so is by creating an advisory board that is composed of small-lot stockholders.

The concept of an advisory board also works for all types of stockholders. To gain a broad level of participation, consider including a cross-section of the smaller and larger individual stockholders, as well as institutional stockholders. The only people to exclude from such a board are reporters and analysts, since they may inappropriately release information into the marketplace that is presented to the advisory board on a confidential basis. This type of board can not only pass along information from the marketplace to the company, but can also be used in the reverse direction, as a sounding board for prospective management activities. If the later approach is used, be sure to have everyone on the advisory board sign a non-disclosure agreement.

Another option is to periodically meet with analysts to learn their opinions about the company. They are well educated in the intricacies of the market, and can provide valuable information about why a company's stock trades at a certain price and what the company can do to improve the situation.

The information gleaned from investors may be so important that the board of directors should hear about it. The IRO can send this information to the board in a periodic report, cover it as part of her standard quarterly report to the board, or include it in a board-only intranet site.

##  SURVEYING INVESTORS

If the IRO elects to survey all stockholders, then the best approach is to use a standardized survey form. One part of this survey is designed to locate areas of stockholder concern about the company (such as the stock price, management capabilities, and dividends) and pinpoint areas in which they have reduced knowledge about the company (such as its products and services). The questionnaire can even delve into specific publications, such as any perceived inadequacies of the annual report, fact sheet, or industry overview documents.

An equally important section of the survey can ask investors about their investment strategies. This may include questions about how they track the stock, whether they now plan to buy, sell, or hold the stock, and whether they have a goal for the stock price. Also, the survey can ask investors what elements of the company story brought it to their attention, and whether those elements still apply to their investment decision.

A final part of the survey can ask detailed demographic information about the responding investors, such as their ZIP codes, age, and marital status. If they provide their phone numbers, it may be useful to conduct a more detailed follow-up interview by phone to probe more deeply into their responses.

Examples of questions from actual stockholder surveys are as follows:

- Why did you decide to buy our stock?
  - Business results
  - Growth potential
  - Dividend yield
  - Geographic location
  - Corporate governance
  - Management
  - Recommended by a broker (Name of broker _____)
  - Recommended by analyst (Name of analyst _____)

- How long do you normally hold an investment?
- What do you think would increase the attractiveness of our shares?
  - Increase dividend
  - Better business results
  - Share buy-backs
- On a scale of 1 to 5, how would you rate the risk level of our stock?
- Would you be interested in a dividend reinvestment plan?
- If you are also a customer, on a scale of 1 to 5, how would you rate the company's capabilities in the following areas:
  - Customer service
  - Product quality
  - Products
  - Service quality
  - Value
- On a scale of 1 to 5, how would you rate the company's investor relations activities and publications?
  - Annual meeting
  - Annual report
  - Fact sheet
  - Web site
- What other information would you like to receive either in the annual report, other publications, or our Web site?
- Does the annual report provide adequate information on the financial and operating activities of the company?
- On a scale of 1 to 5, how would you rate the company's transfer agent?
- Would you attend a regional investor meeting with our management team?
- What would make it easier for you to attend our annual shareholder meeting?
  - Hold it on a weekend
  - Videotape the meeting
- Please complete the following demographic information:
  - Your occupation_____
  - You age_____
  - Your postal code_____

Many companies prefer to issue an entirely new set of survey questions each year. However, it makes sense to use a core set of questions in every survey, so that the IRO can measure responses to these questions on a timeline. If there are significant changes in the responses, then the IRO should make the senior management team aware of the issue.

An additional consideration is how to issue the survey to investors. One option is to obtain a set of preprinted peel-and-stick mailing labels for the investor mailing list (see the Locating Investors section). However, this is an expensive option for larger companies with thousands of investors, especially when the costs of postage and paper are included. A simpler alternative is to create the survey through any of the online survey services on the Internet, such as www.surveymonkey.com. Then paste a link to the survey into the investor relations part of the company Web site and provide a notice to investors about the survey in the annual report, proxy statement, and other mailings. By using this electronic alternative, the cost of maintaining and processing a survey is nearly zero, and provides continuing feedback from investors.

When conducting an investor survey, especially one involving calls to customers, it might make sense to use a third-party surveying firm. These organizations are skilled in extracting information from people they call, much more so than the investor relations staff. Also, calling a large number of investors is an extremely tedious chore for the in-house staff. Finally, respondents may be more forthcoming in their answers to a third party, because they are not dealing directly with the company.

A likely result of an investor survey is that many investors have few opinions at all. In many cases, investors inherited the company's stock, or acquired it a long time ago. In either case, they probably do not monitor company activities, and simply do not care about it very much, as long as its stock price performs reasonably well. Though this may seem like a depressing result of a time-consuming survey, the IRO should just eliminate the responses (if any) of this group and focus on more valid feedback received from other investors.

Also, it can be difficult to determine which survey responses are from the most important investors, since individuals with more time on their hands are the most likely to write lengthy comments. A major investor is probably the busiest respondent, and so has the least time for an in-depth analysis. Thus (and unfortunately), a great deal of judgment is needed to sort through the types of responses received.

Besides a formal survey, the IRO should also make it as easy as possible for investors to contact the company with information. Here are some alternatives for doing so:

- *800 number.* Prominently display a toll-free phone number in the investor relations section of the company Web site, which routes either directly to the IRO (in a smaller firm) or to the department receptionist (in a larger firm). Linking callers directly to a voice mail service is a significantly less palatable alternative, since there is a risk of not checking the voicemails, of losing voicemail recordings, or of investors preferring to speak to a real person when they call. If voicemail is the only practical way to use an 800 number, then at least include a notice on the voicemail message, stating how long the company may take to call back regarding any messages left.

- *Comment form on Web site.* Include a comment form within the investor relations section of the company Web site, in which investors can make free-form comments and forward them to the IRO's e-mail address.
- *Proxy form.* Include space in the annual proxy form for shareholder comments and questions. This will very likely result in change of address comments, but may also yield useful pointers that the IRO can act on. This is one of the better methods for eliciting information from shareholders.

Though surveys are easy to administer, it is difficult to ascertain the validity of the information received. When in doubt, the IRO should not take action on a specific comment until she receives corroborating comments from multiple qualified sources.

 ## LOCATING INVESTORS

To some degree, monitoring the market means keeping in touch with individual shareholders. Unfortunately, some stockholders prefer anonymity. These stockholders, known as *Objecting Beneficial Owners* (OBO), have arranged to have a custodian at their brokerage firm hold their stock for them, so that the ownership appears to be anonymous. It is nearly impossible to gain ownership information from a contact at the holding brokerage firm, so the IRO will have to recognize that some stock will never be traceable.

Conversely, an investor who has not arranged for custodial ownership is called a *Non-Objecting Beneficial Owner* (NOBO). It is quite easy to obtain contact information for all NOBOs. NOBO reports are issued by Broadridge Financial Services, Inc. The simplest way to obtain NOBO information is to request it from Broadridge through the company's stock transfer agent. To complete a NOBO request form, the stock transfer agent will need the company's name and CUSIP number, the record date desired, the intended use (informational or mailing), and the type of report media desired. The request must be signed and dated by a company officer. The fee schedule is approximately $0.165 per shareholder for the first 10,000 shareholders, after which the price drops to $0.115 per shareholder.

For an extra $15 per thousand investors, Broadridge can provide this NOBO information on peel and stick labels, which makes it much easier to mail out surveys and related information directly to investors.

If the IRO only wants to determine the number of shares held by shareholders, then a much less expensive alternative is to request a Share Range Analysis report from Broadridge. Again, it is best to order this report through the company's stock transfer agent. The cost of this service is about $50.

It is also possible to locate institutional investors through their quarterly Form 13F filings, which requires investors with more than $100 million in assets under management to disclose their positions within 45 days of the end of each quarter. Form 13F requires disclosure of the names of institutional investment managers, the names of the securities they manage and the class of securities, the CUSIP number, the number of shares owned, and the total market value of each security. However, some funds structure their investments to avoid triggering reporting requirements, maintaining just under the minimum asset threshold or by establishing a number of smaller funds. Also, an investor can build a position and liquidate it within a reporting period, so that the IRO never knows that the investor is there. Investors take these steps to avoid reporting in order to mitigate the possibility of copycat investing that may affect the stock price.

A useful side benefit of actively tracking investors is the ongoing correction of stockholder accounts. Investors constantly move, resulting in incorrect addresses and shares whose owners cannot be traced. Consequently, a company sends expensive proxy information to the wrong addresses, as well as dividend checks that are never cashed. If a company issues dividend checks, then it can gain some perspective on the extent of this problem by adding up the number of uncashed dividend checks. To correct these problems, ask the postal service to provide forwarding address information when sending out a stockholder mailing. Also, include space on the proxy form for investor comments, which usually results in some address or ownership correction responses. It is especially important to track down investors with large stock holdings, so be prepared to pay a locating service to find these individuals when their contact information lapses.

## MONITORING THROUGH A STOCK SURVEILLANCE SERVICE

A stock surveillance service tracks trade settlements and uses this information to back into share ownership information by tracing which custodial banks tend to settle trades for certain investors. However, the information they provide is by no means exact, since they are interpreting information, not precisely quantifying holdings. Their services are expensive, so they cater more to larger-cap firms. Given the high cost of this service, it is more useful to companies that are subject to attack from shareholder activists and need up-to-the-minute information about stockholdings.

## MONITORING THROUGH A STOCK TRANSFER AGENT

The IRO can ascertain some general information about stock ownership changes through reports provided by the stock transfer agent. To do so, review the transfer sheets that usually accompany the monthly billing. These show some types of stock sales and purchases. Look for patterns of continual stock sales or purchases by the same stockholder over time. If this is happening with large amounts of stock, then the IRO should make senior management aware of an ongoing change in company ownership.

## BLOOMBERG TERMINALS

Over a quarter-million people in the investment community obtain investment information from Bloomberg terminals, for which they pay a monthly fee to Bloomberg L.P. With a Bloomberg terminal, an IRO has access to an overwhelming amount of information, including stock prices, historical charts, analyst coverage and ratings, earnings releases, lists of comparable companies, and relative valuation models. This is not a cost-effective solution for the IRO of a smaller company, but a large IRO department may conclude that a single Bloomberg terminal is worth the considerable monthly cost. Contact www.bloomberg.com for more information about its Bloomberg Professional service.

## ELECTRONIC MESSAGE BOARDS

A message board is an anonymous forum on which anyone can post messages that can be read by all site visitors. There are numerous message boards on which people pass along tips, comments, and outright lies about a company. Examples of Web sites containing such boards are Yahoo!, Motley Fool, and Raging Bull.

A small minority of people using the site post the vast majority of all messages on these boards. The theme of messages posted generally trend toward the extremes, with short sellers posting negative comments and bulls posting the reverse. Thus, the "information" in these postings is strongly slanted toward the needs of the posting individuals, and does not necessarily reflect any form of reality.

Given the motivations of people posting on message boards, it is evident that browsing message boards to gauge the market's reaction to a company may yield some extremely skewed information. Though it is possible to glean some valid information from a message board, it is difficult to discern which items are legitimate and which are pure speculation. Consequently, the IRO should only review message boards as a supplement to more valid information sources.

If information posted on a message board appears to require a response, do not do so through the message board. This can have adverse legal implications, since any message posted by a company officer on a message board can be considered an official form of guidance by the company, and is therefore subject to control (and penalties) by the SEC. A better approach is to respond through a more traditional communication channel, such as a press release or 8-K filing. Even then, never reference the posting, or imply that the information is being provided in reaction to a posting. Instead, merely state the facts of the situation, and let the investment community make up its collective mind regarding the appropriate stock valuation to assign to the company.

##  ACTIVITY CAUSED BY TRADING STRATEGIES

Sometimes, there will be surges in trading volume that appear to the IRO to be completely incomprehensible. There have been no press releases or SEC filings, and yet there is significant activity that appears to be coming from multiple parties. What is going on?

The cause may be *technical analysis*. Investors may be basing their trades on a variety of stock price points or volume levels, rather than on new information about the company or the market. For example, institutional investors may automatically buy more stock if the price drops to a predetermined level, or sell off shares at a preprogrammed high point. Also, if the price represents a new high point below which there had previously been considerable resistance, investors may buy more shares to ride the new price jump. Another variation is to buy into a stock when its moving average price changes sufficiently. Speculators tend to focus on the 10-day and 20-day moving averages, while traditional firms focus on longer moving averages, such as the 50-day and 200-day averages.

A possible cause of trading volume is the activity of *rebate traders*. Rebate trading involves buying or selling short a stock directly from an electronic communications network (ECN), and being paid a rebate by the ECN for the transaction (the ECN makes money by paying a credit to liquidity providers and charging a slightly larger debit to liquidity removers). This strategy works best with high-volume stocks, so that the trader can buy or sell in large volume without altering the stock price. The trader then waits for a minor uptick in the price and closes out the trade, pocketing the rebate. The strategy is shown in the following example.

## EXAMPLE

Munificent Fund is willing to buy the shares of Placid Corporation in the price range of $15.60 to $15.80. Its trading algorithm ("algo") issues a string of 500-share orders and buys at $15.60, which are spotted by the computer of Rebate Trader Corp. The Rebate Trader's computer now jumps ahead of the Munificent Algo by one cent, with a bid to buy 500 shares at $15.61. Rebate Trader buys the shares at $15.61, and collects its fractional rebate from the ECN. The Rebate Trader computer then offers to sell at $15.61. The Munificent algo will likely buy the shares at that price, at which point Rebate Trader earns another rebate from the ECN.

As a result, Munificent has paid $0.01 per share more than it would otherwise have paid. Rebate Trader earns no profit on the trades themselves, but collects a rebate on both trades. ▪

A possible cause of price swings is the *predatory algorithm*. Algorithmic trading systems usually slice a large order into many smaller ones that are fed into the market as orders are filled. Order volumes are frequently for just 100 or 500 shares. Many of these algo orders are pegged to the National Best Bid or Offer (NBBO); this means that a potentially large volume of algo orders will follow a price up or down, potentially creating large price movements on minimal trading volume. Some traders have created predatory algo strategies to take advantage of this linkage between algos and the NBBO, as shown in the following example.

## EXAMPLE

M unificent Fund has an algo order that is pegged to the NBBO, with discretion to buy shares up to a maximum of $15.80. It is buying the stock of Placid Corporation in blocks of 500 shares. The current market price of Placid shares is $15.60. Pirate Fund sees the trading volume and suspects that an institutional investor is behind the orders. Pirate places an order for $15.61, and Munificent's algo matches the price. Pirate continues to run up the price until Munificent reaches its maximum of $15.80 and stops further trading activity. Pirate then sells the Placid stock short at $15.80, on the assumption that the stock price will now fall. The price subsequently drops back to $15.60, and Pirate covers.

Thus, Pirate makes money on the series of transactions, Munificent loses money, and Placid's IRO can only wonder why the stock price is fluctuating so much on minimal trading volume. ■

If institutional investors hold a large proportion of company stock, it is likely that these shares are being traded through *dark pools*. Despite the name, there is nothing cloak-and-dagger about dark pools. A dark pool provides institutional investors with a liquidity pool that is not displayed on the order books of the major stock exchanges. By initially restricting the visibility of these large trades, an investor is less likely to cause adverse price movements in the stock. These trades are still included in the consolidated trading volume posted for a security. Thus, dark pool activity does not impact pricing, but can be a major source of trading volume.

There is nothing that the IRO can do about these sudden changes in price and volume, but it may be worthwhile to attempt deciphering the types of activities causing the changes, if only to have some knowledge of what is controlling the price of the stock.

 **SUMMARY**

Of the various monitoring techniques noted in this chapter, the IRO should, at a minimum, subscribe to an Internet monitoring service and maintain close relations with the best-connected investors. These two activities require little expense or time, and will reveal a considerable amount of quality information. Surveys can be relatively inexpensive, especially if posted on the company Web site for online access by investors; however, the information they provide can be suspect, depending on the types of investors filling out the surveys. Finally, a Bloomberg terminal is an excellent asset, but also an expensive one that smaller firms may not consider to be cost-effective.

Various trading strategies can also cause a great deal of variability in a stock's price and trading volume, such as rebate trading and predatory algorithms. There is nothing the IRO can do about these activities, other than to ascribe some proportion of total activity to them and then concentrate on evaluating the remaining stock activity.

The IRO must exercise a considerable amount of judgment in evaluating any types of information received. Much of the information coming from the investment community is qualitative in nature, not quantitative, which makes it extremely difficult to decide which items to act on. In general, the IRO should assign the greatest weight to input received from those individuals having the most experience in the marketplace and the least weight to anonymous comments. Only when there is a large volume of the same type of anonymous comment should the IRO take action.

# CHAPTER NINETEEN

# Blue Sky Laws

B LUE SKY LAWS ARE passed by the individual states to prevent unscrupulous securities dealers from committing fraud by selling bogus securities to investors. The *blue sky* term comes from the concept that an unscrupulous person could "sell the sky" to someone without the presence of proper regulation. This chapter addresses the general requirements of blue sky laws, their implications for securities dealers, and how this impacts the investor relations officer (IRO).

##  BLUE SKY LAW REQUIREMENTS AND IMPLICATIONS

Blue sky laws require that securities originally offered for sale be qualified and registered with the proper state authorities, and that their prices and terms be consistent with statutory guidelines. The usual guidelines, which are based on the Uniform Securities Act of 1956, are:

- The issuer of a security is engaged in business, is not in the organizational stage or bankrupt, and is not a blank check, blind pool, or shell company that has no business plan or purpose.
- The security should be sold at a price reasonably related to its current market price.

- The security is not part or all of an unsold allotment to the securities dealer as an underwriter of the security.
- The company has a minimum asset base.

Thus, for a securities dealer to sell a company's stock, the stock must conform to both SEC regulations and the laws in the state where the dealer is located. If the security does not conform with the local blue sky law, then (as stated in section 410(a) of the 1956 Act),

> Any person who offers or sells a security is liable to the person buying the security from him, who may sue . . . to recover the consideration paid for the security, together with interest at six percent per year from date of payment, [court] costs, and reasonable attorneys' fees, less the amount of income received on the security, upon tender of the security, or for damages if he no longer owns the security.

This legal requirement is clearly of massive concern to securities dealers, who may be forced by investors to take back securities previously sold to them. Of course, this would only happen if the securities subsequently lost some portion or all of their value, resulting in significant losses or even bankruptcy for the dealer. Thus, compliance with blue sky laws is absolutely critical for the establishment of a state-level market in a company's securities.

This legal requirement is not a problem for any company whose stock is listed on a national exchange, such as the American Stock Exchange, NASDAQ, or New York Stock Exchange. In these cases, states give a "manual exemption," so that the stock is automatically cleared for trading. This exemption was created under the National Securities Markets Improvement Act of 1996.

If a company is only listed on the over-the-counter market, then the situation is more complex. Most of the states allow a registration exemption if a company registers and annually renews that registration through either Standard & Poor's, Moody's, or Fitch's Investor Service (the specific entity varies by state). This registration involves a multpage filing that includes historical financial statements, a description of the business, and the names of all executive officers. However, some states still require direct registration, which usually requires the services of a local attorney. The states that currently allow no registration exemption are:

- Alabama
- California
- Georgia
- Illinois
- Kentucky
- Louisiana

- New York
- Pennsylvania
- Tennessee
- Virginia
- Wisconsin

Individual state requirements change constantly, so have a local securities attorney update this list from time to time.

##  BLUE SKY ADVICE FOR THE IRO

Given the broad range of state blue sky laws, the primary advice for the IRO is to engage local counsel in every state where a company intends to sell its securities, to verify that it has complied with the local regulations. In addition, be aware of the local blue sky laws whenever going on a road show, since both brokers and investors are very likely to bring up the issue at that time.

# CHAPTER TWENTY

# Proxy Solicitations

A PROXY IS A written authorization given by a stockholder to cast his or her vote at a stockholder meeting. Or, to be more precise, it is a power of attorney authorizing a specific vote on a stockholder's behalf. It is generally used to approve a slate of company directors and the company auditor, but can also be used for a variety of additional motions.

The investor relations officer may be involved in the proxy solicitation process, since it involves direct contact with stockholders. If so, she has a choice of doing so entirely by mail, or by online proxy voting, which has recently been approved by the SEC. This chapter outlines how the proxy solicitation process works.

## PROXY SOLICITATION CONCEPTS

Every public company holds at least one shareholder meeting per year, and may also need to conduct additional shareholder meetings for the approval of selected items, such as a new class of securities or a change in the company's articles of incorporation. These meetings are governed by the law of the state in which a company is incorporated, sometimes requiring that an annual meeting be held within a specified time period following the company's prior annual meeting.

Prior to that meeting, a company must issue a proxy solicitation to its voting securities holders, disclosing a broad range of information about both the company and any proposals it wishes to bring to a vote. The proxy itself is any shareholder consent or authorization regarding the casting of that shareholder's vote, which is accompanied by detailed solicitation materials.

The SEC's Rule 14a-3 identifies the types of information that must be included in the materials used for proxy solicitations. The general categories of this information are as follows:

- The date, time, and place of the meeting
- The deadline for submitting shareholder proposals for inclusion in the proxy statement and form of proxy
- Statement of whether proxies can be revoked, and the method for doing so
- Explanation of any dissenters' rights of appraisal for any proposals to be voted upon
- The interests of directors and officers in the matters to be voted upon
- Itemization of all voting securities and their principal holders
- The record date for determining which shareholders can vote
- If directors are being elected, their relationship to the company
- The compensation of directors and officers
- The fees billed by the auditor to the company for auditing, information systems design and implementation, and all other services
- The details of any bonus, pension, benefits, or similar plans to be voted upon
- The details of any securities to be authorized for issuance, or existing ones to be modified
- The details for any extraordinary transactions, such as mergers and acquisitions
- The details of any property to be acquired or disposed of
- The details of any changes to the articles of incorporation or charter
- If this is for the annual shareholder meeting, the company's annual report (for which the most recent Form 10-K can be used)

These materials are issued alongside a *proxy card*. The proxy card is essentially a voting card, which clearly states the name of the security holder being solicited, the matters to be voted upon, and a means for approving, disapproving, or abstaining from each matter. A sample proxy card is shown in Exhibit 20.1.

**Exhibit 20.1**   Sample Proxy Card

ABC COMPANY

PROXY SOLICITED BY THE BOARD OF DIRECTORS

FOR THE ANNUAL MEETING OF SHAREHOLDERS TO BE HELD [DATE]

The undersigned hereby constitutes and appoints John Smith and Jason Billups, and each of them, the true and lawful attorneys and proxies of the undersigned with full power of substitution and appointment, for and in the name, place and stead of the undersigned, to act for and to vote all of the undersigned's shares of the no par value common stock ("Common Stock") of ABC Company, a Colorado corporation, at the Annual Meeting of Shareholders (the "Meeting") to be held in the [location, address] on [date and time], and at all adjournments thereof.

The undersigned hereby revokes any proxies as to said shares heretofore given by the undersigned and ratifies and confirms all that said attorneys and proxies, or either of them, lawfully may do by virtue hereof.

The undersigned hereby acknowledges receipt of the Notice of Annual Meeting of Shareholders, the Proxy Statement and the Annual Report furnished therewith.

THIS PROXY WHEN PROPERLY EXECUTED WILL BE VOTED IN THE MANNER DIRECTED HEREIN BY THE UNDERSIGNED SHAREHOLDER. IF NO DIRECTION IS MADE, THIS PROXY WILL BE VOTED "FOR" THE ELECTION OF THE NAMED NOMINEES, "FOR" THE PROPOSAL TO RATIFY THE SELECTION OF ABC AUDITORS AS THE COMPANY'S ACCOUNTANTS, "FOR" THE PROPOSAL TO RATIFY THE COMPANY'S 20XX EQUITY INCENTIVE PLAN AND AS SAID PROXIES DEEM ADVISABLE ON SUCH MATTERS AS MAY PROPERLY COME BEFORE THE MEETING.

Using a **black ink** pen, mark your votes with an **X** as shown in this example.  Please do not write outside the designated areas.  ☒

**A. Proposals—The Board of Directors recommends a vote FOR all the nominees listed, FOR proposal 2, and FOR proposal 3**

**1. Election of Directors**

| | | |
|---|---|---|
| 01 – Abraham Calamy | ☐ FOR | ☐ WITHHOLD |
| 02 – Brian Dennison | ☐ FOR | ☐ WITHHOLD |
| 03 – Charles Entelmann | ☐ FOR | ☐ WITHHOLD |
| 04 – David Franklin | ☐ FOR | ☐ WITHHOLD |
| 05 – Enoch Gervis | ☐ FOR | ☐ WITHHOLD |

**2. Ratification of ABC Auditors as the Company's Independent Auditors**

☐ FOR   ☐ AGAINST   ☐ ABSTAIN

**3. Ratification of the Company's 20XX Equity Incentive Plan**

☐ FOR   ☐ AGAINST   ☐ ABSTAIN

*(continued)*

## Exhibit 20.1 *(Continued)*

**B. Nonvoting Items**

**Change of Address**—Please print your new address below.

<br><br><br>

**C. Authorized Signatures—This section must be completed for your vote to be counted. Date and sign below.**

| [address label] | Please sign exactly as name(s) appear hereon. Joint owners should each sign. When signing as attorney, executor, administrator, corporate officer, trustee, guardian, or custodian, please give full title. |
| --- | --- |
| | ———————— <br> [date] |
| | ————————  ———————— <br> Signature 1    Title |
| | ————————  ———————— <br> Signature 2    Title |

All materials sent to shareholders must be carefully reviewed in advance for errors. The SEC's Rule 14a-9 states that a misstatement or omission in the proxy materials must have been material in order for a shareholder to have a cause of action against the company. A "material" misstatement or omission is considered to be one that causes a substantial likelihood that a reasonable shareholder would consider it important in deciding how to vote.

Shareholders may periodically petition the company to add proposals to the proxy statement to be voted on at the next shareholders meeting. In order to be accepted for inclusion, the submitting shareholder must be the owner of a class of security that will be able to vote on the proposal, has owned the securities for at least one year, and owns the lesser of 1 percent or $1,000 in market value of those securities. Further, the shareholder must continue to be a security holder through the meeting date. Even if the shareholder meets these requirements, the company does not have to include many types of proposals in its proxy statement. Here are some of the more common reasons for excluding a shareholder proposal:

- It would violate any laws to which the company is subject.
- It would result in some form of discrimination.
- It is materially misleading.
- It is too vague or indefinite.
- It relates to the submitting shareholder's personal claim or grievance against the company or another person.
- It relates to that portion of a company's business that is less than 5 percent of its total assets, net earnings, and gross sales for its most recent fiscal year, but not if it is significantly related to the company's business.
- It relates to matters that are beyond the company's control.
- It relates to the ordinary business of the company.
- It was submitted in the past year, and did not receive a significant number of votes during the earlier balloting.
- It relates to a specific amount of dividends.

Despite the considerable number of available exclusions, many companies include all shareholder proposals in their proxy statements that would not result in illegal activities, on the grounds that these proposals usually receive only a very small percentage of shareholder votes. Management is allowed to state in the proxy materials which proposals it supports, as was the case in the preceding exhibit.

Once a company has assembled all materials for the proxy mailing, it sends the materials to the SEC for approval, but only if the materials involve voting for issues other than the election of directors, the appointment of auditors, or the approval of a plan or related amendments. The SEC has 10 days to respond that it plans to comment; if so, the SEC usually issues a comment letter within 30 days. If the SEC does not respond within 10 days, then the company can proceed with printing and mailing the proxy materials to its stockholders. If there is no need to submit the information to the SEC in advance, then the company can print and mail the proxy materials and file them with the SEC at the same time.

Also, the board of directors must set a *record date*, which is used to identify those shareholders eligible for notice of and voting at an annual meeting. This record date will vary, depending on the state law under which a company incorporates, but generally cannot be more than 60 to 70 days prior to the meeting date. The directors must also fix a *mailing date* for the proxy materials and a stockholder *meeting date*. Again, the number of days notice for the meeting date will vary by state law, but is typically required to be at least 10 days after the mailing date. Many companies mail proxy materials up to a month before the meeting date, in order to give sufficient time for stockholder votes to be returned in the mail.

A third-party printer almost always creates the proxy materials. The printer forwards them to Broadridge, Inc., which mails them to the stockholders of record. Broadridge can tally votes that are mailed back by stockholders, or the company or its stock transfer agent can do so. Once all votes have been received, the designated person or entity creates a summary-level report of votes cast, certifies that the information is correct, and issues a report on it at the stockholders' meeting.

The shareholders' meeting is almost always in-person, at a specific, designated location. However, it is also possible to have an entirely *electronic shareholder meeting*, if allowed by the corporate law of the state in which a company is incorporated. If allowed, the electronic shareholder meeting has no physical location. Instead, shareholders can vote electronically or by fax, and question-and-answer sessions between management and shareholders are by conference call.

This is a painfully slow process, because investors have many days in which to return their proxy cards. Also, because the vote tallying process is manual, the company needs to continually recompile ballots through the most recent date in order to see how votes are trending. Finally, it requires a large amount of printing and mailing expense. An electronic variation on this process is more efficient, and is described in the next section.

## ONLINE PROXY VOTING

The SEC has adopted a *notice and access model*, under which it allows companies to use the Internet to make proxy materials available to voting securities holders. Key introductory extracts from the rule are as follows:

> We are adopting amendments to the proxy rules under the Securities and Exchange Act of 1934 that provide an alternative method for issuers . . . to furnish proxy materials to stockholders by posting them on an Internet Web site and providing stockholders with notice of the availability of the proxy materials . . . Issuers that rely on the amendments may significantly lower the costs of their proxy solicitations that ultimately are borne by stockholders.
>
> The notice and access model that we are adopting provides an alternative means for an issuer to furnish proxy materials to its stockholders. The proxy materials include (1) notices of stockholder meetings; (2) Schedule 14A proxy statements and consent solicitation forms; (3) Forms of proxy (i.e., proxy cards); (4) Schedule 14C information statements; (5) Annual reports to security holders; (6) Additional soliciting materials, and; (7) any amendments to such materials that are required to be furnished to stockholders. The new rules permit any issuer to use the notice and access model to disseminate its proxy materials to all types of stockholders, whether registered or beneficial owners, and with respect to any solicitation except those related to business combination transactions.

The rule states that a company must send a notice 40 calendar days or more in advance of a stockholder meeting date, telling them of the availability of the proxy materials on a Web site. The notice must include a prominent legend in boldface type that states:

> Important Notice Regarding the Availability of Proxy Materials for the Shareholder Meeting To Be Held on [date].
>
> This communication presents only an overview of the more complete proxy materials that are available to you on the Internet. We encourage you to access and review all of the important information contained in the proxy materials before voting.
>
> The [proxy statement] [information statement] [annual report to security holders] [is/are] available at [Web site address].
>
> If you want to receive a paper or e-mail copy of these documents, you must request one. There is no charge to you for requesting a copy.

Please make your request for a copy as instructed below on or before [date] to facilitate timely delivery.

In addition, the notice must state the following:

- The date, time, and location of the meeting
- A clear identification of each separate matter to be acted on and the company's recommendations regarding those matters
- A list of the materials being made available at the specified Web site
- A toll-free telephone number, an e-mail address, and a Web site address where stockholders can request a copy of the proxy materials
- Any control or identification numbers that the stockholder needs to access his or her proxy card
- Instructions on how to access the proxy card
- Information on how to obtain directions to attend the meeting and vote in person

What does the revised proxy solicitation process look like? The company lists a unique control number and a Web site address on a label that it attaches to a proxy notification, which it mails to stockholders of record. The stockholders then use the control number to gain access to the indicated Web site, where they can access the proxy materials and enter their ballots. The Web site automatically tabulates all votes, which one can access online, both at a detail and summary level.

The SEC has a few additional requirements for this process, which are noted in the following bullet points:

- Companies are not allowed to furnish the proxy card together with the initial notice for a solicitation. Instead, the company must post the proxy card on the Web site with the proxy statement and any annual report.
- There is a chance that stockholders may be tricked into disclosing personal information to individuals purporting to represent the company. To avoid this problem, the SEC encourages companies to include a statement in their proxy notices that stockholders are not required to provide any personal information.
- The SEC estimates that 19 percent of all stockholders will continue to request paper copies, so there will still be an ongoing need for the traditional proxy materials distribution and vote tallying procedures. In particular, the new rule allows companies to send a paper proxy card at least 10 calendar days

after sending the electronic notice. This later mailing can include a copy of the proxy statement and annual report.

- The SEC requires that the proxy materials posted on the stockholder-accessible Web site be posted in two formats. One must be in a format substantially identical to the paper version of the materials (such as a PDF document). The second version must be available in a readily searchable format, such as HTML, which may also incorporate hyperlinks between various parts of the document.
- Some stockholders are *beneficial owners*, which means that an intermediary holds their stock. In such cases, the company has no identification information regarding the beneficial owners, and only has an obligation to provide notice to the intermediary (such as a broker). Thus, the intermediary must prepare its own notice and distribute it to those beneficial stockholders registered with it. The intermediary can request paper proxy documents from the company on behalf of its beneficial stockholders.

There is a risk that companies could underestimate the number of stockholders they expect to request paper proxy documents, requiring an additional (and expensive) print run of those documents. Thus, it is advisable to significantly overestimate the number of stockholders requesting the printed version during the first year of implementing this program, in order to ensure that the demand for printed documents can be fulfilled with a single printing. Once a company develops a history of the proportion of stockholders requesting paper documents, it will then have greater assurance in budgeting for the correct number of paper documents.

Though online voting certainly presents the opportunity for cost savings, an even greater benefit is the massive increase in the feedback loop from investors to management. The company can monitor the online voting in real time, and can reasonably expect to see the bulk of the voting completed within a few days of the initial notice being delivered to stockholders. This is a vast improvement over the traditional model, where results trickle in for weeks after the initial mailing of proxy materials and require constant recompiling of the vote results in order to identify voting trends.

In addition to this notice and access model, the SEC has instituted the *full set delivery option*. The full set delivery option is similar to the traditional proxy delivery process that generally involves mailing paper copies to shareholders, except that it also requires the company to post its proxy materials on a Web site and to send a notice (or incorporate the information required in a notice into its proxy materials) informing shareholders of the Internet availability of the proxy materials. However, because the full set of proxy materials being provided already includes a proxy card, the company is not required to provide another means of voting on the Web site.

 ## PROXY DISTRIBUTION PROCESS

The proxy distribution process must be initiated well in advance and coordinated with multiple parties. Use the following procedure to do so:

1. Contact the company's stock transfer agent three months in advance of the annual meeting and request a copy of their meeting questionnaire form (see Exhibit 20.2).

**Exhibit 20.2**   Sample Meeting Questionnaire Form

The following information is needed to start the process for your special/annual shareholder meeting.

1. Record Date _____

2. Mail Date _____

3. Material Delivery Date _____ (must be at least one day prior to mailing date)

4. Meeting Date _____

5. Is [stock transfer agent name] to tabulate votes?   Yes _____        No _____

   If yes, forward to [stock transfer agent name] the security position listings from any of the following if received: Cede & Co., Chase Manhattan, Proxy Trust.

6. If [mailing facility name] is to do the mailing, which of the following material will be sent?

   _____   Annual Report                                _____   Business Reply Envelope

   _____   Proxy Statement/Notice of Meeting            _____   10-K

   _____   Notice of Internet Availability              _____   10-Q

   _____   Proxy Ballot                                 _____   Other _____

7. For voting purposes, what percentage of the outstanding shares constitutes a quorum?

   \_\_\_\_\_ 51%      \_\_\_\_\_50%      \_\_\_\_\_33%      \_\_\_\_\_Other

8. What proposals will be voted on the proxy card?

   _____   Directors                                    _____   Merger

   _____   Auditors                                     _____   Reverse/Forward Split

   _____   Name Change                                  _____   Other _____

9. We will send your meeting materials by overnight delivery service two days before your meeting date.  What is the address where the meeting materials should be sent?

Address: _____

2. In filling out the form, set the record date to be at least 20 business days later than today's date (see the discussion of SEC Rule 14a-13 below). After determining the record date, set the mail date to be between one and two weeks following the record date. At the earliest, set the mail date to be one business day after the record date. Then set the meeting date, which should be at least 30 days following the mail date, or 40 days for nonroutine proposals (see the discussion of broker authorizations following).

3. Note on the questionnaire whether the company is authorizing the stock transfer agent to tabulate votes, and identify what types of material will be sent. Also note the percentage of outstanding shares that constitute a quorum, and identify the types of proposals that will be voted on.

4. Contact the financial printer to print and mail all materials. These materials should include the proxy statement/notice of mailing, 10-K report, proxy card, and business reply envelope. The envelope is provided by the company's stock transfer agent, which tabulates votes.

5. Send the Form 10-K, proxy statement, and proxy card to the printer. Call the printer to confirm receipt.

6. Confirm delivery of the printed materials by the financial printer. The printer should issue a certification statement that the materials were mailed, such as the version shown in Exhibit 20.3.

7. Just prior to the annual meeting, the stock transfer agent will finish tabulating shareholder votes and issue an oath of inspectors of election

**Exhibit 20.3**   Mailing Certification

Date

I, [name], certify that the material for ABC Company was mailed to Shareholders of Record on [date], via United States First Class Mail. The material consisted of a Form 10-K, A Notice of Annual Meeting of Shareholders and Proxy Statement, a Proxy Voting Card, and a Business Reply Envelope.

Sincerely,

[name]

[Certification of Notary Public]

**Exhibit 20.4**  Oath of Inspectors of Election

We, the undersigned, being duly sworn, depose and say that we will faithfully execute the duties of Inspectors of Elections at the Annual Meeting of the Shareholders of ABC Company, to be held on [date], with strict impartiality and according to the best of our ability.

[name]

Stock Transfer Agent

[Certification of Notary Public]

(as shown in Exhibit 20.4), a notarized summary of votes received (as shown in Exhibit 20.5), and a detailed report by individual proxy received.

SEC Rule 14a-13 stipulates that notice be given to all brokers at least 20 business days prior to the record date, to inquire whether other persons are the beneficial owners of the company's securities, and to determine the number of proxies and other materials to supply to the record holder for these beneficial owners. Thus, the record date must be set no earlier than 20 business days (essentially one month) from the current date. Also, when determining the meeting date, 30 days following the mailing date is *only* sufficient when such routine proposals as director elections and approval of auditors are being proposed, since brokers typically have discretionary voting power to vote for these proposals on behalf of shareholders, and can do so quickly. If there are nonroutine proposals, such as changing the number of authorized outstanding shares, name changes, mergers, and stock splits, then the interval between the mailing date and meeting date should be closer to 45 days, since brokers (who do not have authority to vote on such matters) must defer to the shareholders, which requires more time.

Barring the need for an accelerated annual meeting date, it is reasonable to build extra days into all phases of the proxy timeline, thereby avoiding issues with printing and mailing delays.

An important point regarding the distribution of proxy materials is that the company is *only* obligated to send materials to those brokers in whose accounts customers are holding the company's securities. The brokers are then obligated by Section 14(b) of the Exchange Act to forward the materials to those

**Exhibit 20.5**  Report and Certification of Inspectors of Election

We, the undersigned, being duly appointed Inspectors of Election of the Annual Meeting of the Shareholders of ABC Company, on [date], do hereby report and certify the results of ballots cast as follows:

**PROPOSAL 1: Election of Directors:**

|                    | FOR        | WITHHELD |
| ------------------ | ---------- | -------- |
| Abraham Calamy     | 13,709,757 | 290      |
| Brian Dennison     | 13,709,757 | 290      |
| Charles Entelmann  | 13,709,757 | 290      |
| David Franklin     | 13,709,757 | 290      |
| Enoch Gervis       | 13,709,757 | 290      |

**PROPOSAL 2: Ratification of ABC Auditors as the Company's independent auditors:**

| FOR        | AGAINST | ABSTAIN |
| ---------- | ------- | ------- |
| 13,709,947 | 0       | 100     |

**PROPOSAL 3: Ratification of the Company's 20XX Equity Incentive Plan:**

| FOR        | AGAINST | ABSTAIN |
| ---------- | ------- | ------- |
| 12,116,329 | 0       | 390     |

As of the record date, there were 26,186,991 common shares issued and outstanding. A quorum consists of 51% of these shares outstanding, which are 13,355,197.

The number of shares voted for proposal 1 by proxy is 13,709,757.
The number of shares voted for proposal 2 by proxy is 13,709,947.
The number of shares voted for proposal 3 by proxy is 12,116,329.
The total number of shares voted is 13,710,047.
Therefore, we do have a quorum for the Annual Meeting of Shareholders.

[name]

Stock Transfer Agent

[Certification of notary public]

customers. Thus, this final level of distribution is the responsibility of the brokers, *not* the company.

 ## NYSE RULE 452

The SEC has approved an amendment to the New York Stock Exchange's Rule 452, which governs the level of discretionary voting by brokers of shares held in street name when the owners of those shares have not instructed the brokers how to vote the shares. The amendment no longer allows brokers to vote on uncontested director elections without instructions from the shareowners. This amendment is critical for any public companies that have shares held in street name, because the Rule governs *all* brokers.

The amended Rule 452 has an impact on shareholder meetings, especially for companies having a large proportion of retail investors with their holdings in street name. It is less of an issue where there is a high proportion of institutional investors, since they vote their own shares and do so with a high degree of regularity. Here are some of the problems that may arise:

- *Activist shareholder success rate.* If an activist shareholder submits a shareholder proposal, it now has a greater chance of success, since broker votes used to favor the agenda supported by management. The IRO now have to practice much greater outreach to shareholders to counteract the efforts of activists. The voting recommendations of proxy advisory firms to institutional shareholders will also likely have a greater impact on voting results.
- *Quorum.* Since brokers cannot vote without instructions, there is a risk of not achieving a quorum at the next election. This will be a particular problem for companies having minimal institutional ownership, since share ownership may be spread among a considerable group of investors. A solution is to always include a routine matter, such as an auditor ratification, in every shareholder meeting. Brokers can still vote on routine matters, so their votes on such items contribute greatly toward a quorum.
- *Responses to notice and access method.* When a company switches to the notice and access method of distributing proxy materials over the Internet, there is a marked drop in retail investor participation in the voting. The voting decline may be substantial enough to warrant a switch back to delivering a full set of proxy materials in the mail.
- *Voting rules.* If a company requires a majority of all outstanding shares to vote in favor of a proposal, it may be difficult to obtain sufficient votes to do

so. The best solution is to switch to plurality voting, where the winning proposal is simply the one with the most votes—no absolute majority is required.

## SUMMARY

The traditional proxy solicitation process spans a broad period of time, requires painstaking scheduling of activities, and results in the waste of a great deal of paper. While there is no real solution to the duration of the process, a company can deal with the second item by paying close attention to a detailed proxy procedure. Under the SEC's notice and access model, a company can eliminate some of the paper waste by allowing stockholders to access proxy materials on a designated Web site, rather than by mailing the materials to them. Stockholders can also conduct online voting under this rule, resulting in the rapid feedback of voting results to the company. The recent introduction of NYSE Rule 452 may trigger a shift away from the notice and access model so that companies can be assured of sufficient votes to attain a shareholder quorum.

CHAPTER TWENTY-ONE

# Dividends and Stock Buy-Backs

A KEY STAGE IN a company's growth is when it begins to accumulate more cash than it needs for its ongoing operational and acquisition plans. At this point, the board of directors may elect to find new uses for the excess cash, such as a dividend or stock buy-back program. The board should obtain the advice of the investor relations officer (IRO) before enacting such programs, since either use of cash may have an impact on investor turnover, as well as the price of the stock.

 **TRANSITION TO A DIVIDEND**

When the board of directors initiates a dividend payment program, it may not realize that a substantial proportion of the company's stockholders may sell their shares, resulting in an entirely new set of stockholders with different investment performance criteria.

The reason for this change is that, until the point when a company issues dividends, it is presumably classified as a growth stock. A certain type of investor acquires and holds stock classified as growth stock, with an expectation that the stock price will continually grow in conjunction with the expanded economic fortunes of the company. Once the board authorizes the issuance of dividends, growth investors assume that the company's growth is slowing down, so the company now has no better use for its excess cash than to return it to investors. Their reaction is usually to sell their holdings to a new group of investors who are primarily motivated by the size and perceived longevity of the dividend. Also, if there was a growth premium associated with the stock, that premium will vanish, likely resulting in a one-time decline in the company's stock price.

Because of these changes, the board should consider using excess cash to pay down any remaining debt before issuing dividends. By doing so, the company will still be classified as a growth company, and will likely retain its existing investors. As a side benefit, debt reduction also eliminates interest expense, and therefore increases net income. It also increases the size of credit lines that will be available for unexpected occurrences, which, in turn, reduces investors' perception of the company's overall level of risk.

## DIVIDEND POLICY

If the board of directors elects to proceed with a dividend issuance, it should consult with the IRO in developing a dividend policy that coincides with the board's long-term expectations for the company.

An excellent initial decision is to begin with a relatively small dividend. Issuing any dividend, no matter what size, creates an expectation among a company's new income-oriented investors that a dividend of the same size or larger will be issued at regular, predictable intervals. If the board were to authorize an excessively large dividend, the company might quickly find itself struggling to support a large and continuing cash outflow. By instead beginning with a smaller dividend, the IRO can likely issue a series of press releases that point out the company's ongoing ability to gradually support a larger dividend—which is excellent news for investors, and which will likely lead to a gradual increase in the company's stock price.

Another argument in favor of a small initial dividend is to consider the worst-case scenario—where a company cancels its dividend. This implies a cash crisis, unless the IRO can present a cogent case that the company is investing the cash in an activity that will result in outsized profits. The trouble is that the current set of investors are primarily concerned with income, not growth, and so they will likely sell their stock even if the company's reason for diverting cash from dividend payments is entirely valid. If there is indeed a cash shortfall, then the income investors will very likely sell their stock. When this happens, the stock price will probably drop considerably, until it appears to be a bargain for value investors. This new group of investors will then buy stock at a much lower price, and count on a company turnaround to restore profits and presumably increase the price of their shares. Another problem with a canceled dividend is that the IRO may be placed in the uncomfortable position of continually responding to investor queries about when the dividend will be reinstated—resulting in a continual stream of negative announcements. In short, a small, sustainable dividend mitigates the risk of a dividend cancellation in the future.

One type of dividend to be avoided is the special dividend. It does nothing to permanently increase the stock price, since it represents a one-time outflow of cash, for which the stock price will promptly increase (when the dividend is announced) and then fall (after it is paid). Investors will assume that the special dividend will not be repeated, so they will not bid up the price of the stock in expectation of any additional special dividend on some unannounced date in the future.

Once the board decides on the correct dividend size, it should work with the IRO to communicate this information to investors. A simple statement of the amount and timing of a single dividend is not a sufficient degree of investor communication. Instead, the statement should itemize the expected timing of dividend issuances and the basis for the amount of dividends to be paid in the future, so that investors can more accurately calculate the value of the stock related to its stream of future dividend income. When explaining the basis for the amount of future dividend payments, it helps to be as detailed as possible. For example, indicate the exact percentage of company earnings or cash flow to be paid as dividends.

The company's overall theme of investor communications will likely change as part of the dividend policy, since the IRO must now reposition the company as being an income investment, rather than a growth investment. This calls for a complete reevaluation of the message to investors, which will require the input of the entire management team.

A useful side benefit of having a dividend policy is that this presents an opportunity for the IRO to communicate with investors. This may take the form of a cover letter that accompanies each dividend payment, or perhaps a short message that is printed on the check stub. In either case, the message tends to be short, and may simply be a request to access the company's Web site, where more detailed information about the company's status or plans may be posted.

Another benefit of the dividend is that it can be used to compensate investors for the perceived disadvantage of owning nonvoting stock. For example, if a company issues two types of stock, with Series A stock having super-voting rights and Series B having vastly reduced voting rights, then the presence of a dividend solely on the Series B stock may be a sufficient inducement for investors to bid up the price of the Series B stock, which might otherwise be considered of reduced value.

A useful best practice to offer investors is a dividend reinvestment plan (DRIP). This plan allows the company to plow the dividends of consenting investors back into more company stock, usually at a discount from the market price, or at least without any brokerage commissions. This may be perceived by investors as a significant benefit, and may result in a higher-than-average level of investor retention (as well as less cash outflow to pay for dividends).

## STOCK BUY-BACK ALTERNATIVE

A stock buy-back program sends a different message to investors than a dividend issuance. By buying back stock, the board is telling investors that it feels the stock is currently undervalued. This action also tends to increase earnings per share, which, in turn, can lead to an increase in the stock price.

## EXAMPLE

Wastrel Corporation has 10,000,000 shares outstanding, and those shares currently trade at $5 each. Wastrel reported earnings of $2,800,000 for the latest fiscal year, which is earnings per share of $0.28 ($2,800,000 earnings, divided by 10,000,000 shares). If Wastrel's Board approves a $2,000,000 buy-back, then the company can withdraw 400,000 shares from circulation, which changes the number of shares outstanding to 9,600,000. Earnings per share now increase to $0.29 ($2,800,000 earnings, divided by 9,600,000 shares).

The best way to establish a strong case for a minimum stock price is for the board to approve a long-term repurchase program that allows for preapproved stock purchases at a specific trigger price. For example, if the board authorizes the company to buy back shares whenever the market price of its stock drops to $5, then this establishes a floor of $5, below which the stock's price is unlikely to drop. This tends to reduce the variability of the price, and may attract a group of investors who are less tolerant of risk. The key component of such a buy-back program is a long-term commitment to it, since its nonrenewal may trigger a sudden price drop that will result in some investor turnover.

However, a buy-back may not have the desired effect if so many shares are withdrawn that it impacts the perception of overall liquidity. An investor may consider a major reduction in float to increase the risk of holding the stock, since it may be more difficult to maintain an orderly market in the stock. If so, this higher perceived level of risk may drive a decline in the stock price.

A long-term, well funded stock buy-back program is a great source of publicity for the IRO, who can use it to continually issue press releases regarding how many shares have been repurchased, how much money is still authorized and available for additional buy-back activity, and how long the program has been running.

A company can run afoul of its bank credit facilities with a stock buy-back program. Banks frequently disallow stock buybacks as a condition for a loan or line of credit, on the grounds that the company is simply extracting cash from the bank in order to pay its investors. The wording of a credit facility usually restricts the issuance of dividends, and a stock buy-back program can be construed as the issuance of dividends.

## SEC CONDITIONS ON STOCK BUY-BACKS

A stock buy-back program can cause a company to contravene the Securities Exchange Act of 1934. In its Section 9(a)(2), the Act states that it is illegal:

> To effect . . . a series of transactions in any security registered on a national securities exchange . . . with respect to creating actual or apparent active trading in such security, or raising or depressing the price of such security . . ."

This is an obvious problem, since a stock buy-back program absolutely will at least keep the price of a stock from dropping below the program's trigger price. Fortunately, the SEC's Rule 10b-18 provides a safe harbor from liability for manipulation under the preceding Section. However, to obtain safe harbor coverage, the repurchase program must satisfy (on a daily basis) the following four conditions:

1. *Centralized purchases.* All purchases on behalf of the company must be made by a single broker/dealer on a single day. This means that the company should authorize a single broker/dealer to handle virtually all repurchases.
2. *Purchasing boundaries.* Companies cannot bid or purchase the day's opening transaction, nor can they do so within the last 30 minutes of the close

of the trading session. However, companies with a public float value exceeding $150 million and average daily trading volume over $1 million can bid or purchase within 10 minutes of the close of the trading session. Also, bids and purchases are allowed in after-hours trading, as long as the company does not enter the opening bid, and the purchase price does not exceed the lower of the closing price in the equity's principal market, nor any lower bids subsequently reported in other markets.

3. *Purchase price.* The purchase price may not exceed the highest independent bid or the last independent transaction, whichever is higher. If the stock trades on the OTC Bulletin Board system or the pink sheets, then the price cannot be higher than the highest bid obtained from three independent dealers.

4. *Purchasing volume.* The daily purchasing volume cannot exceed 25 percent of the average daily transaction volume (ADTV) during the four preceding calendar weeks. However, the company may make one block purchase per week without being subject to this limitation, as long as the company makes no other purchases that day. Also, the block purchase cannot be used to calculate the ADTV (which would otherwise likely increase it).

If the repurchase plan does not meet one of these conditions, then the safe harbor is removed from all repurchases made on the day when the condition was not met. Also, the safe harbor is not effective if the company is aware of material, nonpublic favorable information. Therefore, the company must be current in its disclosures before engaging in repurchasing activities.

The safe harbor is also not available (with some exceptions) during a merger transaction with another company, which spans the period from the public announcement of the merger until either the completion of the transaction or the completion of voting by the target company's shareholders.

In short, the SEC has designed the requirements of the safe harbor to keep a company's repurchase activities from unduly impacting the price of its stock, both by controlling the timing and size of purchasing transactions.

##  DISCLOSURE OF A STOCK BUY-BACK PROGRAM

Item 703 of the SEC's Regulation S-K requires that a company report in its quarterly Form 10-Q and annual Form 10-K reports the results of its stock repurchase program. The information must be presented in the tabular format shown in Exhibit 21.1.

**Exhibit 21.1** Reporting of Stock Repurchase Program

| Period | Total Number of Shares Purchased | Average Price Paid per Share | Total Number of Shares Purchased as Part of Publicly Announced Program | Maximum Number of Shares that May Yet be Purchased Under the Program |
|---|---|---|---|---|
| Month 1 | 57,000 | $5.19 | 503,000 | 1,997,000 |
| Month 2 | 120,000 | 4.32 | 623,000 | 1,877,000 |
| Month 3 | 41,000 | 3.99 | 664,000 | 1,836,000 |
| Total | 218,000 | $4.51 | 664,000 | 1,836,000 |

A footnote to the table should also disclose the date when the repurchase program was announced, the dollar amount or share total approved for the program, and the expiration date of the program. If the company has also decided to terminate the program prior to its predetermined expiration date, then this should be described in the footnote.

Given the limitations of the safe harbor, and the subsequent reporting required under Item 703, a company must have a system in place for recording the timing, volumes, and prices at which all shares were purchased.

A public company engaging in stock repurchases must be current with the disclosure of all material, nonpublic information of a favorable nature that might have a positive impact on the company's share price. Alternatively, the company can refrain from authorizing stock repurchases until such time as it has disclosed this information. The fact that the company intends to begin a stock repurchase program is itself a material event, so it should disclose the pertinent facts of the program prior to initiating any repurchases. A sample press release follows:

> ABC Corporation announced today that its board of directors has approved a stock repurchase program pursuant to which up to $20 million of its outstanding common stock may be repurchased from time to time. The duration of the repurchase program is twelve months. Under the program, ABC could purchase shares of common stock through open market and privately negotiated transactions at prices deemed appropriate by management. The timing and amount of repurchase transactions under this program will depend on market conditions and corporate and regulatory considerations. The purchases will be funded from available working capital. The purchases are to be made subject to restrictions relating to volume, price and

timing, in order to minimize the impact of the purchases on the market for the common stock.

Without taking these precautions, there is a risk that the company could be accused of stock manipulation, as described in the preceding section. Adherence to the previously described Rule 10b-18 is the standard approach for avoiding stock manipulation charges. In addition, the company can create a Rule 10b5-1 plan, under which it issues written instructions to its broker/dealer, stating the number of shares to be repurchased, the price at which the repurchase is to be made, and the date(s) of such purchases, or a formula resulting in similar instructions. The company must ensure that the plan is well documented and is being followed by the designated broker/dealer. Also, it would be best if the company does not attempt to modify the plan once it is in place; a better arrangement is to set a predetermined termination date for the original plan, after which the company can make adjustments to a replacement plan, and activate the new plan for a specific period of time.

By adhering to both Rule 10b-18 and Rule 10b5-1, a company raises excellent defenses against charges of stock manipulation.

## ODD-LOT SHAREHOLDINGS

When a shareholder owns fewer than 100 shares of company stock, this is known as an *odd lot*. A company must incur a minimum cost per year for each investor, which primarily comprises the cost to print and issue the annual report and proxy statement and to compile votes from the proxy statement. It is very cost-ineffective to incur this cost for the holders of odd-lot shares, so it makes sense to have an odd-lot share repurchase program. Alternatively, a company can offer a direct stock purchase plan for odd-lot shareholders, which allows them to increase their holdings above the odd-lot level while incurring no transaction fees.

An alternative to the odd-lot share repurchase program or the direct stock purchase plan is to conduct a *reverse stock split*. For example, a 100 to 1 reverse stock split will result in less than one share for anyone who originally held fewer than 100 shares, which the company can buy out with a cash payment. However, this is an expensive alternative that calls for a shareholder vote and the replacement of stock certificates with ones showing the reduced number of shares. A somewhat less expensive alternative is the *reverse-forward stock split*, where the reverse split is used to eliminate odd-lot shareholdings, followed by a forward split to bring the remaining shares back to their original amounts. This approach only impacts odd-lot shareholders, and is essentially transparent to all other shareholders. However, either type of stock split requires a shareholder vote, and so is only an alternative if a large proportion of the shareholder base is composed of odd-lot holders.

## EXAMPLE

Wyvern Corporation has 350 odd-lot shareholders out a total shareholder base of 1,200 shareholders, with 10,000,000 shares outstanding. The 350 odd-lot shareholders each own an average of 50 shares, totaling 17,500 shares. The board of directors feels that this is too high a proportion of odd-lot holdings, and so conducts a shareholder vote to approve a 100:1 reverse-forward stock split, with incremental shares being paid off at a price of $8.00 per share. The shareholders approve the measure.

After the initial reverse split part of the transaction, the number of shares outstanding declines to 100,000. After the reverse split, the 17,500 shares originally held by the odd-lot shareholders have declined to 175 incremental shares, for which Wyvern pays a total of $1,400.

Wyvern then initiates the forward split, which multiplies the remaining 99,825 shares by 100, yielding a total number of 9,982,500 shares outstanding. This exactly matches the original shareholdings for each of the remaining investors. ▦

## SUMMARY

When making the decision to issue a dividend, the IRO should counsel the board regarding the ramifications of setting too high a dividend, as well as how the dividend will change the composition of company investors. Also, if the board decides to implement either a dividend or stock buy-back program, be sure to post on the company Web site a history of dividend payment dates and amounts or a history of stock buy-backs. This is useful information from the perspective of telling a story to investors that the company has a long-term, proven strategy in either area that it intends to follow in the future. If the board decides instead to adopt a stock buy-back program, the IRO should stand in favor of a long-term program that establishes a floor below which the company will buy back shares. In both cases, the main emphasis is on the implementation and continuing support of a durable, long-running program that investors can rely on.

If the shareholder list is cluttered with a large number of odd-lot holdings, then there are several methods available for buying out these shares. Doing so eliminates the cost of periodic mailings to the odd-lot shareholders.

# CHAPTER TWENTY-TWO

# Outsourcing Investor Relations

T IS A RARE public company that has not used an investor relations consultant at some point in its life. Consultants have backgrounds in public relations or Wall Street, or once worked as IROs themselves, and so can offer a considerable level of expertise across a broad range of functions. This chapter explores the types of consultant skills available and how to manage the relationship with a consultant.

## SKILL SET OF AN INVESTOR RELATIONS CONSULTANT

Hiring an investor relations consultant is an excellent idea for firms that do not have the resources to build an adequate in-house investor relations function, or that have few contacts in the investment community. They can provide a wide array of services, including the following:

- *Analyst coverage.* Consultants usually have contacts with a significant number of analysts. They can present the company to the subset of those analysts whom they feel will be most likely to initiate coverage.
- *Board advisor.* The board can appoint a consultant to be its investor relations advisor. By doing so, the board gains an independent perspective on the effectiveness of their company's investor relations activities. The

consultant could also engage in various projects for the board, such as a survey of major investors.

- *Communication materials.* Consultants can formulate the entire range of company communication materials, including press releases, conference call scripts, annual reports, fact sheets, and investor presentations. They can also provide advice regarding the types of communication to use in the event of mergers, restatements, or proxy battles.
- *Crisis communications.* Some consultants specialize in dealing with crisis situations. For example, a company may need advice in dealing with a widely reported product failure, criminal investigation, or hostile takeover. These consultants have experience in dealing with the media that can mitigate the impact of these events.
- *Disclosure knowledge.* Consultants should have an excellent knowledge of the SEC's disclosure rules, and can assist a company by setting up the policies and procedures needed to ensure compliance with those rules.
- *Investor days.* If a company conducts an investor day where it brings an array of company managers together for presentations to the investment community, then a consultant can assist with invitations to analysts and investors, as well as manage the event logistics.
- *Investor feedback.* Consultants can conduct periodic surveys of selected investors in order to obtain feedback about their perceptions of the company.
- *Presentation coaching.* The quality of a road show is founded upon the excellence of the presentation materials and the abilities of those executives presenting the information. Consultants can offer considerable advice to upgrade the contents and format of the materials, and can improve the speaking capabilities of the presenters.
- *Press releases.* A common consultant task is writing press releases, or at least reviewing those releases written by company employees. The result should be polished and concise releases.
- *Public offerings.* Consultants offer the greatest return for their fees in the area of public offerings. They can assist in setting up road show meetings for an initial or secondary public offering, as well as shepherd a presentation team through the multitude of meetings needed to complete an offering. Several of the largest consulting firms make this their primary area of expertise.
- *Regulatory updates.* Some consultants monitor the most recent regulations promulgated by the Securities and Exchange Commission, and will issue periodic updates to their clients regarding how these changes will affect their investor relations operations.

- *Valuation analysis.* Consultants can offer advice regarding the establishment of a comparative peer group, and other methodologies for creating a valuation analysis.
- *Web site updates.* Some consultants employ specialists who either design investor relations Web pages themselves or who can provide detailed advice regarding the contents, presentation, and navigation elements of such pages.

Some of the larger investor relations firms advertise themselves as full-service shops, offering all of these services. However, even the largest firm realistically offers just one area of specialization, and has backfilled its core strength with additional staff to give the appearance of broad expertise. There are two main areas of specialization, which are capital raising and public relations. The largest firms have realized that they can charge the highest fees if they specialize in initial and secondary public offerings, since clients will raise more funds by using their services. Other firms have a strong public relations focus, and so specialize in communications materials, Web site updates, presentation coaching, and so on. Because of this level of specialization, a company should consider employing at least two investor relations firms.

Consultants may also specialize in a specific industry, such as technology, health care, or energy. Some industries have special terminology or are only followed by a small number of analysts or investors, so it really makes a difference to employ a firm with deep industry knowledge and contacts. Be sure to query prospective consultants about their clients to discern the industries in which those clients are clustered.

A consultant may only arrange investor meetings and road shows for a certain industry. This is an exceedingly valuable skill. This consultant assists with advising which cities to visit, setting up meetings with investors, and making follow-up contacts after a road show for feedback.

An alternative is to use an investment bank to arrange meetings with potential investors. The investment bank may have a large number of quality contacts. However, it may only put the company in contact with its favored accounts, which tend to be short-term holders that generate the most fee income for the bank—not the more prized long-term holders who only occasionally use the bank's services.

A micro-cap company may find that a few local experts with specialized skills are sufficient for their needs. However, larger companies that need expertise in a broad range of skills will need the services of a more established organization with multiple staff, such as the Financial Relations Board or

Capital Market Communications. Sole proprietors may agree to an hourly rate, but the larger firms will want a monthly retainer that starts in the range of $25,000 and increases precipitously from there. A few firms will accept stock instead of cash, but they are a small minority.

In short, any part of the investor relations function can be outsourced, though few firms can handle the entire array of activities. Instead, a company may find that it must employ several firms to ensure that it has access to a sufficient level of expertise. The next section addresses how to manage these outsourcing relationships.

##  MANAGING THE CONSULTANT RELATIONSHIP

Even if a company fully outsources its investor relations function, it is still necessary to appoint an in-house manager of the consultants who have been assigned to handle the work. This person is responsible for coordinating the activities of all consultants and approving their work. The in-house manager should have a sufficient knowledge of investor relations to understand the various work products of the consultants. Also, since the investor relations function is normally positioned to report directly to the CEO or CFO, the in-house manager should be a sufficiently senior manager to directly coordinate consultant efforts with either of these executives.

The proper level of control over a consulting firm is to require it to make a monthly report of its activities. This can include a listing of all contacts made on behalf of the company, the dates of those contacts, the names of the contacts, and topics discussed. Or, if specific work products were completed, the in-house manager should review how the results compare to the initial work request.

If consultants are to take over the bulk of the investor relations function, then the in-house manager must be committed to making them a fixture within the company. They should have a representative present at many company meetings in order to fully understand the inner workings of the company.

A consultant should have its own internal procedures to ensure that information is released on behalf of the client company only after the information has been thoroughly reviewed and approved. To do so, there should be an approval form for each release that notes the source of the information, who prepared and approved it, any recommended changes to it, and when it was released. An internal compliance officer should periodically examine these approval forms to ensure that all procedures are being followed.

There is a potential downside to outsourcing investor relations work, which is that confidential company information is now being placed outside the company. Though a consultant rarely breaches confidentiality, it may be an issue if the information being disclosed is of an extremely sensitive nature. Since it is generally easier to control confidentiality if information is kept in-house, the in-house manager could consider shifting only nonsensitive work to a consultant.

Another risk is that a consulting firm may be hired to perform a specific function, and then attempt to broaden the range of its services in order to increase its fees. This risk can extend to the consulting firm completely taking over the investor relations function, possibly including the ouster of the IRO who hired the firm. Though attempting to expand their role is common enough, it is a rare situation indeed for a consultant to attempt to replace the IRO.

 ## NATIONAL INVESTOR RELATIONS INSTITUTE

The National Investor Relations Institute (NIRI) is a professional association of approximately 4,000 corporate officers and investor relations consultants who are responsible for communications between companies and the investment community. Its mission is to advance the practice of investor relations, as well as the professional competency and standing of its members.

NIRI has 33 chapters in the United States that conduct periodic meetings and seminars for members. NIRI also runs an annual conference at which a variety of educational topics are presented. NIRI has a bookstore on its Web site, which is located at www.niri.org, on which it posts a broad array of investor relations publications and articles. NIRI also publishes the *Investor Relations Update* each month, as well as the *IR Mentor* on a quarterly basis. Finally, its *NIRI Weekly* electronic newsletter sends out seminar notices and links to media articles that are related to investor relations.

NIRI is an excellent source of information for anyone wanting to learn more about the profession, to meet other professionals in this field, or to locate consultants.

 ## SUMMARY

A public company will probably establish a relationship with an investor relations consultant at some point during its life—either as a complete substitute for an in-house investor relations function or to provide expertise in a specific functional area.

The greatest value added from a consultant relationship is in the arena of initial or secondary public offerings, since it can yield a larger amount of funds received per shares issued. Many other consultant capabilities fall into the domain of public relations, where their greatest expertise is in writing communication materials, upgrading Web sites, and providing coaching for presentation skills. These are two entirely different skill sets and may require the retention of two investor relations firms, each specializing in one of the areas.

# CHAPTER TWENTY-THREE

# Investor Relations Metrics

T HE IRO IS CONSTANTLY quizzed by investors and analysts about a variety of metrics, and so must have a thorough knowledge of a number of measurements. This chapter provides sufficient information about metrics for an IRO to construct a complete reporting framework, as well as to provide explanations for a number of reporting situations.

## INTERNAL AND FINANCIAL METRICS

The IRO should use a set of measurements to gauge the performance of her company in its relations with investors. The following bullet points contain a number of possible metrics from which to choose:

- *Average bid/ask spread.* Investors want to have the smallest possible transactional cost when they buy or sell a company's stock. This occurs when there is a very small difference between the bid and ask prices of the stock. The smaller the spread, the more seamlessly investors will be able to alter their holdings.
- *Average holding period.* The IRO always wants to increase the average holding period for her company's stock. The reverse situation, where there is considerable churn, causes more price volatility.

- *Corporate governance quotient*®. This measurement is created by Institutional Shareholder Services (ISS) and is posted on the Profile page on the Yahoo! Finance Web site for the 8,000 larger companies that are followed by ISS. It evaluates the strengths, deficiencies, and risks of a company's corporate governance practices and board of directors. The scores are based on 63 corporate governance variables that are targeted at a company's board of directors, audit, anti-takeover provisions, and executive and director compensation. Scores are compared to a relevant market index, such as the S&P 500 or Russell 3000, or to an industry peer group.
- *Institutional/retail/insider investor mix.* Retail investors have far smaller holdings than institutional investors, but tend to retain their holdings for a much longer period of time, which helps to reduce price volatility. Insider investors also tend to have extremely long holding periods. Consequently, the proportions of stock held by all three of these groups is a useful metric. In addition, since institutional investors can make up a large majority of all stock held, the IRO should consider a more detailed analysis of this group, showing the percentage of total float held by each entity, its net change in stockholdings over the past quarter, and an estimation of its investing strategy (e.g., hedge fund, index, growth, or value).
- *Investors by geographic region.* The IRO can determine the success of a road show by comparing the geographic distribution of shareholders to the locations of recent road shows. It is even more important to use this distribution analysis to plan the locations of the next road show. If there are areas with sparse stockholder representation, then these are prime targets for a road show. Conversely, it makes little sense to plan a road show into an area with high investor concentrations, since the local investor base already has sufficient knowledge about the company.
- *Float.* This is the number of registered shares available for trading. A large float can accommodate large daily trading volumes, which leads to increased price stability. If the price is stable, then the perceived risk is reduced, which may lead to more demand for the stock and a resulting increase in its price.
- *Market cap category.* A company will attract different groups of investors, depending on the size of its market capitalization. There is a considerable difference of opinion regarding the exact capitalization range that qualifies a company for each progressively higher market cap category, but here are some rough ranges to use:
  - Micro-cap, under $250 million
  - Small cap, $250+ million to $1.5 billion

- Medium cap, $1.5+ billion to $5 billion
- Large cap, $5+ billion

- *Number of analysts following the company.* Analyst reports about a company are among the best possible sales tools, so gaining analyst coverage is a prime IRO responsibility. For this metric, include any analyst who has issued a report during the past 12 months. Also, consider splitting the metric into the total number of analysts who have issued buy, neutral, and sell recommendations. A similar metric is to track the number of new research reports generated within a specified time period.
- *Number of market makers.* This metric applies only to over-the-counter stocks, but is critical in that situation for ensuring a reasonable amount of trading activity.
- *Number of requests for information.* Investor relations activities should gradually increase a company's profile throughout the investment community. As this happens, the number of requests for financial information will increase and should be tracked. Since many companies now make their reports available on their Web sites, it is easy to count the number of downloads for each report through the Web site's statistics software.
- *Number of road show presentations.* This is a measure of the volume of activity and does not indicate the results of a road show. Also, it does not indicate the number of people to whom the IRO's team presented during the road show. Nonetheless, it is a common measurement of overall investor relations activity. More precise metrics related to road show presentations are the number of shares purchased following a road show, the number of people added to the investor relations mailing list, and the road show cost divided by the resulting number of shares placed (for which a reasonable goal is $0.05 per share).
- *Number of round lot stockholders.* If a company is listed on a major exchange, it must meet a minimum requirement for the number of round lot stockholders. A round lot stockholder is any entity owning at least 100 shares of a company's stock. If the number is close to the minimum required by the listing exchange, then this is a critical ongoing metric for the IRO to watch.
- *Stock exchange de-listing price.* All of the major stock exchanges, with the exception of the American Stock Exchange, will de-list a company's stock if its bid price is consistently below $1. If a company's stock price trades near this level, then this metric becomes exceedingly important!
- *Short interest ratio.* This is the number of shares being sold short, divided by the average daily volume of shares traded. For example, if the number is three, then it would take three days of average trading volume for short

sellers to cover their positions. This is a useful metric when tracked on a trend line, since the IRO can tell when short sellers are taking an increased interest in the company.

▪ *Stock relative price performance.* The IRO should certainly track her company's stock price performance relative to one or more stock indexes that most closely match the size of the company. This comparison should be for the year-to-date, as well as for the past year, three years, and five years. It is quite possible that a stock's relative price performance will come up as a topic of conversation during a road show or other conversations with the investment community, so the IRO should have this information available.

▪ *Trading volume.* On a long-term basis, the IRO can significantly boost the volume of trading in her company's stock through ongoing road show presentations. High trading volume equates to enhanced liquidity, which attracts more investors. Consequently, this is a valuable metric to track.

The preceding metrics address issues over which the investor relations department has some control. The IRO should also be aware of the more common financial and industry metrics that investors use to evaluate a company, which are as follows:

▪ *Cash flow per share.* This is usually defined as cash flow generated before financing costs and taxes, divided by the number of shares outstanding (and which may be called "operating cash flow per share"). The IRO should be well aware of this number, since many investors will ask for it. This is an excellent metric for determining the underlying health of a company, because it ignores a number of GAAP (generally accepted accounting principles) standards that obscure a company's true condition.

▪ *Current ratio.* Investors may occasionally ask about the ratio of current assets to current liabilities, since it gives an approximate measure of a company's ability to pay its current bills from current assets. It can be skewed by too much illiquid inventory (which is included in the numerator), so an alternative measure is the quick ratio, which excludes inventory from the numerator.

▪ *Economic value added (EVA).* This shows the incremental rate of return in excess of a firm's total cost of capital. It is calculated by multiplying a company's net investment by the difference between its actual rate of return on assets and its percentage cost of capital. It is used by sophisticated investors, who usually limit this calculation to their investments in larger companies. This is not an issue for a micro-cap company.

- *Industry indicators.* Investors tend to focus on different indicators for each industry, since a certain metric may have a major impact in one industry, and none at all in another. For example, the price of gasoline is enormously important in the airline industry, while the number of housing starts has a major impact in the home improvement supply industry. The IRO should be aware of whichever industry indicators are commonly acknowledged to be important in her industry.
- *Institutional capture rate (ICR).* This measures the proportion of trading in company stock that is attributable to long-term investors, and is best viewed on a trend line to determine long-term changes. This metric can also be viewed from the inverse perspective—a low ICR is indicative of high volatility in shareholdings, with no intent by shareholders to retain ownership for long. The ICR is calculated by taking the greater absolute value of shares bought or sold by institutional investors and dividing them into total trading volume over the three-month measurement period. The institutional investor activity comes from their quarterly 13F filings; since the 13F information is only updated on a quarterly basis, this is the reason for only measuring ICR on the same quarterly basis.
- *Price/earnings multiple.* This is the single most commonly used financial metric. The goal of a high price/earnings multiple is not based on a single spike in a stock's price. Instead, it should be for the highest possible sustainable multiple, which avoids peaks and troughs in the price. This is a moving target that must be periodically adjusted, since the values assigned by the market to an industry can shift considerably over time.
- *Revenue per share.* A growth-style investor wants to see a constant increase in the level of revenue per share, and will promptly sell if there is a decline in the rate of increase in this measurement. Revenue per share is a significant metric if there are a significant number of growth investors in the investor base.

A good way to summarize these metrics is to create a quarterly scorecard that compares a company to its peers, using the most relevant mix of the preceding measurements. For example, the scorecard could compare trading volumes, market capitalizations, stock prices, and short interest ratios for the most relevant set of companies, as well as their results based on the price/earnings ratio and cash flow per share, accompanied by a variety of profitability measurements. A more qualitative type of information to include in the scorecard is a selection of comments made by earnings call attendees for the entire peer group, to see what industrywide issues are being recognized by the investment community. An example of such a scorecard appears in Exhibit 23.1.

**Exhibit 23.1**   Peer Group Comparison Report

| Measurement | Subject Company | Peer A | Peer B | Peer C |
|---|---|---|---|---|
| **Share information** | | | | |
| Stock price | $5.50 | $11.00 | $2.35 | $6.85 |
| Daily trading volume | 52,000 | 81,000 | 24,000 | 60,000 |
| Float | 15M | 20M | 9M | 18M |
| Market capitalization | $233M | $420M | $102M | $321M |
| **Valuation** | | | | |
| Price/earnings multiple | 20.3x | 26.2x | 18.1x | 19.0x |
| Market cap/revenue multiple | 4.0 | 5.0 | 3.5 | 4.0 |
| **Financial Results** | | | | |
| Revenue | $58M | $84M | $29M | $80M |
| Gross margin % | 40% | 47% | 38% | 42% |
| EBITDA margin % | 11% | 15% | 8% | 10% |
| Net profit margin % | 7% | 10% | 4% | 8% |

This peer group comparison report reveals that the financial results reported by each company directly translates into its valuation multiples and stock price. Though there is rarely such a perfect relationship in the real world (since qualitative factors are also involved), a comparison report does provide a wealth of information regarding why a company's stock price behaves in a particular manner.

Investors and analysts may use other metrics to track a company's stock. If so, it will be easy enough to discern them; just conduct a road show and write down every metric that the attendees ask about. If a new metric repeatedly comes up for discussion, then include it in the standard list of metrics to be tracked.

 **PEER METRICS**

The IRO *must* be aware of peer metrics. These are the metrics being used by the peer companies against which the investment community benchmarks a subject company. If a metric is consistently used by the peer group, then the IRO needs to include it on a regular basis in the company's external reports. Investors and analysts need this information in order to form comparisons between the performance of the clustered companies. For example, if a consulting firm finds that its peer group is reporting the average billable percentage for their consultants, then it should do so, too.

When making comparisons between a company's metrics and those of its peers, the IRO should by all means highlight those in which the company is outperforming its peers. However, the IRO should also be aware of any areas of underperformance, since she will certainly receive inquiries about them during quarterly earnings conference calls or other meetings with the investment community.

If a company has multiple business segments, then consider breaking out peer metrics for each of the segments. Investors will appreciate having greater clarity into a company's financial results. However, this may also result in a significant change in the overall company valuation, which may not be an increase. For example, if additional metrics detail reveals that a significant part of a business is located in a low-multiple industry, a company may see its overall valuation decline.

## COMPANY-SPECIFIC METRICS

A small number of metrics may give investors unique insights into a company's operations. The IRO should severely limit the number of unique metrics that a company uses, because few metrics yield a discernible distinction from the peer group over a long period of time. Before presenting a new metric to the investment community, the IRO should consult extensively with the management team to determine whether the company can realistically report exceptional results with that metric on a long-term basis.

The IRO should clearly define these metrics, since investors and analysts may not have seen them elsewhere. Better yet, post the definition of each unique metric in the investor relations section of the company Web site.

An example of a company-specific metric is the number of its major customers. This is an especially critical item for smaller companies whose revenues may be derived from a small number of large customers. Investors can be scared away by a perceived overreliance on just a few customers. Accordingly, the IRO should be aware of the amount of revenues attributable to the top few customers and consider reporting on this information to an even greater extent than is required in the MD&A section of the quarterly and annual reports.

As another example, a company may have an unusually high percentage of management or employee ownership. If so, the IRO should absolutely report this percentage, because it shows that the management team feels the company is still a good investment. This is an especially powerful metric if managers are continuing to add to their stock ownership positions. However, if the IRO is aware that some managers may reduce their holdings in the near future, then she should begin to reduce the emphasis on this metric.

## METRICS CONSISTENCY

The IRO should retain all metrics for as long a period of time as possible. It is not acceptable to constantly swap out metrics in favor of the latest one that paints a company in the best possible light. The investment community is very experienced at spotting these changes, and will want to know why the old measurements were dropped. Further, if a company has a long history of altering its metrics, then they will eventually stop following the stock, because it is too hard to measure the company's results on a consistent basis.

Another issue is when companies use the same metrics for a long period of time, but alter the underlying definitions of those metrics in order to enhance their reported results. This is also not acceptable, for the same reason just noted. If the IRO has a valid reason for altering the definition of a metric, then she should address it during a conference call, post the new definition in the investor relations section of the company Web site, and retroactively change the metric calculation for previous reporting periods, so that the calculation is consistently applied.

There will occasionally be unusual charges or gains that skew reported metrics. When these are significant changes, the IRO should normalize the results by stating the original results and what those results would have been if the unusual items had not occurred. This is necessary in order to avoid an unwarranted stock price change that would have otherwise been caused by the unusual item. Some IRO's might feel that an unusual gain gives them a one-time stock price boost, and so is better left undocumented. However, this approach also results in higher expectations for the future that the company cannot achieve, and that will simply result in a guaranteed stock price drop at some point in the future. Consequently, it is better to normalize metrics whenever possible.

Finally, the IRO must carefully consider whether to initially report a metric at all. Once a company starts reporting information, the market expects to continue seeing it on an ongoing basis. If it eliminates the metric entirely, then the usual supposition is that the company's performance has declined, and it wishes to hide this information. The IRO must then issue extensive explanations about why the metric is being cancelled. Thus, it is better to carefully consider the long-term implications of reporting additional information prior to releasing it to the marketplace.

## EXPLAINING RESULTS

The calculation and reporting of some financial and operating results require special judgment, since they can mislead the investment community unless presented properly. This section contains several examples of these situations.

Revenue can be misleading when a company is acquiring other businesses. For example, a company has $10 million of revenue, but at the end of its fiscal year, it acquires another company that has $5 million of revenue. Clearly, it will only report $10 million of revenue in the current year but will experience a 50 percent increase in the following year. The solution is to report, as an ancillary figure, a revenue run rate of $15 million. For any company that is acquiring other entities on an ongoing basis, the revenue run rate is a critical financial metric.

Explaining sales can also be a problem when they fluctuate by season or promotion. In these cases, quarterly results can vary so dramatically that investors will have no idea what is going on unless fully educated by the IRO. If seasonality is the problem, then it helps to report the rolling historical 12-month performance, which averages out all seasonality. Or, if investors want to know about sales prospects for the upcoming high season, then consider reporting on advance orders in comparison to advance orders at the same time in the preceding year. If sales fluctuations are caused by promotions, then report on the baseline sales level without the promotion. In all of these situations, the goal is to report sales from which unusual fluctuations have been removed.

Sales can also be impacted by the volume of product already present in the sales pipeline. If a company has recently used a large discount promotion to sell large volumes of product to its distributors, it is entirely likely that this action will result in unusually low sales in the near term, while the distributors sell off their excess stocks. The IRO should point this out in order to set expectations for a short-term dip in sales.

Another reporting item that can cause difficulty is the total dollar amount of backlogged sales. Companies can get into trouble by adding nearly completed orders to their reported backlogs; if those orders do not materialize, then the backlog will unexpectedly drop. To avoid this problem, only include in backlog those sales for which there is a signed sales order from the customer.

Profitability can also be an issue, if there are unusual charges that skew the profit figure. For example, a company shows significant losses caused by charging to expense a large amount of stock that it issued in exchange for services. In this instance, its level of reported profit will be substantially lower than its peers. The IRO would be justified in presenting profits before stock-based compensation expense, since it is more comparable to information reported by peer companies.

Unusual payment terms can also cause issues. For example, if a large supplier has negotiated unusually long payment terms, this will adversely affect the cash-flow information shown in the statement of cash flows. Since many investors judge a company by its free cash flow, it is useful to disclose the reason for the unusual payment terms in order to prevent a stock sell-off.

Free cash flow can also be severely impacted by an increase in fixed assets. To keep investors from dumping stock when they see a sudden downturn in cash flow, be sure to explain what assets were purchased, why they are important to the company's strategy, and what kind of return on investment is expected from their use. If this investment is in the purchase of another company, rather than fixed assets, then use the same checklist to explain the company's diversion of cash flow to fund the acquisition.

Another metric requiring interpretation is the cost of the sales department. This can be a weighty expense in some industries, possibly resulting in queries from analysts regarding why so many salespeople are being kept on staff. If so, the IRO should be prepared to explain the average duration of a salesperson's learning curve (when they are least productive) and the potential for future sales growth once they become more experienced.

An issue that impacts both revenue and gross margin is changes in the product mix. When a company reports its results, investors will assume that the same historical product mix is generating the current results. If the mix changes over time, this will likely translate into different financial results, which the IRO should appropriately explain.

The percentage of production capacity utilized can be important in some industries. The IRO should be aware of how changes within the company impact the total amount of its production capacity, since analysts may ask about it. For example, if an airline sells off ten of its airplanes, the IRO should know what this does to its percentage of seats filled. Similarly, if a company consolidates facilities, analysts will ask how this impacts the company's ability to process customer orders.

If a company engages in multiple acquisitions or has a heavy capital structure, then the amount of its intangibles amortization or asset depreciation may swamp its reported profits, resulting in significant ongoing losses. Though a company is required to report its net profit, the IRO should place a strong emphasis on reported EBITDA earnings (earnings before interest, taxes, depreciation, and amortization), which cancels out the impact of the depreciation and amortization. Otherwise, analysts may drive down a stock's target price in the face of continuing losses.

A more infrequent circumstance is when a company is positioning itself to be sold. In this situation, the IRO should consider revealing non-GAAP accounting information that more clearly identifies areas of value. For example, intangible assets, such as patents and trademarks, may appear to have little GAAP accounting value, because only the historical cost of creating those assets can be reported. However, a patent that only cost $25,000 to file might be worth millions to an acquirer. The same situation applies to real estate—a company may own valuable property whose cost is quite low, but that has a very high resale value. Of course, disclosures of this type should be clearly separated from GAAP-compliant information and positioned next to a reconciliation that identifies how the additional information varies from GAAP.

Clearly, a company can be faced with interpretational issues for a wide array of reporting items—sales, backlog, payment terms, acquisitions, product mix, and so on. When deciding on the best explanation to place on these items, the IRO's key goal is to clarify information to such a degree that there is no room for misinterpretation by the investment community.

##  SUMMARY

When presenting metrics information to investors, it is much better to use a set of metrics, rather than a single one. A single metric will change over time, and not always favorably. By using a cluster of metrics, the IRO has a better chance of finding something favorable to present to investors on an ongoing basis. Also, a group of metrics presents a more complete view of a company and its prospects than a single metric.

# Index

CPSIA information can be obtained
at www.ICGtesting.com
Printed in the USA
BVHW080301011019
559855BV00010B/71/P